HOW TO EAT OUT

Giles Coren

**HODDER &
STOUGHTON**

First published in Great Britain in 2012 by Hodder & Stoughton
An imprint of Hodder & Stoughton
An Hachette UK company

1

Copyright © Giles Coren 2012

A CIP catalogue record for this title is available from the British Library

ISBN 978 1 444 70690 1
eBook ISBN 978 1 848 94987 4

Typeset by Hewer Text UK, Ltd, Edinburgh

Printed and bound by Clays Ltd, St Ives plc

Hodder & Stoughton policy is to use papers that are natural, renewable and
recyclable products and made from wood grown in sustainable forests. The
logging and manufacturing processes are expected to conform to the
environmental regulations of the country of origin.

Hodder & Stoughton Ltd
338 Euston Road
London NW1 3BH

www.hodder.co.uk

This book is dedicated to the guys in the basement – rarely well-paid, rarely well-treated, and rarely white – who do the washing up. Because no matter how good or bad the food, or what the service is like, or which blasted interior designer did the stupid refurbishment, the greatest thing of all about eating out is that someone else does the dishes.

Contents

1	IN THE BEGINNING ...	1
2	CHINESE	16
	How to Tell a Good Chinese Restaurant	26
3	DIM SUM	28
	How to Stay Healthy in a Chinese Restaurant	39
4	STILL IN THE BEGINNING	40
5	BURGERS AND STEAKS	49
6	PIZZA EXPRESS	60
	Lay Off the Bread	72
7	ITALY	74
8	INDIAN	84
	Always Order the Fish	96
9	I WAS A WAITER ONCE TOO, YOU KNOW	97
10	REMAINING ANONYMOUS	104
	How To Complain	118
11	MY FRENCH YOUTH	120
12	FRANCE TODAY	134
	How to Get the Most from Your Local	144
13	BOOKING	146
14	HAVING 'FUN'	150
	Book a Table, Not a Restaurant	160
15	LEGALLY	162
16	BLOGGERS	170

	How to Deal with Food-Poisoning	174
17	MOCK DOG, SIR?	176
	Avoid Restaurants with a Waiter Posted Outside	181
18	THE VEGGIE OPTION	182
19	A WEEKEND AWAY	190
	Tip!	198
20	EASYJET'S PORCINE PLASMA 'SPECIAL'	199
21	JAPAN	203
	How to Get the Most from a Sushi Bar in Britain	216
22	SALT	220
23	WHO IS THIS AL FRESCO?	223
	Insist on Tap Water	230
24	IN HOGARTH'S FOOTSTEPS	232
25	CROATIA	239
	How to Order Wine	243
26	LE MENU DÉGUSTATION AND A SICK BUCKET	244
27	HAND DRYERS	246
	How to Complain about the Wine	250
28	PUDDING IS FOR WIMPS	252
	How to Choose a Restaurant for a Date	256
29	THE HEALTH FARM	258
	Be Nice to the Staff	263
30	THE SUPERSIZERS GO . . .	264
	Take a Doggy Bag	282
31	DON'T YOU EVER GET BORED OF EATING IN RESTAURANTS?	284

IN THE BEGINNING . . .

The place I am trying to get back to, in everything I do and everything I eat, is the Gourmet Rendezvous on Finchley Road, North West London, on a rainy evening in November, 1979. Maybe 1980. Any night around that time will do.

We're just walking in, my mother, father, sister and me, having parked at the bus stop right outside (my mother will not walk any further than the width of a pavement, she would rather turn around and go home and eat cheese on toast than park even on the far side of the road), and while my father stands in the doorway, shaking down the umbrella he has used to keep the rain off my mother's hair in the ten-yard walk from car to restaurant, the rest of us stand almost in the middle of the small room, exposed, waiting for him to take control.

I'm in blue jeans, brown sandals and a grey sweatshirt with Mickey Mouse on it. So is my sister. Except maybe her sweatshirt is red. Maybe it has Minnie Mouse. Our hair, bowl cut, over the ears, mine much darker than hers, is very slightly wet because on the way from the car to the restaurant door, only a pavement's width, as I said, my mother was briefly distracted by a picture of a house with a swimming pool in the window of the estate agent's next door, and as she veered off suddenly to look more closely at the details he swerved with the brolly to keep her dry, and Victoria and I, unexpectedly uncovered, stood momentarily in the rain.

Then my dad is stabbing the brolly into the umbrella stand by the door, and coming past us to throw his hand in the direction of the restaurant's owner and to greet him by name so loudly that the room goes a little quiet. Whoever the owner was talking to before is left for dead, the plates he was about to set down are cast aside, and he comes to greet my father. The table whose service has been interrupted looks mildly annoyed, but then they notice that the man being greeted is Alan Coren, and they appear delighted.

My sister and I squirm, but we love it really.

The owner shows us to a table (I don't know his name – I only know that the owner of the Mandarin, five doors down, is called Michael, and that we don't go there anymore because he likes us too much, and is always trying to give us free things, which is embarrassing), but my sister and I hang back, certain that my mother will reject the table on the grounds of position, draughts, light, any number of mysterious evils. And, indeed, as we move towards our corner she scans the room like a presidential security agent, assessing the other available tables for value as if noting potential hiding places for a sniper or bugging device. But, to our relief, she does not seem on this occasion to think that they have any special invisible qualities that our intended one does not have – some magical property that the establishment knows about and is trying to keep us from enjoying – and appears satisfied.

We're certain that people are staring at us. They think we are scoping the place, have taken a dislike and are about to leave. They can hardly know that my parents come here at least once a month, and that this happens every time. Even when there's only two of them.

Eventually, we sit. It's such a relief. (It must be as much of a relief for the people I eat meals with now, as I go through the same process myself, every time I walk into a restaurant, re-experiencing every time the same suspicion that I am somehow being diddled out of a better spot just round the corner, determined to get the very most I can out of the couple of hours I will spend here).

My mother reaches into her handbag, rummages, then looks up.

'Did you bring the fags?' she says.

'I brought *my* fags,' says my dad.

There is some chunter about the ownership of the fags: My dad picked them up from the hall table. Ah, now, those were my *mum's* fags. My dad's fags were on the bedside table. No, those were my dad's *bedroom* fags. His actual fags were on the hall table, which is why he brought them. And so what were the fags my mum saw in the driver's side pocket of the Mercedes when she got in the car? Those were his *car* fags, they stay in the car for emergencies (such as traffic jams so bad that he has smoked the entire pack of office fags he had put in his jacket for the journey). He would give my mum as many fags as she wanted, of course, but she should remember to bring her own next time.

My sister and I listen, mystified. On the top shelf of the far cupboard in their bedroom are always four cartons, at least, of ten packs each. Eight hundred fags. They are communal, marital fags, but only up until the moment when one member of the marriage extracts a packet, at which point they become personal fags, and are fiercely protected. In not very many years, maybe five, maybe six, they will be the first fags I smoke myself, and a couple of years after that, my sister's first fags too.

(We know where they are because when our father is lying on the floor of the telly room, getting every answer correct on *Mastermind* or *University Challenge*, and he upends a packet and finds it empty and cries, 'Fags!', we race to be the first upstairs and back again with a full packet – he lets us tear off the cellophane and pull the gold paper plug from the box.)

Here in the restaurant he pulls a pack of Nelson from his pocket. The old admiral's face is as sour and one-eyed as ever. The IRA will bomb the factory in a year or two – the first and only time our family is personally affected by the Troubles – and my parents will go over briefly to Piccadilly, with its wide, flat, double-bed box, before settling at last upon Silk Cut, the brand that he will smoke till the end, and which my mother is almost certainly smoking as she reads this paragraph.

He pulls one cigarette out halfway, and offers it to her. Then flips his brass zippo with a big manly gesture as if breaking a sawn-off shotgun, thumbs it twice and on the third gets a flame to light her up.

His own cigarette he taps three times on the flat of the yellow lighter, rather aggressively, to settle the tobacco – a gesture left over from the days before 'cork tips' – throws it into his mouth like a cocky sailor to thrill his children (a sleight of hand on his part, the cigarette only leaves his fingers as it enters his lips), and lights it.

The owner arrives and offers an aperitif. My parents never, ever have an aperitif. My father always says, 'I think we'd rather go straight to a bottle, wouldn't we?' and everyone always would. Normally, then, he peruses the wine list very quickly and orders something he knows already and can pronounce without fault – never the cheapest, but never too flashy. Except in Chinese restaurants, and especially at the Rendezvous, where he always says,

'We'll have a bottle of Wan Fu.'

He pronounces it with a sort of Kung Fu accent, quickly, the 'n' almost silent, the 'Fu' a noise like a tennis racket swishing through air. He wishes deeply that he could speak Chinese, and every other language on earth, so as never to be at a linguistic disadvantage anywhere, to anybody. But he can't, so he makes up for it with strong pronunciation of the words he does know.

His only actual sentence is 'N'gai, mai dan!', which means 'my bill, please', but is not much use because he can only say it at the end of the meal, by which time the establishment will have sussed that he isn't Chinese. (It is also Mandarin, he says, so these Cantonese probably wouldn't understand it – the implication being that there is a kind of Chinese that he speaks better than they do).

Then we set to reading the menus, just for fun, because we always have the same things. And when the guy comes back with the wine bottle with its red writing on a white label with a picture of a pagoda and the words 'Wan Fu' on it (which mean, I think, 'white wine' or possibly 'French wine' – I'm not sure, and you certainly won't find it in a Chinese restaurant in Britain today, for I have asked in every single one of the hundreds I have reviewed, and never been met with anything but that special blank stare which is still China's major export), he sets to ordering:

'We'll have two seaweed, two grilled dumpling, two spring roll . . .'

My father orders two of everything to avoid arguments about who is entitled to what, and also to give him the opportunity to concatenate a multiple integer with a singular noun, which strikes him as sounding more Chinese. When he cannot speak the language in a restaurant (which is every restaurant apart from French, and obviously British, except there weren't any British restaurants in 1979), he reckons that to make the same solecisms in English as his host is tantamount to meeting him halfway.

In Italian restaurants he orders, 'Spa-GE-ttti al booooro, per my dorrrrterr Beektorrria, and a for a mia the bolo-nyay-zeh!' He doesn't know he's doing it, and the waiter doesn't notice, but my sister and I chew napkins with embarrassment. (*NB: I would give anything, anything, to be sitting there at the*

Villa Bianca in Hampstead with him now, hearing him do it one last time.)

'. . . and two sesame prawn toast.'

'And crab and sweetcorn soup!' I shout.

'And chicken and sweetcorn soup,' shouts my sister. Who doesn't like the idea of crabs, but doesn't want to not have something that I am having.

'And after that we'll have moo shee pork for four,' says my dad. Oh, you should hear him say 'moo shee'. He makes it sound so Chinese. He makes those two words sound like Confucius explaining an ancient truth to a roomful of disciples.

'MOOO-ooShhhEEE . . . pok!'

We just think he's mispronouncing 'mushy pork' and wonder why. Truth is, he prefers Peking duck, which also comes with pancakes and at our family Chinese meals was the other massive course one always had between a hill of starters and a mountain of mains, but he can't make such a big cultural bridge between himself and the mysterious land of bamboo and pandas by just saying, 'Peking duck'.

It's funny. In Chinese restaurants in the 1970s there were very few Chinese words on the menu. It was anglicised Cantonese dishes all the way, described in language intended to make the food sound as bland and accessible as the stuff one ate at home – lemon chicken, chilli beef, pork dumpling, egg fried rice – so my dad didn't get as much of a chance to roll his tongue round the language as he would have liked. But as tastes became more refined – as recently as the last ten years – and there was an explosion first of dim sum restaurants and then places devoted to regional Chinese cuisine (regional! As if China were a huge place made up of all sorts of different people, eating all sorts of different things!), far more Chinese words started to appear, and I find myself now demanding, without looking at a menu, *'har gao, cheung fun, gailan, char siu pao . . .'*, motivated by exactly the same impulses as my father: to impress upon the staff how cosmopolitan, adventurous, cultured and confident I am. Not like the rest of these big-nose whiteys who wouldn't know a shark's fin if it rose out of the bath water and snaffled their goolies.

And now I'm sad. The last meal I had in a restaurant with my father was Chinese. Just me and him at The Royal China Club on Baker Street, the very best of its kind back in 2007 (I have other favourites now). I had taken him to Harley Street for his chemo, or blood tests, or something, I forget. It always made him incredibly miserable, and I thought to cheer him up with the prospect of Chinese food, as he used to do for us.

The restaurant was only 400 yards or so from the medical centre, the sun was out, I thought we might walk. He didn't put up much protest, but after a couple of minutes I noticed he wasn't beside me, and turned to see him leaning against a wall, not looking too bad, but saying that he just needed to get his breath back. I've worried ever since that I was dragging him into a meal he didn't want, and a sort of emergency block-walking exercise regime that couldn't have been more pointless.

And then in the restaurant I think I probably ordered all show-offily, using the Cantonese names (only to impress him, of course, the staff couldn't have cared less), demanding all sorts of crazy things he should taste (thinking that now, right at the end, was a good time to get him to try new things) and I have a feeling I ordered a spicy tripe dish, the smell of which alone turned him green.

Thing was, after a life of gourmandising, he wasn't interested in food anymore. He complained of foul tastes in his mouth, and made 'bleurgh!' faces at most things. But I think I was convinced that if he would only eat better stuff, and more adventurously, that he might, somehow, I don't know, die a bit less.

So I ordered steamed lobster balls on chilli flakes and shanghai dumplings in shark fin soup with a fleck of gold leaf on top, big piles of healthy choi sum in garlic, steamed turbot, rare wagyu beef dressed with soy, turnip fritters . . . and my ill father, who'd been on a drip all morning, weighed nine stone but still had a silk hanky in the top pocket of his tweed jacket, said, 'it looks delicious, Jig' and we had a glass of Meursault or something, and he ate . . . hardly anything.

You see, he wasn't interested remotely in all this terribly authentic posh stuff from organic ingredients, prepared in the ancient way, with refinements born of the new Hong Kong cuisine of the early 21st century. I think he just wanted to be back at the Gourmet Rendezvous, with spring rolls and prawn toast and a bottle of Wan Fu on their way, only 40, the newly appointed Editor of *Punch*, and not dying of cancer.

So back we go.

And he's ordering, 'Sweet and sour pork, beef in oyster sauce, Kung Po prawn, chicken and cashew nut, and can you do two portions of plain chow mein noodles (pronounced *noodoo*) and beansprouts?'

Course they can, they always do.

'And toffee apples!'

'And toffee bananas!'

The guy gathers up the menus. I wish I could remember his name. He had big spectacles, slightly tinted. White shirt, black trousers, biggish teeth. Quite lively hair for a Chinese man. In my mind I confuse him with the father of my best friend at the time, Alex Goulden. But Mr Goulden (Roger, I think he was called) was a dentist. There's no way he was moonlighting at a Chinese restaurant on Finchley Road. He was Jewish. He drove a Porsche.

While we wait, they bring two meshed warming stands with tea-candles inside (we had a couple at home, for takeaways, but they tended to burn through the aluminium boxes) and my sister and I pass the time hovering our hands over the flames and seeing who can last longest (I always win – by cunningly holding my hand not quite over the flame).

My parents stub their fags in the bamboo ashtray and light a couple more (they're not making it up in *Mad Men*, you know – when people smoked back then, they really smoked). The rain is still falling outside. You can hear buses going past, but you can't see them because of the net curtain over the window. Inside, the light is yellow and warm. The room is a perfect square. Maybe 14 tables, 40 people altogether. Light brown walls, possibly cork, possibly bamboo (don't imagine that it is time alone which makes me forget – even reviewing restaurants now, writing them up the day after, or that very afternoon, I get the physical details wrong – I aim for my descriptions to be true rather than necessarily correct). There might be a handful of red paper lanterns, there might not.

My sister and I nurse tall glasses of Coca Cola. We don't get it at home. At home it is always Shloer (delicious but suspiciously appley) or own-brand fizzy apple juice from Sainsbury's, or Waitrose (newly-opened in the basement of the John Barnes department store not 100 yards from where we sit), or Corona cherryade or limeade from the milkman. Corona is great – our very lifeblood – but actual Coke is like being on holiday.

The seaweed comes, and we fall on it. My dad stubs his fag, my mum also, but reluctantly, laying a penny over the tip so that it goes out nicely and can be relit in a minute.

There is the smell of very hot copper and tar. So familiar then. Not smelt now in years (the smoking ban in restaurants became law in the very week of my father's cancer diagnosis – like a sick joke, like a cosmic stable door swinging closed as the cells of his body galloped away to their terminal mutations).

We're crap with chopsticks, and the seaweed goes

everywhere. We shovel it in using sticks held together to make a single two-pronged fork, and most of it falls through the gap between them. It's bright green and sugary and crunchy like sweeties, with a little bit of salt to make you feel grown up. Our dad says that it isn't really seaweed at all, but shredded cabbage. We both go, 'Eueueueurghhh!' but carry on eating just the same. I've no idea why cabbage should have been seen as intrinsically more revolting than seaweed.

The sesame prawn toast is golden and fat: lovely fried bread with magical pink flesh and a dusting of meaty seeds. How it's made and where it comes from is a mystery. The spring rolls are hot, hot, hot (always burn the roof of your mouth and make it all smooth and weird) with exotic vegetables in them and what my dad says is bamboo (yeah, chin rub, Jimmy Hill, like you can EAT bamboo!) and weeny prawns, and you get to dip them in fluorescent jam that must be made of the same stuff as Kia-Ora. Like all the best foods, it glows in the dark.

The dumplings are a bit grown up, we dodge them. We roll our pancakes and grip them tight so they don't fall to bits. We slurp our cola. We watch our dad with his chopsticks eating every single last morsel from every plate, even though there is too much food for eight people, let alone four, and by the end he's even prising up noodles that have fallen and dried and welded themselves to the tablecloth and popping them into his mouth and sloshing them down with the third bottle of Wan Fu.

And there's noise from all the other people eating, and all sorts of neighbours of ours come and go, and you can't see for the smoke from fags and pans and the steam from pots, and then they bring toffee apples and bananas in roiling caramel and a big glass bowl of iced water and the guy plucks the chunks of fruit from the boiling sugar with special long, metal chopsticks and plunges them into the water so that they set hard, and the straggles of dripping toffee set suddenly, as if frozen in time, and when he puts it on your plate there's a long strand of toffee hair, with a flat underside from sitting momentarily on the meniscus of the water bowl, and it snaps in your mouth like the best thing ever, and you just wish it would never end, and that mealtimes could always be like this.

But they aren't. In fact, they hardly ever are. Meals at home are just eating. Top 1970s grub, no doubt. But just food.

If my mother cooked then it was lamb in plum sauce, beef stroganoff, stuffed pimentos in tomato sauce, pork chops with tarragon and cream, rice and peas (our favourite), cholent with pickled cucumbers, chocolate rum cake (made with sponge fingers which were the closest thing to sweeties you'd find in our larder but if you ate one raw from the packet, by God, there'd be trouble), apple strudel, cherry strudel . . . or if it was the nanny it was hamburgers, or spaghetti with Buitoni Bolognese, or fish fingers and peas or shepherd's pie, and then butterscotch Angel Delight with hundreds and thousands, and it was all fine.

But it was usually just us at table during the week, just me and my sister. In our big suburban house in a silent street in the middle of nowhere. There wasn't the bustle and fun of chopsticks and waiters and boiling toffee and funny-looking diners at other tables to laugh at and give silly names to.

I mean, there were curly-wurly straws and a fluffy ginger cat and the Snoopy jug full of squash and the two Snoopy glasses, and always the hope that my dad would be back early from work, leaping around the kitchen and pulling faces and dropping all sort of bonkers presents on us that had come in to the *Punch* office as press freebies – on a good day an Asterix book or a batting glove signed by Clive Lloyd (that was a *very* good day), on a bad day a Dutch children's magazine or a jazz record.

But mostly it was just us and the nanny. And the rules. So many rules:

No elbows on the table.

No talking with your mouth full.

No eating with your mouth open.

No drinks with soup (why?)

No tearing, only cutting.

No mixing two types of cereal (again, why? All I wanted in the world when I was eight years old, the only thing I truly desired, was a bowl of Coco Krispies with a spoonful of Ready Brek sprinkled over it. But I wasn't allowed. And nobody would tell me why. It was like some weird, distant relative of kosher. Some terrible thing would happen if two brands of cereal were mixed. Maybe they were worried I might just have too much fun, and turn into a monkey.)

No leaving of any food, ever.

No getting down from the table without asking. And don't bother asking if you haven't finished what's on your plate. Including the thick, blooky wall of fat from the outside of the pork chop. Or you're sitting here till morning.

Eating at home was about discipline, morality and calories. Then endless tooth-brushing. Followed by tooth inspection (lined up like two little Von Trapps by the Captain's whistle) and a bath which had to be over by the time the *Six Million Dollar Man* had started or I wasn't allowed to watch it (a weird rule, since by far the best bit of the whole show was the opening credit sequence).

But in a restaurant, especially at the Gourmet Rendezvous, all bets were off. Holiday rules applied. You could have ice in your Coke, you could chuck food around a bit (just like Chinese people do!) without it being too much of a big deal, you could fidget and wriggle and play games (word games, as opposed to, say, tennis), and because the food was communal you could get away without finishing everything, although you always did finish everything.

Best of all, though, our parents were there. The whole family was together. They weren't at work or out having fun without us. We weren't stuck with only each other for company, or the nanny, or the housekeeper, in a big house in Cricklewood with wolves living down the back stairs.

Which was why the worst thing ever was if my dad strode out of the house to go to work yodelling, 'We'll all go out for Chinese tonight!' and then we didn't.

I think he always thought he meant it. He loved more than anything the thrill he could create in his children by making rash promises ('we'll get McDonald's on the way home!', 'we'll go to the zoo!', 'we'll play Monopoly!', 'we'll all move to America!') but was entirely unaware of the flipside disappointment created when there was no delivery – which was equivalent roughly to the negative of the original excitement level, squared. Or even cubed.

When he said, 'We'll all go out for Chinese tonight!' the rest of the day passed in a haze of dizzying greed and anticipation. If it was a school day, I would walk a foot taller than usual (and thus be nearly as tall as everybody else). I was untouchable. I was having Chinese later on. I was having little piggy chunks in batter deep fried and covered in sweet and sour sauce the colour of Aquaman. I was going to be using chopsticks. I was going to be drinking a Coke. Maybe two. Maybe even three if my parents lost count. When these mugs were tucked up in bed after boiled egg and soldiers ('bleurgh!') I would be in a loud, smoky room, slurping noodles while my dad talked to the man in Chinese!

And if it was the holidays, then I would spend the long, lonely, friendless day with my sister on the landing, playing Lego and saying, 'I'm going to eat twelve pieces of prawn toast!' And she would escalate immediately to, 'I'm going to eat infinity pieces of prawn toast!' And I'd up that to infinity plus one. And then she'd try wearily to explain again the concept of infinity and the impossibility of adding to it, which always blew my mind.

And then eventually, what felt like aeons later, there would be the sound of the garage door sliding shut, and his footsteps along the side of the house, the hefty turn of his key in the door, the decisive wipe, wipe, wipe of his brogues on the mat and we'd come running downstairs.

'Daddy! Daddy! When can we go? Can we go now? Can we go now?'

'Go where?' He'd say.

And we'd remember now, only now, that this was always going to happen.

'To the Gourmet Rendezvous.'

'The Gourmet Rendezvous? Ah, kids. I'm whacked. We'll go another time. Mummy's going to roast a chicken.'

'Oh,' we'd say.

'Come on, what's the matter? You love roast chicken. We can have Chinese any time. But it's raining outside. You don't want to go out.' (*We do, we do, we want to get wet when you chase Mummy with the umbrella, we want to watch the rain on the window, and hear the buses splashing through it while we burn our mouth on the first spring roll*).

'But you said!'

'Come on. Enough now. Restaurants are for people who don't have lovely roast chicken at home. Now, who wants to run upstairs and get me a packet of ciggies?'

And off we'd go, slower than usual, to get them.

My poor dad. He couldn't possibly know that the disappointment he'd engendered was massive, existential, terminal. And we could not express it without appearing to be ungrateful for the chicken. It's not that there was anything wrong with roast chicken. It was very nice. On any normal day you'd look forward to it. But not when you'd been promised Chinese. Not when you'd been offered a carnival. This being the 1970s, the age of convenience, my mother quite often cooked the chicken in a new-fangled polythene 'roaster bag' to keep the oven from getting dirty, and I always thought, 'But if we go for Chinese, then there'll be no mess in the kitchen at all!'

But it wasn't the thing to say. So we'd sit down, grumpily, for the chicken. And we'd eat it. With our mouths closed. With a glass of quite weak orange squash. And then butterscotch Angel Delight with hundreds and thousands. And then tooth-brushing. And tooth-brushing inspection. And then bed.

CHINESE

Nowadays, of course, I can have Chinese whenever I want. Except I don't. Because then I wouldn't eat anything else at all. When Chinese food, in a recent survey, finally overtook Indian as the most popular takeaway in Britain, the common taste fell almost into line with my own, although falling just a little short.

Because I would go further than saying I prefer Chinese food to Indian and insist that I prefer Chinese food to every kind of food. Indeed, I prefer it to pretty much every kind of thing. I much prefer Chinese food to the ballet, for example, or to trousers. I also prefer Chinese food to football, cars, quilted toilet roll and Italy.

Chinese food is pretty much the best thing in the world. And there is no point eating anything else unless you absolutely have to for your job. If I were not a restaurant critic I would eat only Chinese food. And if ever I am eating out for purely social reasons, I am always a little sad if I am compelled to eat anything else.

Only the other day I was meeting a friend who lives in Bayswater for a spot of supper, and for the couple of hours before I set off from North London we exchanged emails about where we might go – the new Russian-backed sushi joint (likely to be overpriced but great for picking up prostitutes), the Venezuelan tapas joint, the new New British place (for a boiled pork chop and lots of Farrow and Ball 'railings') – and even as I drove over there I was sending and receiving texts every five minutes about possible changes of venue: maybe that weird German place with the Jagermaister and the accordion and the young neo-Nazis? Or what about just a burger?

And although a full ten minutes went by when we were certain we were going to go to a perfectly serviceable Lebanese on Westbourne Grove, my joy was unconfined when the phone went bleep again and I read, 'Fuck it, let's have Chinese.'

I punched the air. I always punch the air when I'm going to have Chinese (even if I'm simultaneously driving and texting at the time – it's a good job I have three hands). Oh, the zip and ping and yabber of it. The puffs of steam, the golden crackle of fried pastry, the yelp of strong pork with a little ginger, the sour tickle of pink vinegar on a plump prawn dumpling, the slobber of greens, the shrill, demented cry of hoi sin sauce on cucumber and fatty duck. And to know that your friend craves it too, craves Chinese and only Chinese, means that you are as one, and there need be no talk when you rendezvous, only eating.

We went to one or other of the fine establishments on Queensway that are rammed with scrawny Cantonese students stripping roasted ducks with the efficiency of cats, and extended families of blubbery Persian tweenagers poking gold-plated Nintendo DSs with pudgy fingers, and ate like gods.

But that was downtime. It's not so often that a new Chinese worth the name comes around for review and when it does, I'm just cock-a-hoop.

As a kid, I was a sucker for Chinatown, and it still feels properly exotic to me even now. Not Chinese exotic, of course. More American. New York, Los Angeles, Chicago. At dusk, in winter, with the neon signs twinkling, steam pumping from the vents, the restaurants lighting up and 100-year-old busboys squatting to smoke fags in the gutter, it feels like the beginning of a really good noirish thriller. Or *Gremlins*.

In daylight I love the colourfulness of the restaurant façades ('taste' simply doesn't factor here). I love the pagoda thing, the cartoon-portentous gates at the end of Gerrard Street, the lanterns everywhere, the fact that it seems always to be Chinese New Year. (Is there a day in the Chinese calendar which is *not* traditionally celebrated by 18 people having a fit inside an air-conditioning duct painted to look like a dragon?)

I love that it's always rammed with Chinese tourists. Do Chinese people simply travel the world visiting Chinatowns, like some kooky game of international stepping stones? ('And here we are in Munich – you can tell because the dragon's wearing lederhosen . . .')

But I don't eat there anymore. By all the gods, no. Compared to the much-improved modern London restaurant norm, most Chinatown restaurants are so unwelcoming. They don't even look like restaurants do now. They are brightly lit, foggy, not hugely clean, have no interest in producing quality and are very aware of catering principally to tourists.

In recent years, they've even started doing that awful tourist resort thing of standing outside and telling you to go in (they do it in Brick Lane, too), reckoning that enough white people are so scared of different-skinned foreigners that they'll do what-ever they're told. It's one of the great paradoxes of world catering that the keener a restaurant is to get you to go in, the more horrid they will be to you once you're sitting down.

It wasn't always so. Until the middle Nineties eating out in Britain was often such a grim, unfriendly and poisonous business that Chinatown seemed quite nice by comparison. Twenty-odd years ago, when I lived nearby, I used to eat there three or four times a week. But I was a kid then, with an iron stomach, and only wanted to eat the set meal ('gweilo-fleecing autocrud', as they call it in the trade) of crabmeat and sweetcorn soup, deep-fried poo-farmed shellfish mashed into various shapes, random aerial vermin and pancakes, chicken in black bean, beef in oyster, egg fried rice, toffee apples and a bottle of Bulgarian Sauvignon.

You could get the lot for £9, but I'd go up to £11 for table-cloths, unsplintered chopsticks and a spitoon. Those places are still there, I'm sure, and just the same as when I liked them, but the national standard has left them behind and nobody with any sense uses such establishments anymore (unless specifically looking to recapture the innocence of childhood and the strange wonder of those 1970s nights).

Instead, one goes to any of the growing number of new 'regional' Chinese restaurants that have sprung up all over the capital in the last four or five years, everywhere from Bayswater, Fulham and Shoreditch, to Stoke Newington, Epping and Lavender Hill, without much caring for the historic Soho centre of things Chinese. For it is the great refrain of the well-travelled modern gastro-poseur, that London Chinese restaurants have come of age and the full glory of China's many regions is at last represented on our menus.

But to say, as people do, on the basis of a handful of restau-rants, that the Chinese food available in Britain is diversifying in any significant way, and the traditional old Anglo-Cantonese prawn toast and Peking roadkill joints are being seriously chal-lenged by the rougher-edged, spicier, more authentic regional cuisines of Shanghai, Sichuan, Hunan, Moon Lan Ding and Ding Dang Dong, really isn't true.

First of all, there are simply hundreds of local Chinese cuisines, possibly thousands. If you consider that we are all prepared to acknowledge such a thing as, say, Niçoise cuisine, which comes from a town with a current population of around 350,000, then there is no reason why there should not be – working on a population ratio – at least three thousand fully individuated Chinese provincial cooking styles. So to suggest that the recent appearance of four or five regional dining options represents anything more than the polishing of an ancient turd is ridiculous.

Secondly, it's only happening in London. It's about twelve restaurants. It is nothing. It is a blip. It is an insignificant pustule no more visible from space than the Great Wall of China (which turns out not to be, after all). It is a thing just significant enough to allow a small handful of restaurant critics to frot themselves silly with exotic details culled from Wrongopedia and show off about how they love eating eyeballs and bollocks.

So when a place opened last year that professed to be the first serious arrival in Britain of Dongbei cuisine, I had no option but to pretend that I had travelled there extensively and was the man best placed to decide how this manifestation of its cooking measures up (and as it had arrived in, of all places, Chinatown, there was a chance that I would also be able to herald Chinatown as the new Chinatown).

Ah yes, Dongbei, in the far north-east, hard by Southern Russia and North Korea, where I spent so much of my distant youth. The old rust belt, the industrial heartland, the cold winters, the climate that allows for no rice growing and thus a wheatier cuisine of bread and pasta . . .

Yawn, stretch, but we know all that. The truth is that Manchurian Legends (as the place was called) was the standard-issue, fiercely lit, multi-storey Chinatown café where they can't find your reservation in the book, drag you up to the empty top floor and sit you at the laughably awful table by the roaring extractor fan, then seat your guests, when they arrive, on a different floor altogether and don't tell you, and you waste half an hour waiting for each other. Then they bring you one brightly coloured plastic menu crusted with food and God knows what other effluvia (the pages are wipe-clean, but nobody has), and three stapled photocopies. Then, soon as you've ordered, they bring everything at once, really, everything, so that your table disappears under a deluge of different dishes which all look basically the same, and then disappear. Literally, disappear. The only waitress went and hid behind a screen in the otherwise empty room so that one had to get up and go and shout down a corridor if one wanted so much as a beer or a spoon.

In short: Chinatown as I have known and loved it these 30-odd years.

The cooking was good in parts. Although the butchery that comes before the cooking was hellish. As if they had used not a knife but a sledge hammer. Duck and chicken dishes came with the chopped meat all fiendishly still attached to small shards and sometimes great splintered spades of bone. It reminded me most of all of Jamaican butchery, which involves putting a live goat through one of those machines tree surgeons use for shredding whole branches to mulch. The lazy, unskilled butchery of impoverished cultures uninterested in beauty.

We started with some jellyfish, as I always do. It is the edamame of the sea: not filling, great texture, good mainframe for spice, good with beer, perfect appetiser. Here it was set off with plentiful chilli and fresh coriander, and relatively safe in the kitchen for having no bones.

Then came a mixed grill that involved in large part the bones one normally throws away after they've finished flavouring the stock, but covered with dry, choking spice and served for money. Albeit, not very much money. A bare and meatless breastbone covered with chilli is only a pound, or maybe a pound 50 – obviously, you can't tell from the bill because this is Chinatown so they don't itemise it except (maybe) in Chinese (and I didn't take a menu because they were in short enough supply as it was).

In amongst the red, dry and fiery carnage was a redeeming skewer of delicious chicken hearts, though, which pleased me enormously.

Sweating heavily from the spice already, I ploughed into bang

bang king prawns served in their own weight of rough-chopped red and green chillis, fiery green beans with minced pork and more shovelfuls from the tip of the European chilli mountain, a much milder dish of braised pork belly (the deep fat full of good barnyard stinkiness) on glass noodles and a sauce of staggering brownness, and a wonderful, wonderful plate of small chicken schnitzels lightly battered in a pale agrodolce sauce (I use the poncy Italian word because 'sweet and sour' would send your imagination down the wrong track).

Actually, thinking on it, the sea-spiced three vegetables was well done too, the aubergine smooth and sweet like set custard, and both the stir-fried baby chicken and the duck with lotus root would have been good too, if it weren't for the horrendous ossuary they had given the name of meat.

The dumplings were evil though. Where a rice dumpling can be a thing of lightness and beauty, these doughy sacks of wheat were like chewing on the Michelin man's scrotum, and we resorted to sawing into the skins for meat and surviving on that alone, discarding the inch-thick husks.

I dunno. The waitress was charming enough when she did show up. It's not their fault they don't like white people. We can be awful. I'd stick us up in the roof and not tell us when our friends had arrived too, and feed us a lot of old bones.

So forget Chinatown. Again. The big Chinese opening of 2011 was meant to be the Grand Imperial Chinese restaurant at the Thistle Grosvenor Hotel in Victoria. Or the Grosvenor Imperial Thistle at the Grand Chinese Hotel. Or something. So many names of such great portent, it is hard to separate them. I should have known from that alone just what a miserable afternoon I would have there. But I live in constant hope of good new Chineses opening, and this one looked at least worth a try.

It started off miserably, the depressing hotel in which the

restaurant is housed being itself covered in cardboard while some sort of miserable works were carried out, so that you surface from the miserable Tube station onto the miserable pavement, and walk round and round the builders' hoardings until you find the hidden door, rammed and jostled at every step by lemur-eyed tourists wheeling giant plastic caravans full of brightly coloured outerwear, who have been locked in an endless holding pattern since disembarkation from the Gatwick Express, waiting for some scrawny, chain-smoking hotel-hawker to lure them to his 12-star terraced flophouse behind Paddington and boil them down for soap.

Once you are inside, the hotel lobby sort of bleeds into the restaurant through an empty bar, where the head waitress asks, 'Can I help you?' in a tone that makes it clear the question is meant as a threat.

The room is vast and painted partly gold. Gold alcoves house giant vases, there are vast grey marble columns reaching into a ceiling so high the great chandeliers appear like distant constellations. The lovely tablecloths are inlaid with gold. It's getting to be like Enobarbus's description of the barge of Cleopatra . . . until the head waitress comes back with a senior waiter in tow, and the horror show begins. Slamming down big, shiny menus, they pull stiff napkins out of porcelain rings and wedge them down into our laps with all the decorousness of James Herriot intruding into the posterior privacy of an unwell heifer.

The woman asks for our drinks order, and I say 'tea'. She says nothing, just goes and gets it. But they have at least ten different teas on the menu here. Why does she not ask what kind I would like? Or even, heavens to Murgatroyd, suggest one that she thinks I might like? I know this is a new and expensive Chinese restaurant and one should not expect actual human warmth, but is a little civil interaction too much to ask? It is a dull autumn Wednesday, the room is empty but for a lonely Dutchman drinking beer with ice in it, and two Japanese ladies who think it's a shop. You haven't got time even to acknowledge we're alive?

Apparently not. As she pours our tea she is barking loud Chinese right in our faces, presumably meant for the ears of the man behind her. Although, as it is spat right in my face, I briefly wonder if she is in fact insulting me directly in heavily accented English that I cannot follow.

She brings the express dim sum menu, which names 12 dishes and allows us five to share at £20 for the pair of us. It's good value, but I want to try a wider range of dishes and ask if that is possible. She says not. Only five. When I express my disbelief for the third time she breaks down and admits that there is also an à la carte dim sum menu, and goes to get it with a great huffing and puffing. Clearly the 'express menu' is 'express' not because they fear we might be on a tight schedule ourselves, but because they want us to, 'Eat up big nose and get the HELL out of my restaurant!'

As I order my dishes, the waitress says nothing, and in pauses where I am mulling the options she taps her foot. Actually taps it. For she has much better things to do, and I am wheat-eating European scum.

When the food comes up from the kitchen, the two high-ranking Chinese government assassins (possibly) do not even deign to bring it to us, but leave that filthy business to the busboy. His job, traditionally, is to bring the food to them, so that they can bring it to us. But as he stands holding the tray, waiting for them to take it, I see them nodding him on towards us (as they mutter and kvetch in the corner), telling him to chuck it at us himself. The restaurant is more or less empty, but we are filthy, dairy-smelling gweilos, and we can go and hang ourselves.

Busboy puts a plateful down. Now, we have ordered eight things, some unfamiliar. I want to know what they are. So I ask him. He says 'dumplings'. I know that, I tell him. But what is inside them? He says pork. But I doubt that. They are not pork-shaped. They are finned. They will have lobster in them. I let him go. He mutters to the Oriental Rosa Klebb who comes by a minute later and says 'lobster inside'.

It's such a shame they have to be like this. Why can't they be nice? Why is friendly service so rare in a centrally located Chinese restaurant? It can be lovely in the suburbs. I'm sure in your local they are all over you with the free fortune cookies and weird purple after-dinner liqueurs, so why not here?

The food was good: light, fluffy *char siu pao* (those little white rice puffs of barbecued pork); *har gao* (prawn dumplings), beautifully translucent and containing not chopped but whole shrimp; a peppery foie gras and beef dumpling with just enough fat from the liver to mellow the tightness of the beef; and soup dumplings, *xia long pao*, that were perfectly made and weighted.

The lobster dumpling was plain and exquisite, as were the scallop *cheung fun* (rice-flour cannelloni) which were light and translucent again, and with scallop that was barely cooked, retaining all its sweetness and zip.

For pudding they do chocolate dim sum. That was really why I'd come. I had heard about it on Twitter and Esther was really quite excited. So I ordered the mixed chocolate platter and the coconut doughnuts. With evident glee, the waitress told us that would take at least 20 minutes.

Now, in a restaurant where they give a flying lee ho fook about their customers they would have told us about this delay at an apposite moment earlier on, perhaps when we were order-ing. Or at the very least have written it on the menu. But, no. What they want you to do here is to not have the chocolate dim sum, and to just naff off. So we did. Which was a shame. But we'd sat there in their giant golden room being treated like crap for the better part of 40 minutes, and that was enough.

How to Tell a Good Chinese Restaurant

YOU CAN TELL a good Chinese restaurant, quite simply, by looking through the window and seeing how many Jews are eating in there. It's much more useful than checking if it's full of Chinese because, to be honest, the Chinese are not always so fussy as is sometimes supposed. And also because one out of every five inhabitants of this planet is Chinese, so it's a statistical banker that 20 per cent of the clientele of any restaurant, of any kind, will be of that persuasion, regardless of its quality.

Furthermore, most Chinese restaurants are in China, where a place being full of Chinese is really not going to tell you much at all. Although, I grant you, looking for large numbers of Jews in a restaurant in China is going to be a joyless task, since China is a very long way away from anywhere that Jews live in any quantity, so any Jews that do happen to be in town will have recently flown in and be suffering from jetlag something terrible. And you want they should go out in this humidity? Nobody told them about the humidity. Just a little soup on room service, thank you, and tomorrow we'll maybe see some restaurants.

But in London, Leeds, Manchester and above all New York, it is a reasonable system. Indeed, it is often said that the three great dishes of Jewish cuisine are chicken soup, salt beef and Peking duck.

There are all sorts of reasons why this might be. First of all, there are some similarities in the cooking: the Chinese, like the Jews, do not use dairy in their cooking, and both cuisines share a dependency on chicken and noodle dishes flavoured with onions, garlic and celery (I'm thinking of the overcooked, mildly flavoured food of Canton, rather than the richer, spicier cooking of Shanghai or Sichuan).

Best of all, the bone-dry, disembodied blandness of crispy aromatic duck is very much the way many Jews have experienced roast chicken all their lives, at the hands of mothers terrified that anything less than three hours in a very hot

oven
will not kill the
bacteria.

It is true that pork, prawns,
lobster and other trayf (non-kosher
ingredients) do feature heavily in Chinese
food, but they are very often mashed up, mixed
with other things and covered in sauce. So they don't
count. There is an oft-cited verse in the Torah which
explains that unclean animals are forbidden, 'except in
situations of life and death or when, with all the additives and
food colouring, you swear to God you thought it was chicken'.

Theorists on this matter (and they do exist, see 'New York Jews
and Chinese Food: The Social Construction of an Ethnic Pattern' by
Gaye Tuchman and Harry G. Levine in *Contemporary Ethnography,*
1992: Vol. 22, No. 3) also point to the relatively low status of Chinese
immigrants in early 20th-century America, which allowed Jews to feel
more comfortable in their restaurants than in those of the Italians or, for
obvious reasons, the Germans or the Poles.

NB. Many Jews, perhaps on account of the whole 'chosen people'
thing, and a general unwillingness to confer credit on other nations,
believe Chinese food to be merely an offshoot of Yiddish cuisine. A
plump Jewish gastronome of my acquaintance, by the name of Maurice,
frequently phones, wanting to take me to a new   Chinese restaurant
he has found, 'which does terrific kreplach.'

Kreplach, in the Old Country, meant dumplings filled with chopped
meat and served in chicken soup, but these days it is more often
Yiddish for dim sum. Except in the sentence 'you should try the hot
and sour soup with kreplach', when it means 'won ton'.

Only the other day, as it happens, Maurice phoned with
just such a recommendation, and added, 'They do a good
kneidl also. The one with the barbecued pork inside.'

It is lucky for you that I am one of the world's very
few trilingual English-Yiddish-Cantonese speakers
and am able to tell you that he was talking
about the char siu pao, or you
wouldn't have a clue what
was going on.

DIM SUM

One of the many things that makes Chinese the perfect food for me is my lack of patience. And the Chinese are the least patient people in the world. If you've ever been trampled to the ground at Kowloon harbour by hordes of tiny executives scrambling for the Hong Kong ferry, then you'll know what I mean. To the casual Western stroller, fortuitously positioned at the front of the queue and looking forward to a seat in the bow with a good view of the bay, it comes as a bit of a surprise when the barrier goes up and they suddenly surge past, around and over you. They'll knock you to the ground without a thought in their hurry to get to work, and then it's like being unseated at the Canal Turn at Aintree, as they race over your body, weeny feet stomping on your ears as they sprint for the line.

But that's the Cantonese. It's why they invented the dim sum trolley: so you can walk into a restaurant and be eating within less than a minute (if the pudding trolley comes first then you start with pudding), and out again in five.

It's an experience you can replicate in London at a number of places, such as Chuen Cheng Ku in Wardour Street, where I began my dim sum life in the 1980s with my Chinese friend, Wong.

CCK is a proper trolley joint. No menus, no ordering, no waiting, no daft little ponce telling you the specials of the day.

You just sit down and within seconds something edible is coming past on wheels.

It was Saturday and Sunday mornings only back then. And you wanted to be in by 11 a.m. to be sure of a decent seat and no waiting. And it was quite important to get the right table. You didn't want to be funnelled off to one of the side rooms for white people or, heaven forfend, sent upstairs. No, it had to be the main dining room, and then as close to the door of the kitchen as possible to catch the trolleys as they first emerged. By the time they have been round the room even once, some of the finer dumplings will be starting to deteriorate, and the choicest morsels will be gone. There is a section at the back that looks rather nice but has two steps leading up to it which flummoxes a dim sum trolley as disastrously as it does a dalek, and you will get no attention at all up there. Likewise, avoid corners, counters, large tables of boisterous people. Eating in a dim sum trolley joint is all about position and vision, a complete view of the terrain, no surprises from behind, unobstructed sightlines, similar to being a sniper.

For years I didn't know the names or ingredients of anything I was putting in my mouth. There were just guys with steamed dumplings, guys with steamed long dumplingy things that weren't dumplings, guys with little saucers of curried and spiced braised things that looked like squid and snails and whelks and the feet of flying and floating things, and huge parcels made out of leaves, girls with fried stuff, girls with roasted animals, girls making soup on little weeny wheely kitchens, and girls making porridge on similar things, and girls selling turnip cakes and girls selling puddings and we just ate and ate and ate.

And then gradually the names found their way into my brain: *har gao, siu mai, congee, cheung fun, char siu bao* . . . which is just how language works for a baby. The words for things come along when you need them, and only then.

Able now to order what I wanted in Chinese, I was ready for the dim sum boom that began at Royal China in Bayswater and stretched through Hakkasan and Yauatcha to the myriad top-notch dim-summeries we have today.

It happened around the cusp of 1999/2000 and led me to wonder if people weren't getting the wrong end of the stick about the impending 'Chinese century'. There was me, thinking it was all about the world's most populous nation marrying modern technology and market economics to a communist disregard for intellectual property to create a sustainable competitive advantage that will make it the world's biggest economy and radically restructure the global business system, with a simultaneous development of the world's largest army becoming the world's scariest military force by investing the fruit of that economic surge in high-tech bargains from the Russian arsenal, and everybody else thinking it was about barbecued pork buns, sticky rice in lotus-leaf parcels and shredded yam puffs.

Suddenly, without any warning, London was in the throes of a dim sum revolution. At the very mention of a modern/traditional Chinese interior makeover and small eats sanctified by spurious ceremonial flimflam, restaurant critics, punters and restaurateurs alike were rolling over on their backs, woofing three times and paddling the air.

For some reason, people unmoved by the Chinese buying up of every spare bit of soil from Mombasa to Hawaii were going all noodly over Shanghai dumplings: 'Ooh, ooh, look, they've actually put the soup *inside* the dumpling, those wily buggers – how on earth do they do that?'

(As it happens, they do it exactly the same way my grandmother used to put the *kneidlach* inside her chicken soup, only the other way round. And I'd like to see Johnny Shanghai putting soup inside a *kneidl*, by the way. It's all very well with your rice gluten flour, my friend, but you just try pulling your fancy shapes and shenanigans with matzo-meal. And a prohibition on pork and shellfish. You know what you'd have? Chicken soup with *kneidlach* is what. My grandma would have been the dim sum queen of Stanmore.)

As long as it was silent slave-workers pushing big steel trolleys round the stadium-sized floors of Chuen Cheng Ku to an almost exclusively non-white clientele (at about £3 a dish), dim sum remained a Sunday morning diversion palatable only to those who worked out that to eat well you had to sit at one of the tables by the kitchen door and bang the trolley-girls with a stick as soon as the hinges creaked.

But then Royal China opened on Queensway and the queue began to form which is there to this day. The critics started naming it (with gleeful unstarriness) their favourite spot for weekend lunching. Further branches opened. Hakkasan came. Hakkasan won a Michelin star. Yauatcha came. And now all you have to do is renovate an old space with black lacquer and lanterns and bind up some A5 dim sum menus to dish out at lunchtime with your full carte, and everyone who is anyone will say you are the hottest ticket in town.

So I, obviously, grew tired of it all. They had taken my special thing and made it, yuk, popular. In protest I left the country. Briefly. And headed for Hong Kong, where it all began. Hong Kong, the dark heart of these 'little heart-touchers'.

And dark that heart most certainly is. Hong Kong is Hades with great catering. From a corner suite high in the Peninsula Hotel in Kowloon I looked down at the bay and at Hong Kong Island, black and glowering like the Los Angeles of Ridley Scott's *Blade Runner*. Lit with rude neon and full of greedy people breathing raw smog, it looks beautiful from the Peninsula in the way that the fires of Hell must look picturesque (even Christmassy) to the angels looking down from Heaven. I left the hotel only to eat.

But first, in order to stand the heat, into the kitchen. Yip Wing Wah, the dim sum master in residence at the Peninsula's Spring Moon restaurant, who oversees the making of 3,000 dumplings a day, offers short courses in the art, and I learned from him a few of the basics.

A high-protein flour is mixed with an ordinary flour and kneaded with almost boiling water to a much tackier consistency than, say, Italian pasta. More like Blu-Tack. Then you roll a ball the size of a large marble, whack it with the flat of a chopper, spread the chopper through 360 degrees to make a perfect flat little circle, drop a spoonful of, say, chopped prawn and coriander into it and then fold it into a beautiful scallop shell or dimpled crescent moon. (At least, you do if you are Yip Wing Wah. If you are me, you end up with a thing that looks like a stillborn vole half-eaten by its mother, and you count yourself lucky you didn't lose a finger.)

Then you fill 20 steamer baskets with the 60 dumplings you've made in ten minutes (or one basket with the three you've made in an hour) and stack it on to one of the holes in the lid of a vast drum whence steam rushes as if from some Venusian geyser. Despite the *Generation Game* comedy of my culinary ineptitude, the dumplings tasted amazing straight from the drum, with a bright squeakiness I've encountered only very rarely in restaurants, when I've had that treasured table by the kitchen door and plucked them from the trolley as soon as they entered the dining room (bad form, it turns out, in dim sum etiquette).

Dim sum is all about impulse: see it, grab it, eat it. A potentially lethal attitude to bring to a hotel kitchen. With my own dumplings swallowed, I turned to some of Wing's other specialities and hijacked dozens of the finest *char siu sau* imaginable, straight from the oven, and taro puffs of abalone, mushroom and yam paste, woven like angels' hair. In every way this was the very Platonic ideal of dim sum, no, of food itself, to which all else must aspire.

When they finally threw me out I rolled down to the quay for the thrilling ten-minute ferry ride across tanker-chopped waters (which would have been shark-infested if the scarily polluted water were not, essentially, sulphuric acid) to Hong Kong Island, and made straight for One Harbour Road at the Grand Hyatt, where a Swedish-Chinese millionairess recently converted to Judaism told me the best dim sum on the island was to be had. Always take the gastronomic advice of Jewish Swedish-Chinese millionairesses. They do not put up with rubbish.

Here, in a vast swirling dining room with 40-foot (13-metre) window-walls on to, yes, the bay, I ate quite stellar *congee* (rice porridge) with pork and preserved duck eggs and *har gao* enlivened by the addition of shark's fin and sweet Chinese ham, and a single large shark's-fin dumpling in soup. Around me, the richest and smartest of Hong Kong's rich and smart chowed down in what is the dining room of a hotel really no more interesting than a Novotel. But in Hong Kong, you go for the food and the air-conditioning, not the charm.

Spring Moon and One Harbour Road represent the very top end of dim sum eating, with waiters in white tuxes taking orders from the menu and delivering dishes on silver trays. For a more grittily real experience you want to follow the hordes of office workers who knock off a few minutes early at lunchtime to beat the queues for Maxim's on the second floor of City Hall in Central, just by the Star ferry.

A red and gold room the size of a football pitch, Maxim's throbs with the bustle of dozens of chariots pushed by chattering women who sing the praises of their wares in a desperate bid to unload and return to the kitchen for a fag break (everyone in HK speaks English apart from the dim sum waitresses). Here, punters sit in circles (as is traditional) and observe semi-seriously the rules of precedence (host sits opposite most honoured guest, guests descend leftwards in order of social seniority or age), signalling for more tea by inverting their pot-lids, and so on. A ham sandwich from Pret this most certainly ain't.

Denser and oilier than the yuppie dim sum I described earlier (as less expensive manifestations of any cuisine always are), the food was nonetheless lovely. Swede cakes, fried baby *cheung fun*, and 'stinky' bean curd were all brilliant and well worth the queue and the din.

Although dim sum is strictly speaking a Cantonese thing, I had a great Shanghainese example of it at the low-key basement restaurant Wu Kong in Tsim Sha Tsui, which, I discovered only after I got home, is a favourite restaurant of Ken Hom. And there were numerous happy encounters with randomly accessed niblets from street stalls, none of which killed me or cost an amount large enough to mean anything when rendered into sterling.

When I got back to London, something very strange had happened. The dim sum boom had filtered downmarket, chained out, gone national.

And most of them were called Ping Pong. At first, there was just the one outlet, on Great Marlborough Street, close to the top of what used to be Carnaby Street. Possibly still is Carnaby Street. I assume it's still there. But I wouldn't know for sure, never having been, on account of not being Japanese.

This Ping Pong brought itself to my attention initially thanks to the immense queues I saw outside whenever I drove past. I'm not a big fan of queuing for food, generally. Especially not when I suspect that people are queuing mainly because a place is cheap. I'll wait ten minutes for a dim sum lunch at Royal China at the weekend, and I'll fidget for three minutes in a Camden kebab line when drunk, but that's about it.

Gradually, though, I started to hear good things about Ping Pong. But almost exclusively from friends of mine in their mid-twenties – an age I remember well, when anywhere which served a meal you could keep down for less than £12 was worth multiple return visits.

But I am a snob when it comes to dim sum, as to most things. And on top of that, I had now made dumplings in a Hong Kong kitchen. So I knew the importance of newly made rice gluten dough, freshly killed prawns, and how precious each second is between the moment the bamboo steamer comes off the steam, and the moment it hits your table.

For the first minute, you can lift each dumpling from the box with your chopsticks entirely fusslessly. As the second minute ebbs away you start needing to jiggle each dumpling to shift the little perforated lining of greaseproof paper. After four minutes, you have to hold the paper down with a finger and pluck the dumpling off it like a leech from a jungle commando's arse. Any longer than that, and you're shaking the limp paper rag like a Seventies amateur photographer drying a Polaroid, until a dumpling finally wings off and sticks to the wall. Then you're like a Staffordshire bull terrier shaking a Burmese cat by the neck until . . . Ooh, I do love a simile.

And when you do get it off, by now several minutes since the thing was cooked, the shell is going to be thick and claggy, it's going to stick to your teeth and the walls of your mouth and positively defy chewing. And the filling is going to be lukewarm and wan. And that's what I always suspected you would get at Ping Pong, because that is usually the way with chains.

I used to like Dim T, for example, when it first opened in Hampstead. But then it spread to Highgate and beyond, chains popping up everywhere like mushrooms in a turdfield, and the dumplings started to be made centrally and come in frozen from I don't know where to satisfy this voracious dumpling empire, and were good only for throwing at the wall to see if they stuck (which they do), and so I don't go there anymore. And certainly wasn't planning to see if Ping Pong were marginally better.

But then I noticed that they had built a Ping Pong in Hampstead, on the site of what used to be ZeNW3, and I knew that I had no option now but to give it a try. Poor old Zen. I loved Zen, even when it was rubbish. Which it usually was. Rubbish and extremely expensive. But quality and value are not everything. History is important, too.

ZeNW3 opened in 1987, the year I turned 18 and gained my gastronomic majority, and was a revelation. Its bright, white, two-tiered glitz (which won it the *Evening Standard* Best Restaurant Design award in its year of opening) was a beacon of fun in dowdy old Hampstead, which had never before, and has never since, had a restaurant worth making a special trip for. And it became an early backdrop for my adult life.

It was the first Chinese restaurant I went to without my parents. It was the place I went with my girlfriend and ten friends after her father's funeral, when we were 20 and using death as an excuse for drinking for the first time. It was also the first place in which someone came up to me and said, 'Are you Giles Coren, the restaurant critic?' and expressed a desire to sleep with me. Also the last. And anyway, I didn't like the way he did his hair.

From Kentish Town, it was always the nearest posh, bit-like-being-in-town restaurant and so it was there for all those times – dates, mates after work, drunken afternoons – when the usual discussion about where we could go within a mile that was sort of all right and not too expensive would end with, 'Bollocks, let's go to Zen.'

The food standards wavered horribly: sometimes terrific, sometimes shabby beyond belief, and the bill for two was never less than £78. But I went for other reasons. For the bright, white, crisp linen, the views of the High Street, the little shredded pickles on the table to get your taste buds going, for the glamour and rattle of new money and old Jews. And for the water feature running down the main stairs that was said to bring luck, but down which, it was whispered, an old man had fallen in the first year, and broken his neck.

Which was maybe why Zen's luck ran out. That and the food, which started to fail so badly that they started doing sushi (quite terrible sushi) to try to lure people in on the old 'Chinese, Japanese, it's all the same' principle.

So then it closed. And we hoped for something gorgeous to come and fill that fantastic space. And we got . . . Ping Pong.

Ping Pong is big and brown and brutal, with wipe-clean shiny tables that they actually do wipe clean, while you're sitting there, with noxious chemicals that put you right off your supper. Luckily.

The waiters are big ugly Serbian men in t-shirts. The punters have an average age of 23, iPod in one ear while they eat, texting with the non-chopsticks hand, the sort of people who are scared off by washable napkins. Not locals, clearly, but people who have come from elsewhere on the bus.

As for the food, well, it's not the sort of food I really understand. It is that genre of chain store comestible which a restaurateur friend of mine describes as 'just barely good enough for most people'. And I guess these were those people.

I mean, a roast pork puff should be a glowing triangle of amber pastry, dotted with sesame seeds, that emits a squeal of steam when you go at it with your sticks. Inside the short, short, meaty pastry should be a hot, sticky explosion of *char siu*, sweet and Christmassy and just a tiny bit piggy. What we got here was three small Ginsters sausage rolls, slightly mulled. Flat, lukewarm, industrial, with an aftertaste of bad breath. But these iTwonks were shovelling them down with glee.

Har gau, plain prawn dumplings, should be thin, opalescent rice skins through which you can just see three small prawns making love, their arses bulging against the dumpling walls like stolen babies stuffed in a pillow case. But these were thick, doughy lumps filled with the most dismal shrimp paste. The scallop ones were no better.

Vegetable spring rolls were, if you want to be generous, comparable to a plate of Morrisons party snacks. Indeed, the whole meal had the taste and texture and general spirit of frozen supermarket nibbles microwaved for the lunch break of a Sheffield call centre's AGM. Except the punters weren't glamorous enough for that.

So in the end, Ping Pong was just as I had feared it would be: another bland corporate clip joint of the kind that iPodperson and BlackBerrywoman have decided is a safer place to risk their drearily earned pennies than a big, flash, in-your-face place which might be terrific, might be terrible, but will at least have a bit of soul.

And a few months later, without fanfare, it closed. At the time of writing it is a branch of the miserable faux-Parisian steak chain, Côte. But by the time you read this it might well be a Gregg's. It will be interesting to see how low it can fall.

And to think I once saw Judi Dench in there.

How to Stay Healthy in a Chinese Restaurant

CHINESE FOOD, EVEN
AT THE top end, can involve a lot of
stodge, a lot of salt, a lot of sugar, and a lot
of fat, mostly pork fat. It can leave you feeling very
heavy, miserable, dry-mouthed and weirdly under-
nourished yet at the same time bloated, fat and wondering
how many weeks you just lost off the end of your life. So start
with a big plate of stir-fried greens – bok choi, choi sum, gai lan,
ping pong, hoo flung dung, it doesn't matter which; nobody knows
the difference anyway, not even the Chinese.
It is important to insist that they bring this first because as soon as
there are fried crispy won tun or steaming fat prawn dumplings or racks
of sticky barbecued pork on the table you're not going to bother with
the greens. But get the greens in when you're still starving (don't have
gloopy oyster sauce all over them or anything, just ask for them with a
bit of garlic and ginger) and you'll gobble them down, feel good about
yourself from the start, be healthier, live longer, and poo beautifully
the next morning. And, because you are full of greens, you will eat
less of the fatty, salty, stodgy stuff now, and have to take it
away in a doggy bag for tomorrow, thus halving the
calorific impact of two meals.
This can also usually be done in Vietnamese, Korean,
Malaysian and Singaporean restaurants. I was
going to do a little spot on 'How to stay
healthy in Indian restaurants',
but you can't.

STILL IN THE BEGINNING . . .

I think part of the reason we thought going out to eat was so thrilling was that our parents seemed to do it all the time without us.

'Where are you going? Where are you going?' we'd squeal, when our mother came to kiss us goodnight, smelling of Madame Rochas and Elnett, which she definitely hadn't put on to eat egg sandwiches in the telly room and watch *Bouquet of Barbed Wire*.

'Just up the road for a bite to eat,' my dad would say, from the landing, reckoning to play down the formality of the occasion and the distance of the destination in order to minimise the fuss, loading a packet of Nelson into each of his outside jacket pockets as he spoke, and one into his inside pocket, then checking his lighter for power with a succession of roguish flicks.

'Up the road', 'round the corner', 'next door' . . . my parents had a battery of terms to convey the nearness of where they were going each night (probably not each night; probably only a couple of times a week), which no doubt were delivered honestly to mean Chelsea or Mayfair or Putney, which did not seem so awfully far away to them, nor do to me now, but which did nothing to fool two children who had never so much as crossed a main road on their own and more often than once had got lost, together, on their own block (truly – after four or five minutes of walking, the vague rumour that if we carried on we would eventually come all the way round to where we started seemed as preposterous as it must have done to the more sceptical members of Christopher Columbus's crew aboard the *Santa Maria*, and we could do nothing but stop a stranger to ask for help).

'There aren't any restaurants up the road!'

'We're just going to Capability Brown, we'll hardly be gone an hour.'

'Capability Brown? That's miiiiiiles away!'

It truly wasn't. It was down at Fortune Green where the 159 buses turned round. It was maybe four minutes by car. Fifteen on foot if you walked it. But nobody did. Up the steep hill of our broad suburban street, right down West End Lane, past Loder's, the newsagent with the cola chews and Milky Bars and small selection of English comics, past the cemetery (where my dad now is), and the little park where local kids, shirtless in summer with their skinny white bodies and tiny pink nipples like the rivets on jeans, would poke you in the eye and steal your pocket money (8p for *The Beano*, 8p for a pack of Monster Munch, 4p for later), past the tyre shop with the big blue carriage doors and giant stacks of shiny tyres outside, past the Nautilus, the best fish and chip shop in the world, where my father used to pick up cod and chips for four to be eaten at the kitchen table on the second-best rainy nights in the world (sometimes we were allowed to eat out of the newspaper, but mostly we had to decant it all onto plates, which weren't nearly big enough so that the giant curling sea beast with its thrashing tail would turn to avoid a plunging fork and swish chips all over the table), past the police station where we sometimes went to look at the horses, and where my dad addressed all the coppers in his special North London voice, saved up from when he was little in Southgate for use with policemen, dustmen and burglars, and then on, down the road, past the Catholic church where

Bessie, our Irish housekeeper, went every Sunday with a scarf over her head and the newer of her two pairs of pointy spectacles, across the bottom of Mill Lane, where my grandparents lived in the 1950s (and where my father, I guess, used to return to in the holidays when he was away at university), and then round to the left, past the petrol station where the man came and filled up the car and my mother always tipped him through the window, and the fire station with shiny red fire trucks and men in brass hats, like in *Trumpton* (it's a strip of estate agents and pizza delivery stations now), then left up past the layby for buses, past the bakery with sugar mice in the windows (still there, astonishingly), up the hill and on the left, with its green awning: Capability Brown.

Not far, on paper. No more than a single mile. But conceptually, to a nine-year-old, miiiiiiiles. The edge of the world, barely known and guarded by dragons.

'I'll miss you!'

'You'll be asleep.'

'I won't be able to sleep.'

'Of course you will.'

'Give me a sleeping pill!'

I knew about sleeping pills because all four of my grandparents yakked them like peanuts. And my mother was an anaesthetist, and I knew that the 'chemist cupboard' down by the back staircase contained enough drugs to kill off a postcode.

So she would go off to the bathroom and come back with my battered yellow tooth mug half full of water, and say she'd dissolved one in it, and I'd drink it down, knowing she was probably fibbing. But only probably.

And as my placebo worked its magic I would lie there, in my dark little bedroom next to my baby sister's bigger one (not fair then, not fair now), with the nanny watching *Celebrity Squares* down the corridor and the housekeeper in her own little bolthole on the other side of the house, making jam or knitting hats or whatever she did with her free time, thinking of what it was like on the inside of Capability Brown, or of Quincy's, which was also just down the road, or of Chez Nico where they went less often, and came back with tales of portions so small that they had to stop for salt beef sandwiches at Harry Morgan on the way home, and of diners being thrown out by the fiery chef in his towering toque for having the wrong shoes, or asking for ketchup; or the Gavroche, which was just like a cruise ship, they said, and where you could have *île flottante* (floating island!) for pudding, and wondering, as I finally nodded off, if my mother would bring back little chocolates this time, as she sometimes did, in dark purple boxes with gold string, which were okay as chocolates went (not in the same league as a Lion Bar) but meant that while she was gone she was thinking about us. And I was amazed by that. How on earth had they had time to remember their children in the staggering, dazzling, wonder-drome of food they had spent the night in, where there were chandeliers and live bands and the men wore white tie, and once, famously, my father punched a drummer who sat down next to my mother in the interval, and the band had to do its second set without a rhythm section.

Poor little us. Little me. Trapped at home while my parents whooped it up. But the more I think about it (looking for some sort of background, some sort of foundation to build this story of the unlikely importance of restaurants), the more places I think of that we did used to go to with them, after all.

There was the Golden Egg in Swiss Cottage where my dad took me after swimming and diving lessons at the Holiday Inn. Vast, low-ceilinged, brown, with a laminated menu, but all I wanted were the pancakes. The big fluffy American-style pancakes with maple syrup and ice cream.

The first time I had them I was disappointed that they were

not like my dad's pancakes – one of the few things he cooked regularly: thin, mottled one side, crisp at the edges, rolled up with lemon and sugar. But then gradually, as I got used to the fluffy pucks at the Golden Egg, I began to be disappointed that my dad's were not more like those.

And there was the American place in Golders Green, no idea of the name, where my mother took me after, what? Piano? Cricket? Extra maths for morons? More swimming? At that place, brown again, higher ceilings, booths, I always had the Wyoming: a hamburger with egg mayonnaise on top, served open, with a cress salad.

Man, I loved that burger. Forking up enough egg mayonnaise and eating it neat to get the thing down to a size where I could whack the other half of bun on it and eat it with my hands. But also enjoying the purity of the clean egg taste before it got lost in the char of the bun and the rivers of ketchup. Was it ever served anywhere else? Did it exist before? Does it exist now? Is there another man or woman on the planet to whom the word 'Wyoming' means a hamburger with egg mayonnaise on it?

I ordered it the first time because one of the things my father and I had in common was Westerns – films, books, action figures (well, the action figures were mostly me, and they were all called 'Gregory Peck') – and a lot of Westerns took place in Wyoming. And in his own children's books, the ones he wrote based on the stories he made up for me at bedtime, the 'Arthur Westerns' (which would have been called the 'Giles Westerns' if Giles were not such a dumb name – good enough for a son but too silly for a boy in a story), Wyoming usually figured. Along with Arizona, Texas and New Mexico.

Tuscon, Dodge City, Seminole . . . they were place names that he brought back from his two years at university in America, along with an 1888 Colt .45, whose cold black iron barrel is glinting now on my own bookshelf as I write, and stories of the giant hamburgers and steaks he used to eat on campus at Yale and Berkeley, which blew his tiny North London mind after twenty years of post-war British eating.

Burgers loomed large, looking back. It was all about going to McDonald's, which opened in Swiss Cottage in 1977 or 8, only the third or fourth in England. There was one in Woolwich and then one in Golders Green, with no chairs, only leaning rests – which meant nobody could make you sit there till you had finished your burger. Except you always finished your burger. That was the thing about burgers. And then there was Swiss Cottage.

But our parents didn't really get it. If we liked McDonald's, they reasoned, then how much better a place where you could get a beefburger (whatever happened to that word?), but also sit down for ages and order from a waiter and have napkins. So instead we went to Strikes. Strikes 1926, I think was its full name. Where the walls were decorated with photographs of the 1926 General Strike for reasons I didn't understand then, and understand even less now.

They served a 'gammon burger', which sounded massive. 'Gammon' had to mean something way bigger than 'huge' or 'ginormous' or even 'humungous', but turned out, in fact, to be a type of ham. Who knew? Who the *hell* knew? I can still taste the disappointment now. The thick, tough, salty, piggy disappointment. And don't get me started on the slice of pineapple.

No wonder Strikes failed. It got swallowed by Dayville's, the ice cream joint next door, which provided their ice creams for a bit, then gobbled the whole enterprise. It stayed being called 'Dayville's 32 Flavours', though, even though it had probably acquired a load more flavours in the takeover.

Directly across the road was Baskin and Robbins, which boasted '31 Flavours'. This was odd because Baskin and Robbins came afterwards. You'd have thought it would call itself '33

Flavours'. The escalation could have gone on all the way to 'Infinity Flavours', until some poor sap opened a place called 'Infinity and One Flavours', and had my sister to answer to.

But this was the 1970s, time of austerity, meanness, downsizing, all sorts of lefty bullshit, and clearly the smart thing to do in those days was to move in opposite someone selling exactly the same product as you, and offer less of it. So Baskin and Robbins swooped in and screamed, 'Hey, look, they might have 32 different flavours of ice cream, but we've only got 31! We've got less flavours than them! Yaaaaaay! Sorry, fewer flavours! Yaaaaaaay!'

As it happens, I counted the flavours in Dayville's once. There were only 24.

And if I thought Strikes was posh, then the Tower Hotel was posh on stilts.

It was where I went for my 11th birthday and my 12th birthday, and very possibly my 13th. My 10th, 9th, 8th and 7th had been celebrated at the Angus Steakhouse in St John's Wood, on the site of the old Lord's underground station (for those of you who navigate not by restaurants but by defunct Tube stations, and have got this far anyway), which was my favourite place in the world. But then it closed down. Or my parents pretended it had closed down when in fact they had grown bored with the whole prawn cocktail, steak, Black Forest gateau thing. (It was hard to tell with my parents and the fibbing. Like when they said that our tortoise, Tortie Malcolm George, had 'escaped' during my sister's fourth birthday party, which was true, I discovered more than 20 years later, only in the spiritual sense in which Jesus, say, or Little Nell 'escaped' their mortal torment.)

Either way, the Tower Hotel was like the Angus Steakhouse with knobs on. And these knobs took the form of waiters in black tie. Black tie! Like at the Cattleman's Club in Dallas. And also deep, thick linen tablecloths, an amazing view of Tower Bridge all lit up like Cinderella's castle and a head waiter who could make a 50p go into a champagne cork by 'magic'. (This magic involved turning away from the table at the crucial moment and making juggling motions with his arm as if cutting something . . .)

I had steak there, too, like at the Angus, but here my father tried even harder than usual to make me have it at least 'medium', rather than 'very well done'.

'Won't you even try it?' he said. 'It's much nicer.'

But I wouldn't. Wasn't interested in the blood element of things. And in the end my dad would roll his eyes, and the waiter would roll them back (his own eyes, not my dad's), and there would be some yuks about how unsophisticated I was, and I would get my meat nicely cooked through.

It was a battle that went on for years. My father just so, so wanted me to eat my steak rare. I think he was genuinely embarrassed to ask for it well done in a posh restaurant. That was the power differential in a restaurant in those days. My father was a famous and successful man, the greatest comic writer of his day, a television star, an Editor, a rich man with a beautiful wife who earned a packet herself, a massive great ten-bedroom house with three live-in staff in what he could easily have called 'Quite near Hampstead' if he had wanted to (the neighbours did, and were horrified when their boasts of living in the same street as Alan Coren were met with, 'Doesn't he live in Cricklewood?'), and yet in a posh restaurant like this (which was really only the refectory of a flash business hotel where City men took their secretaries for lunchtime rumpy) he felt on the back foot, socially speaking, when talking to a moustachioed waiter with a dodgy French accent.

So he ordered his own steak 'blue' or even '*bleu*', which was, he said, even rarer than rare. So blue that the blood hadn't even had time to get red yet. This was how really sophisticated people had it, I was given to understand. And most of all, this was how French people had it.

In France, where we went on holiday most summers, even more of a fuss was made. The first words I learned in French were '*bien cuit*'. I looked them up in a dictionary when I was seven or eight, before we left for a fortnight with some friends of theirs and their supposedly companionable children, to make sure that nobody tried to fool me into eating bloody meat. I discovered also that '*saignant*', which was what they called 'rare' actually meant 'bloody' so that '*bleu*' had to be even worse than that.

And then in the restaurants when I said '*steak frites, s'il vous plaît, très bien cuit*', my Dad would roll his eyes with the French waiter and say, '*Très, très, très bien cuit. Carbonisé. Cramé. Foutu!*' to make a joke of it, and dissipate the embarrassment of my puerile squeamishness.

And then he would order his own so blue that it wobbled on the plate and was cold inside. And he would joke that with a set of spark plugs a good vet could have that up and running around again in no time.

But the odd thing was, for all the embarrassment I caused in restaurants with my demand for well-cooked meat, and all the bloodiness of the navy blue beef my parents ordered to make up for it, when my mum grilled steak at home, or fried it with onions, or roasted a fillet of beef, it always came out at the very least medium, and usually past halfway to well done. Which struck me as very weird. And made me very suspicious of their motives at the Tower Hotel, and everywhere else.

Why did they always ask for it so rare, I wondered, when they obviously knew, as I did, that beef is so much nicer for a proper bit of cooking?

BURGERS AND STEAKS

Steak snobbery and burger snobbery continue to dog me in adulthood, in the form of endless people confiding in me that they know just where to get the best hamburger in London. Or the best steak. Or the best chicken soup in the world. Or telling me the secret of the perfect Bloody Mary. Or the only place in New York you can get Caesar salad the way Caesar actually made it.

I appreciate people's (and I obviously mean men's) need to show off, to demonstrate the extent of their knowledge, the range of their experience, the clarity of their judgment, the overwhelming importance of their opinion. But the application of superlatives to certain dishes (usually the relatively simple sorts of dishes listed above) is dim-witted and vain in the extreme. Men come up to me, dismally self-important little bankers and barristers in their early thirties usually, to name some barman as the maker of the finest Negroni in Europe, with all the grandiosity and pomp of our forefather Adam pointing at a spotted thing with a long neck and declaring it a 'Giraffe'. And it makes me ill.

For the application of superlatives to food is a terrible, terrible mistake. In cooking, the perfect is truly the enemy of the good. It leads only to mental breakdown in chefs and disappointment in diners. We shouldn't need Plato to tell us that things in perfect form do not exist on Earth.

And yet there seems to exist in the mind of every adult male some sort of platonic ideal of a hamburger (I guess because it is often at the core of primal and formative dining experiences: possibly the first thing you ever ate outside your home, safe because not slimy, exotic because not a fish finger). And this intuition of a perfect burger existing somewhere in the supernal scoffo-sphere allows these adult males to tell you that it can be found only in a little place they know in Sioux Falls, South Dakota (which shows they have travelled), or in Lucky Seven (which shows they have property in Ladbroke Grove), or in the Hard Rock Cafe (which shows they are Russian), or at Michael Caine's table at The Ivy (which shows they are Michael Winner), or at Joe Allen (which allows them, when you point out that it isn't on the menu, to smile smugly and say, 'No, but regulars know it is there if you ask for it.')

And it also allows all these wretched chains to pester me endlessly to come and compare their burgers with everybody else's. They have incredibly inflated, superlative-inducing names: Ultimate Burger; Gourmet Burger; Wicked Blinding Mental Burger with Knobs On; and they all boast grass-fed, arse-licked, pan-killed, dry-aged, stone-seared fillet of a half-cow/half-mermaid *Sports Illustrated* cover girl, ground by pixies and char-tickled over baby maple sapling smoke . . . and you get there, and it's just another minced mammal in a bap. And you're either in the mood or you're not. That's how it is with burgers: sometimes they taste like the best in the world, and sometimes they don't. And it has everything to do with you, and how you're feeling, and nothing at all to do with the object itself.

I have enjoyed many burgers. In the late Seventies I thrilled to the smell of a fresh Big Mac from the new outlet on Finchley Road, couriered home at 80 mph in my father's blue Mercedes 220SE convertible, so that it came through the front door with

the whiff of Imperial Leather and five-star petrol, its polysty-
rene box newly popped, the sweet steam rising from the plump
bun . . .

I loved madly the double-pattied Wimpy Half-Pounders I
would eat walking up Cornmarket in Oxford, on my way to
McDonald's at the top of the street (boy, I could pack 'em away
in those days), and also the three Mushroom Double Swisses I
ate there when it turned into a Burger King in 1990, and my
friend Jim and I queued from dawn on opening day, to be the
first inside.

And I loved the half-pounder at Maxwell's in Hampstead.
Classy, because eaten sitting down and with a choice of dress-
ings for the salad. I loved the one I ate there with my friend
Jules in the spring of 1988, the week before he died. And I loved
the ones I had later, after an evening bar shift at the Dome,
because it was open late, with a Long Island iced tea and a
Spanish girl called Paula, who worked as an au pair for a
Hassidic family in Palmers Green.

I loved them all, and at various times thought they were the
best burgers in the world. But what an idiot I would be to send
you to any of those places and expect you to feel the same.

But I think I can just about send you to Byron, since we're
talking about it, which is a rapidly expanding chain owned by
the same people (I believe) who own Pizza Express (a chain
about which I am far less enthusiastic, and of which more later).

I went to the very first one on Kensington High Street not
long after it opened in 2007 or 8, because the girl I was seeing at
the time, who is now my wife, lived more or less upstairs. Even
then, the place looked big and bright and new and all built
around a central grilling area and appeared to be just another
soulless wannabe chain. There was nothing to drag me in especially, until one night, when we were lying around doing nothing
much at all on a sweltering summer evening (she lived right

under the eaves and it was always boiling up there), she said, 'I'd do anything for a cheeseburger right about now.'

I didn't take much notice of the menu. Just ordered the Byron burger: 'dry cure bacon, mature cheddar, Byron BBQ sauce' – my three favourite burger toppings all in one – and then ate it, and thought: 'That's about the best burger I've ever had.'

Otherwise, nothing remarkable to report. The menu says: 'Our hamburgers are ground daily from select cuts of blah blah . . . fully traceable grass-fed Morayshire blah blah? aged for a minimum 21 blah blah . . . buns from a fourth-generation family baker in the East End.' And I'm, like: 'Whatever – that's about the best burger I've ever had.'

The chips were good, too, but the zucchini fries were greasy and I'd rather catch my eye on a rusty nail sticking out from a broken door in Basra than ever eat their onion rings again. But I did think: 'That's about the best burger I've ever had.'

As with any grill house, you're going to leave smelling of burned fat (specifically, of the smell of the breakdown of cow cell structure, the obliteration of bovine DNA by heat) and your clothes are still going to smell of it in the morning. And, admittedly, when I went back and had a plain hamburger with no toppings (just to see), it wasn't nearly so exciting – but then a plain hamburger just ain't.

And I will grant that if you're the sort of person who wants avocado, pineapple, smoked koala and jam on your burger, then you're not going to like that the only choices are between types of cheese on your cheeseburger, the aforementioned Byron, and a chicken or veggie option. But I did think, as I said before: 'That's about the best burger I've ever had.'

And if you're thinking that I was maybe just projecting on to a run-of-the-mill meat patty in a bun the feelings that, secretly, I harboured for the young lady who lived upstairs, well, then I can't do much about that, except say, once again, and notwithstanding my antipathy towards men who make these kinds of pronouncements, that I did think: 'That's about the best burger I've ever had.'

It goes without saying that the 'anything' never materialised.

Now, that's burger-twats dealt with. But I don't want to forget about steak-twats. They're even worse than burger-twats. They're always just back from New York or Argentina or Pope's Eye in Hammersmith and are just desperate to describe the nuttiness, the juice and twang of grass-fed Charolais, the cordite whiff of griddle lines and the rich egginess of the fat, and all I can think is, 'You went to a restaurant and ordered steak?'

What did you have for a starter? Toast? A bowl of Frosties? Some wine gums? Who of any substance orders steak in a restaurant? OK, apart from J.R. Ewing. And that was only because the Cattleman's Club didn't serve anything else.

Steak is the thing that chefs all feel they have to put on the menu because there is a certain kind of punter who will always ask why there isn't a steak on. The kind of punter who doesn't trust fancy foreign fiddling. The kind who is afraid of food. The kind who eats out only once every ten years and otherwise lives on tinned curry, so thinks it is a treat.

But until the quite inexplicable steak-joint boom of the last two years, I honestly don't think I have ordered a steak in a restaurant in ten years. Steak requires nothing except buying, and a brief introduction to heat – it was the first hot dish and cooking it requires no skill beyond what we were capable of a million years ago, when our knuckles still dragged on the floor, foreplay was a tap with a mammoth bone and the most loquacious men of the day said nothing apart from, 'Ug!' Granted, I have met many chefs who would have found such an era intellectually daunting but, come on, surely a steak you can do at home?

Not the steak-twats. They have this dream of anthracitic external blackness and minerality, of coarse saltiness, of a deep, juicy redness revealed when the cut halves of the meat are peeled open and pushed apart; an internal, blushing ripeness, ethereally tender to the touch, yielding a little moisture under pressure, smooth on the tongue, pale in flavour but strong in scent, seeming almost to swell as it enters the mouth.

But it doesn't exist. Not on a plate. The platonic ideals have become confused. If you seek an ecstasy of sexual union, of blood and sweat and salinity, a commingling of bodies, a communion of souls, a vomitous fulfilment of yearning and sorrow, of light and dark, heat and cool, flesh and bone, firmness and yield, sweetness and bitterness . . . you're just not going to get it from slicing a chunk off a cow and heating it over a flame.

And, anyway, cooking steak is just too hit and miss for it to be any sort of benchmark. I, too, dream of a good, big, mature and happy animal, humanely escorted from this mortal grind to a better place, and then hung there for flavour, growing tangier by the day, a thick hand of its rump at room temperature, almost edible as it is, hitting hot coals on either side for a minute or so and then resting, resting, resting, and then gobbled with lots of salt and a glass of claret. I fulfil that dream at home a couple of times a month: same butcher, same farm, same cut, always the same cooking method. And sometimes it's glorious, and sometimes it's just OK. But it's only ever a steak. Never as versatile as pork, or as jolly as lamb, or as soul-enriching as chicken, or as, er, healthy as fish.

And yet steakhouses are popping up all over town just now like mushrooms under trees. New York-style funky ones, good honest British ones, Russian-owned scary ones, and American celebrity chef-owned 300-quid-a-head ones. All part of some bizarre anti-recession but still quite recession-y simple-yet-expensive, 'weren't the 1930s great?' thing.

They're always on about the broiler they've brought in

specially from New York, as if it were a technological import to rival the moment William Caxton got a load of Gutenberg's printing press while on holiday in Germany and thought, 'Oho, there could be a groat or two in this.'

This broiler gets very hot. So hot you can dispose of your murdered wife on it in less than a minute. Atherton invited me into the kitchen and made diamonds on it from a handful of gallstones. When it's really firing, he says, he hopes to kick-start nuclear fusion (the export of these grills to Iran, needless to say, is illegal, although we think the Koreans may have one).

This kind of heat is the key, apparently, to the perfect steak. It's why they use them in New York, where everything is perfect. The steak is whopped on to hot coals to get that proper smoky crust, then it's hoiked up into the broiler for a minute or so at some sun-rivalling temperature, then back on the coals, then a rest, and then out.

You choose your steak these days from a range of cuts of myriad grass-, corn- or beer-fed animals reared anywhere from Hereford to Hobart and aged for anything from yesterday to several years before you were born, and usually including a wagyu described as anything up to '9th Grade', which means it is just now choosing its GCSE subjects.

Generally, they will bring an example of each of these meats to your table – wrapped to the neck in linen napkins, like decapitated infants in swaddling – to show you the marbling. Everyone gets terribly excited and then . . . well, Heavens, it's just a steak.

Places like Hawksmoor and Goodman's in London probably represented the plateauing of the new steakhouse, the thing at its best, done as well as it can be and as well as anyone needs. And then came the Côte chain, a fairly awful ersatz French steak joint from the Richard Caring group that owns The Ivy and Caprice and practically everything else, and you knew that it was all over.

Still, not taking 'NOOOOOO!!' for an answer, that same group brought us 34 in Mayfair, a version of The Ivy, Caprice or Scott's but morphed into sort of a steakhouse. Awful. And more awful still was a place called Cut, first British outlet from a man called Wolfgang Puck, and sent to remind us that steak really is for wankers.

Now, to well-travelled international gourmandisers with drag-along crocodile luggage, shoes hand-stitched from the bum skin of a single Cornish orphan and credit cards named after elements you and I haven't heard mention of since school (Am-Ex Beryllium? That'll do vomitously well, sire), Wolfgang Puck is a byword for . . . well, I'm not sure what for.

He is an Austrian chef and restaurateur who works princi-pally in America, but his name only ever comes up in conversation with men so boring I fall asleep while they're telling me about their latest business trip and daydream restively, as they drone on about Hollywood and film-funding and this darling little caviar hovel they go to in the valley, of unpicking the under-chin seams of their most recent skin-tuck and pulling their faces off backwards over their heads, in a monumental facial wedgie, so that their skull pops up out of their shirt like a gory lollipop, then slapping their floppy face skin over my own and, while everyone is screaming at the horror, running out into the street, hopping into their car and telling their driver, who thinks I am them (and is secretly glad that his employer's new facelift appears to be leaking), to take me to the airport, where I make my escape by . . . oh, you're still talking? And now it's about wristwatches and limited edition vanadium cufflinks? Fascinating.

Puck previously had a place called Spago in West Hollywood which he rolled out across the wealthiest parts of America before moving on to a chain of steakhouses called Cut. The one in Los Angeles is full of celebrities, by all accounts. I am told that Piers Morgan and Simon Cowell all but live there, which is wonderful to know.

From LA, the Cut brand was rolled out to Las Vegas and Singapore (cunningly chosen, aircon-dependent cities in barely habitable climates where sweaty plutocrats can be chilled down to a temperature where they feel like eating big steaks all year round), and now he's opened one in London where he imports all kinds of grain-fed, sugary American beef and serves it in all sorts of exciting American cuts to the people of Park Lane.

Thrilling stuff. But to me Wolfgang Puck will only ever be a spoonerism. Especially when you pronounce his first name as an Austrian would. Volfgang Puck. It's a disaster waiting to happen. And then when you consider that he's called his restaurant 'Cut', it's a consonantal meltdown to obscenity just hovering before your lips. For all his vaunted trans-Atlantic gloriousness, who in the world would dare go into polite society and say, 'Volfgang Puck has opened a new restaurant called Cut?' Slip up and they'd send you to prison.

I went with a couple of friends, had a steak, and was brought a bill for more than five hundred (500) (FIVE HUNDRED) pounds. And I am not paying five hundred (500) (FIVE HUNDRED) pounds of anybody's money for a two-course steak lunch with two modest bottles of wine suggested by the house. Not even Rupert Murdoch's.

Half a grand for a steak and a glass of red. That's a Puck of a lot of money.

So, what did I get for my half G? I got a lobby off Park Lane (purporting to be part of The Dorchester) that was done up very schpraunzy and populated by heavy-bellied visitors from the Gulf in shorts and flip-flops sitting with their legs apart, yawning, in the company of women under blankets who were presumably their wives, daughters, mums, chiropodists . . . it was hard to tell.

I was offered a drink by a pretty young Asian girl who didn't know what sherry was. Or anything else much. So I said I'd have a beer. She asked what kind I wanted. I asked what they had. She looked blank. I said bring me whatever the barman recommends, so she brought me a bottle of Peroni. Nice to see the Pizza Express house lager so far from home.

Then they took us to the dining room. Or, rather, the bit of the lobby with tables in it for eating. We had been refused a lunch spot at anything other than 12.30 p.m. or 2 p.m., but when one o'clock (which we'd tried for) rolled round, the room was still not even 25 per cent full, which means that they just enjoy Pucking people about. I hate that.

From the menu I could see that they lean here towards American corn-fed beef, which is a fine diet for chickens, but unnatural for cows, leading to a malty flavour and melting texture beloved of gumless octogenarian Floridians (being essentially a slab of Horlicks) but a bit whoopsical in the mouth of an Englishman raised on our more robust, grass-fed animals, with their chewy, minerally meat.

Three little burgers came out for an *amuse-bouche*. They were fantastic, sweet, light, rich and gamey, having been made from the bovine equivalent of those fat Texan tourists one sees wobbling around London in pale shorts and white gym shoes, wearing tiny hats on their great pudding heads and slurping iced, chocolate-flavoured lard through a straw from a four-pint paper pot. There was also a crisp little sandwich of raw Big Eye tuna and wasabi mayo, which was equally dreamy.

I had a terrific chef's salad of young seasonal vegetables, and a decent oxtail bouillon with some wondrous bone marrow dumplings, and then an Australian wagyu steak. I had the wagyu really only because they had endless varieties and cuts of steak but the wee differences are all so boring that I just thought, Puck it, I'll have this beer-fed and massaged foie gras of steaks at £76 for a wee six-ouncer, and see if it's worth it. They said the chef would serve it medium rare. I said fine.

But they overcooked it. So that was a waste of time. Close to eighty quid's worth of weirdly fattened Texan tourist accidentally cooked all the way through (not surprising when you read on the menu that all the meat is 'Grilled Over Hard Wood & Charcoal Then Finished Under a 650-Degree Broiler'). It was still perfectly nice in a Garfunkel's sort of way, but rather ruined as a delicacy.

The American ribeye, aged for a million years, yadda yadda, was better, if you like the buttery tenderness of corn-fed meat, and the French fries and onion rings were out of this world. In fact, Pucked-up wagyu aside, the cooking was good. And if I wanted to eat fat, rich food in the company of fat, rich people in a hotel lobby on a dual carriageway, I'd be there every night.

But ninety quid a head for a two-course meal, not counting any liquids at all (no water, wine, coffee, or even pizza chain beer), in a '*steakhouse*'? I'd rather be dead.

Recession? What Pucking recession?

PIZZA EXPRESS

hen I went off to boarding school in 1982 (not far from home, in fact only five miles up the road, a weird choice by everyone concerned, but arrived at democratically, I am told), the main attraction for me was the opportunity to consume Big Macs at will. Or at least as far as an allowance of 30 pounds a term would get me. I think a Big Mac then was 70p (or perhaps 69 – priced to keep it under the daunting hurdle of the big seven-oh). And a term was maybe ten weeks long, so I was counting on one burger more or less every other day, as long as I went without breaktime sweets and, I suppose, whatever else a 13-year-old might want to purchase. But even now I can't think of anything a 13-year-old might desire that can be exchanged for money, apart from hamburgers. (I'm really wanting a hamburger now, as it happens, but I've got writing to do.)

School finished at 4 p.m., dayboys went home, and we lifers had two hours to kill until 'dinner'. And when I put those inverted commas around dinner, it is for all sorts of absolutely correct grammatical reasons. Reasons which made eating something in that time quite essential. My plan, obviously, was always McDonald's.

The problem was that I fell in with a boy called Bob. Bob was tall and blond, with spectacles, and always wore a tie. Honestly. When we changed out of school uniform at four and put on our jeans and t-shirts, Bob put on a shirt and tie and a tweed jacket. His parents were much older than everyone else's. His dad had been an academic and a headmaster and was an expert on Ottoman architecture, and his mum was the daughter of a baronet. They called him Bertie. He was very good at snooker and rock-climbing, supported Chelsea and was a pisspoor opening bat, and was available for the post of best friend (I say 'best' – but of course that erroneously suggests that I had others).

His great weakness, alas, was his opinion that 'McDonald's is rank'. He couldn't possibly understand how I could eat that stuff.

'You know what they make the milkshakes out of?'

'Milk?'

'Ha! You wish. Chicken fat.'

But what about the burgers? The burgers were deli—

'Rank!' cried Bob. 'They're full of sugar. It's food for children. Children and Yanks. It's disgusting. It makes your clothes smell of vomit just walking in there. You go if you want to, but you're on your own.'

I didn't want to be on my own. I was always on my fucking own.

'So where shall we go then?' I asked.

'Pizza Express,' said Bob. 'There's one by Victoria Station, I don't know if it's as good as the Coptic Street one where I eat with my father when we go to the British Museum. And I'm not saying it's the best Italian restaurant in London, but it's pretty good.'

So we went to Pizza Express. And with us a boy called Fleming. Bob ordered two garlic breads for us to share by way of a starter.

Garlic bread? What scary foreign shit was this?

And then he indicated to us that we might order our mains.

This was great. He was just like my dad. Fleming and I both ordered La Reines which were ham, mushroom and, I think that was all, just ham and mushroom, because they sounded safe and were only £1.80. Bob ordered a Napolitana, which according to the menu was topped with . . .

Anchovies? Bleurghh!

And olives? Double bleurghh!!

'It's delicious, if you really want to know,' said Bob, who called his parents by their first names, drank wine at home, stayed up till he felt it was time to sleep, and claimed to have read *War and Peace* twice.

He was the poshest person I had ever met. In his tuckbox, which was wooden and ancient, and marked with the scars of fourteen generations of prep school boarder, he kept not the multipacks of Monster Munch and Chewits that I kept in my not-really-a-tuckbox suitcase that my dad and I had found at the last minute on Portobello Road, but jars of olives and a tin of Patum Peperium.

'Want some?' he had said the first time we met, at the toaster in the dormitory, where I was preparing to spread the house issue seedless raspberry jam.

'What is it?' I said.

'Peperium,' said Bob, like I was a right spazz. 'Gentleman's Relish. It's from Fortnum's.'

I hadn't even heard of Fortnum's. So Bob spread a thin layer of the brown paste onto a piece of buttered toast and handed it to me. I sniffed it.

'Fucking hell!' I shouted. I truly believe that was the first time I swore in my life. 'What is it made from? Dead bodies and dogshit?'

'It's made from anchovies,' said Bob. 'And is quite delicious. You just have to get used to it, that's all. It's an acquired taste. Like caviar and Guinness and Cuban cigars.'

But I didn't acquire it. Not then, anyway. And Bob was left to eat it alone, which he did every day, so that its smell got into our very pores and into the plasterwork and fabric of the dormitory itself, and made the place smell exactly of the smell you get when you dig your finger into your anus, wiggle it a bit and then sniff it. Which, seeing as we all did that all the time, didn't ultimately bother anyone at all.

So where were we? Oh yes, Pizza Express, Victoria Street, 1982. Three 13-year-old boys. Spending four times the price of a slap-up McDonald's scoff, because Bob was too posh to eat out of a bag.

'And we'll have a bottle of the Valpolicella,' said Bob, handing the menus back and not even looking at the waiter as he did so.

'How old are you?' asked the waiter.

'Twenty-one,' said Bob, who looked like the Milky Bar Kid, except with a knitted tie. ('Never say "18", he told me later, that just sounds like you're lying; aim much higher and they won't dare contradict you.')

'Twenty-one?' the waiter repeated, with a smile.

'Yes,' said Bob. 'Twenty-one. In fact, I am very nearly 22. Twenty-one and four-fifths, you might say.'

'Well, you can have beer,' said the waiter. 'But not wine.'

'How very annoying,' said Bob. 'I always have red wine with pizza. It's simply the perfect accompaniment. What kind of beer do you have? Do you have Theakston's Old Peculiar?'

'No,' said the man. 'We have Peroni Nastro Azzurro.'

'Is that an ale?' asked Bob.

'No, it is Italian beer.'

'Hmm, I've not tried Italian beer. Well, you'd best bring us three of those then.'

The waiter left, and Fleming and I stared open-mouthed at Bob. This man would be our leader, our guide, our Virgil. He had ordered beer. I had never had beer. I was still excited about being allowed a Coke at the Gourmet Rendezvous. And they were actually bringing it to us. This would never have happened if I had tried (I, alas, looked so young as a child that I could not get served in a pub even when I came of age five years later; indeed, even at 21, and working in a bar myself, I would be challenged for ID in the pub down the road, trying to get a drink after work).

The waiter brought three bottles, cracked them, and poured them into tall glasses, all still on the tray in his left hand, then put them down in front of us.

The cold, not sweet fizz filled my mouth and slid down my throat. Not as nice as Coke, but I wasn't going to say that. And yet, maybe, there was something in this. It didn't cloy. The after-taste was vegetable. The froth had a yeasty earnestness. It was probably like olives and anchovies and oysters, I would come to enjoy it with time and experience.

'Eurgh!' said Bob, slamming his glass down on the table. 'Lager!'

'I think I like it,' I said.

'Gnat's piss!' said Bob. I'd never heard the phrase before. I thought Bob had made it up. I thought that the 13-year-old boy in the tie who was prepared to be my friend had coined the phrase on the spot to describe an inferior foreign beer of negligible strength. If I'd been gay, it would have been love. But I'm not gay. So it wasn't.

We drank our gnat's piss anyway, and ate our warm, thin, unbelievable pizzas – the base wheaty and crisp, the cheese milky and sweet with a nuttiness where it was browned, the ham salty and firm, the mushrooms sweet, the three black olives, their edge taken off them by the heat of the oven, almost edible – and we ordered another round of beers, but only one more, or it would have gone past the small blue fivers that Fleming and I had each withdrawn from our Post Office savings accounts (Bob had a Coutts chequebook and a silver guarantee card – but I won't go into Bob and his financial arrangements, because this book is not about Bob, although I am beginning to wish that it were).

Bob stood us coffee – milky for us, double espresso for him – and we settled up, didn't tip because Bob said if the fellow had wanted a tip he should have served us the wine we asked for, and we staggered back to school full of beer and pizza singing, 'Peroni beer is gnat's piss! Peroni beer is gnat's piss' to the tune of 'Ring-a-ring-a-roses' as we went.

At the school gates, the duty master stopped us – three giggling, singing 13-year-olds scraping in just under the wire for prep – and said, 'Goodwin, Fleming, Coren! What have you been drinking?'

Fleming and I looked at our feet.

'We have been drinking gnat's piss,' said Bob, looking the teacher dead in the eye.

'Gnat's piss?' replied the beak.

'Yes,' said Bob. 'We ordered wine, but the bastard wouldn't give us any.'

And off he strode into the school, and we hurried along behind him.

That was 28 years ago and Pizza Express has gone completely to fuck since then (as have I). Everyone knows it.

The pizzas have got flabbier and doughier and sweeter as the British public taste, driven by the rise of processed food with its hidden fillers and sweeteners, has regressed to such an extent that only children's food will do, and the '*sugo*', the tomato sauce base for the pizza, is now so jammy you could spread it on toast and call it breakfast.

The toppings have got mingier and crappier and blander as bottom-line sourcing and factory farming cuts the balls off the flavour of everything, and the rapid expansion of the chain in bursts over the 20 years since it was first sold off has led to a situation where such tiny tweaks as lowering the standard number of olives on a La Reine from four to three across the country can save some plutocrat billions of pounds. It's a wonder they put anything on the pizzas at all.

And, of course, the pizzas have got smaller. (It's like the old Jewish joke about the restaurant where 'the food is terrible – and such small portions!') Everyone knows it, and yet the more you say it the more they deny it. They've told me in the past that I am misremembering, that the pizzas looked bigger to me then because I was smaller. They tell me I think they tasted better because my palate was fresher. They tell me I think the quality has declined because my own tastes have become more sophisticated. Pah! I'm still small, and there is nothing sophisticated about my tastes at all.

All we need is proof. I guess there's nothing that can be done to compare quality but the size thing can't be hard to establish. Somebody somewhere must have a plate from the old days. Show me a plate from Pizza Express in the 1970s and I will show you an inch-wide margin when you drop a 2012 Pizza Express pizza on it.

Come on, a hundred pounds to the person who finds me an old plate. You never will. They've destroyed them. There's a mountain of smashed crockery somewhere where evil Pizza Express execs have attempted to hide the evidence over the years. But all we need is one plate. One measly (enormous) plate . . .

Every now and again, to keep my eye in, I have returned to a Pizza Express randomly to see how it's coming along. I remember one in Pinner, seven or eight years ago, where I went after hearing of a relaunched menu, one of the many times they have paid lip service to the notion of bringing back the glory days.

The new pizzas were the 'Rosa', the 'Parmense', and the 'Frutti di Mare' (which was essentially the old 'Marinara' with a poncy new name). Then there was a bruschetta con parma, a pancetta salad and a mozzarella and tomato salad, touted as 'new' because it used sun-dried tomatoes, a fashionable new delicacy just over from Italy. They still used rubbery old pizza cheese for the mozzarella though.

Other innovations included 'art' on the menus and the rank acne of trademark registration symbols all over the page. Three of the pizzas from the earlier, 2000 relaunch (the mercilessly awful Soho, Sloppy Giuseppe and Caprina) had survived, the first two with inexplicable 'TM's over their name, while the hilarious walnut-topped Pizza alle Noci had been put out of its misery.

A new ingredient called 'Peppadew' was written in tiny capitals and has a microscopic 'r' above it. I'd never eaten Peppadew before, so I looked it up. By the admission of its own website it was: 'a savoury fruit which, when processed according to the patented process, uniquely balances hot, spicy and sweet flavours with a crisp mouthfeel'. Scary. Pizza Express had clearly gone for the 'when your business can't be bothered to cook any more call in the cyberboffins' school of restaurant management.

When the waitress brought the first of the 'new' starters, 'Olives Marinate', I counted the olives and asked, just for a joke: 'Is it strict company policy that there must be nine olives per bowl?' She went white and said: 'Oh my God! Are there nine? There have to be ten!' I laughed and said I was joking, but she would not be talked down. The episode ended when she brought a single, tenth olive on its own plate.

The bruschetta was pizza bread on which sat six grilled cherry tomato halves (presumably also an HQ-directed quantity) and a piece of cold, grey ham on top. The pancetta salad was decent rocket with cubes of gorgonzola (in its happiest state, a gorgonzola simply cannot be cubed), with nice ripe pear slivers (four of them) and three bits of what tasted like English bacon, not sweet, dense, pancetta. They had forgotten to dress it.

As for the new pizzas, well, they were as awful as all Pizza Express pizzas have been since the sell-off in 1993. The Rosa was a margherita with more of those gorgonzola cubes on it, and the Parmense had asparagus, ham, and an egg on it. It was the very first month of English asparagus season and I asked where these spears, which had no flavour at all, had come from.

'I don't know, they come frozen in bags,' was the answer. It did not even slightly scent my widdle that evening. The egg, which I had specifically asked to have soft, was boiled hard as a glass eye. As for the pizza Frutti di Mare, I don't know – Pizza Express is no longer a place where I will order the seafood.

It was just all so misguided and dim. Pizza Express did not start being bad-mouthed because it had no new pizzas, it was because its old pizzas had become rubbish. Why kill off the Prince Carlo and the King Edward (ahh, that potatoey base!) when just seeing them on the menu was part of the fun? Excessive corporatisation ruined the chain in the first place. More corporate fiddling is a waste of time. Better food is the thing.

Among the innovations on the menu was a boast that Pounds 1 million had now been raised for the Venice in Peril fund by the 25ps that have been donated on the sale of each Veneziana since 1967. I couldn't help imagining what would have been raised if the tightwads had donated money from a pizza that people actually like? Venice would be 300 ft in the air by now.

Meanwhile, at the very steps of the Palazzo del Pizza Express, the sea of mediocrity lapped louder than ever.

The morning after I wrote about my experiences in Pinner, I got an email from someone at the company which said: 'Following your piece on Pizza Express in *The Times Magazine* I wanted to ask if you would happy [sic] to take an hour to have lunch with our chief executive Harvey Smyth and Helen Benedict who is spearheading menu development at Pizza Express to talk through the article and the points you made.'

I replied, 'Hell, no', and forgot all about it. Then the phone rang, and it was Ms Benedict herself.

'I just wanted to say hello,' she said. 'It's important for us to understand your perceptions of Pizza Express. You've been following us for some time.'

Like an unmarked police car, luv. But you're not the first to glance in your rear-view mirror and then nudge the driver and whisper: 'Lose him!' As long ago as April 2001, the then Chief Executive of Pizza Express, Ian Eldridge, was asked in an interview in *The Independent* about the shrinking of the pizzas at his execrable chain and replied, 'I blame people such as Giles Coren in *The Times* and other chattering classes for this rumour.'

So you see, it's my fault.

Anyway. I told her what a disgrace the pizzas were and how depressing I found the greedy, soulless, samey, high-street-despoiling, Stepford Wife approach to restauration and she took it on the chin and still wanted to meet up.

So I said 'no' again and she asked why not and I explained that the notion of chainification was horrific to me and I wanted Pizza Express to crash and burn and fail and die and for the little restaurants that have been gobbled up by its evil satellites to grow again out of the ashes.

And she still wanted to meet me and so I asked what she did before she came in to 'spearhead menu development', and she said she was 'headhunted from Starbucks'. And I laughed and said she must be joking. And she said she wasn't. And I just laughed more, and said this was EXACTLY WHAT I WAS TALKING ABOUT!

They don't need management consultants and headhunters and somebody who put a Starbucks on every damn street corner of our once diverse, strong-headed, poetic and resource-ful little country, they need someone who knows ABOUT FOOD!

Before her five years at Starbucks, Helen was at Colgate for ten years. Marvellous. I'd as soon have a toothpaste pizza as anything else on the menu these days, frankly. Indeed, Colgate is the only organisation Helen has worked for that makes some-thing I would recommend putting in your mouth.

* Just a word on that 1971 menu: it was sent to me by an octo-genarian reader from Worcestershire called Tim Finney, who sympathised with my attacks on the new menu. The font was just the same as todays, with that familiar circular logo, all swirly like an Art Deco garden gate, but the pizzas, oh, what glory.

Of the 14 named on it, only nine have survived. Three of the disappeared I can remember – the 'Prawn' (prawns, olives), the 'Neptune' (tuna, anchovies, olives) and the much-lamented 'Marinara' (anchovies, garlic, no cheese). But as one who first ate there only in 1982, I was seeing for the first time the 'Pietro' (anchovies) and the lusciously titled 'Onion and Anchovy' (onions, anchovies).

There is a wonderful tinge of brownness to the menu. Almost every pizza is mostly anchovies (7 out of 14 as opposed to the modern ratio of 4/22).

There is a sense of the wonderful convenience of salt-cured fish preserved in oil, in a world where refrigeration is still a namby-pamby luxury for the rich. I was two years old in 1971, and had no notion of a gastronomic atmosphere (so palpable in the menu) which felt like the war had only just ended and you couldn't have extra cheese without stealing somebody else's ration book. And not a thing on the menu cost more than 48p.

Compared with the myriad starters available today, under

'antipasto' on the 1971 list is a single option: olives. They cost 20p and were served with 'gyula', but I am afraid I have been unable to find out what 'gyula' is, or are, or were.

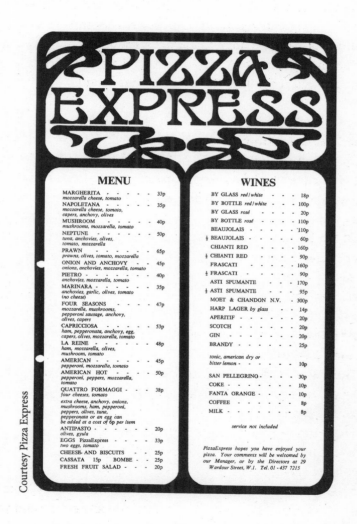

PIZZA EXPRESS

MENU

MARGHERITA	33p
mozzarella cheese, tomato	
NAPOLETANA	35p
mozzarella cheese, tomato,	
capers, anchovy, olives	
MUSHROOM	40p
mushrooms, mozzarella, tomato	
NEPTUNE	50p
tuna, anchovies, olives,	
tomato, mozzarella	
PRAWN	65p
prawns, olives, tomato, mozzarella	
ONION AND ANCHOVY	45p
onions, anchovies, mozzarella, tomato	
PIETRO	40p
anchovies, mozzarella, tomato	
MARINARA	35p
anchovies, garlic, olives, tomato	
(no cheese)	
FOUR SEASONS	47p
mozzarella, mushrooms,	
pepperoni sausage, anchovy,	
olives, capers	
CAPRICCIOSA	53p
ham, pepperonata, anchovy, egg,	
capers, olives, mozzarella, tomato	
LA REINE	48p
ham, mozzarella, olives,	
mushroom, tomato	
AMERICAN	45p
pepperoni, mozzarella, tomato	
AMERICAN HOT	50p
pepperoni, peppers, mozzarella,	
tomato	
QUATTRO FORMAGGI	38p
four cheeses, tomato	
extra cheese, anchovy, onions,	
mushrooms, ham, pepperoni,	
peppers, olives, tuna,	
pepperonata or an egg can	
be added at a cost of 6p per item	
ANTIPASTO	20p
olives, gyula	
EGGS PizzaExpress	33p
two eggs, tomato	
CHEESE- AND BISCUITS	25p
CASSATA 15p BOMBE	25p
FRESH FRUIT SALAD	20p

WINES

BY GLASS *red/white*	18p
BY BOTTLE *red/white*	100p
BY GLASS *rosé*	20p
BY BOTTLE *rosé*	110p
BEAUJOLAIS	110p
½ BEAUJOLAIS	60p
CHIANTI RED	160p
½ CHIANTI RED	90p
FRASCATI	160p
½ FRASCATI	90p
ASTI SPUMANTE	170p
½ ASTI SPUMANTE	95p
MOET & CHANDON N.V.	300p
HARP LAGER *by glass*	14p
APERITIF	20p
SCOTCH	20p
GIN	20p
BRANDY	25p
tonic, american dry or	
bitter lemon	10p
SAN PELLEGRINO	30p
COKE	10p
FANTA ORANGE	10p
COFFEE	8p
MILK	8p

service not included

PizzaExpress hopes you have enjoyed your pizza. Your comments will be welcomed by our Manager, or by the Directors at 29 Wardour Street, W.1. Tel. 01 - 437 7215

Courtesy Pizza Express

Lay Off the Bread

AN EX-GIRLFRIEND EATS nothing all day. She claims she doesn't get hungry. So whenever we meet for dinner she is utterly starving and inhales the entire bread basket and three clods of butter without pausing for breath. Then halfway through her main course she starts poking about and saying, 'I don't know why they give you such large portions, I'll never eat all this!' I just don't know why people eat the bread. You shouldn't be that hungry. Ever. Bread is not a first course. It is a breakfast food, an accompaniment to certain terrines, and the food that in most Western cultures has traditionally stood between the poor and starvation. But in some 50-quid-a-head place with a chef off the telly and a whole range of exciting things to chew on for the next couple of hours, why would anyone want to fill up with bread? Even if it is a hand-milled biodynamic spelt flour roll with cold-pressed virgin cobnut oil, sun-dried tomato, fontina cheese, dark chocolate and the dingleberries of a girl unicorn? It'll ruin the whole damn meal. And make you fat.

And anyway restaurants should be discouraged from all this 'artisan bread that we bake ourselves every morning' because baking is not a restaurant's job. It is a baker's job. And restaurants are never any good at it.

I always tell

them, as
soon as I arrive, to bring
no bread. But sometimes they
do and you must tell them to take it
away. You are not a Victorian orphan. You
are not a medieval leper at the gates of the
big castle. You are not a fucking circus elephant.
What in the world do you want with a bloody
bread roll?

Some critics make a big fuss if they are not brought free bread immediately. But generally it is the ones working for *Time Out*, local rags, or the *Guardian* who have to assume that their core punter cannot afford to eat out anyway and are hoping just to scarf down the contents of the bread basket and run for it.

Or the fat ones who are always so hungry that they'll get a headache before the starters arrive if they are not fed buns. But you shouldn't be that hungry. Ever. It just isn't modern. It is born of that old 'don't eat between meals' fascism that was only ever conceived as a random rule to give Edwardian fathers another reason to thrash the crap out of their children. Any civilised person arriving in a restaurant around 8 p.m. should have had a glass of sherry and a smackerel of something around half past five. If only so that you don't fall on the bread as soon as you sit down like a fucking fox in a dustbin.

ITALY

The closest I have yet come to rediscovering the joys of my early teenage Pizza Express trips was a pizza I had in Rome, at a place called da Baffetto. It's not a great big clever discovery of mine. It was in *The Rough Guide*, or *Time Out* or the *Lonely Planet*, or one of those other guides for poor, thick, young indigent Brits who really shouldn't be allowed any further south than Margate. And it is very famous indeed

They said the pizzas were great, and cheap, and you had to queue, and sometimes share your table with a lot of fat, troughing tourists in pastel-coloured outerwear. And you did, but they were, and I didn't notice the price.

Nobody eating there was Italian, which was a great boon. And the pizzas were big and thin (as the 'Roman style' demands) and the cheese on them was rich and golden and toasted bubbly brown in parts, had a depth and a tang that you don't get in England, and the ham had a bit of gaminess and the mushrooms tasted of mushrooms and the tomato sauce on it didn't taste of jam (lordy, I do not ask much) and there was something about the unsweaty heat of the thing, the dryness and wheatiness of the base, the scent of the oregano and marjoram under the ham, the floral miasma of the tomatoes, that did, truly, remind me of wet afternoons on Victoria Street in the early 1980s.

But everything else I have ever eaten in Italy has been

terrible. Really, terrible. It's an awful bloody place, and they don't know the first thing about restaurants. Or maybe it's just me.

It's an odd thing to admit, I suppose, but I am really crap at finding nice restaurants. Not in England so much – where I have the benefit of the (occasionally useful) opinions of dozens of other critics, hundreds of (generally useless) press releases, and the advantage of having eaten out here day after day for years and years – but abroad. Abroad, I have hardly put a forkful of food in my mouth that I did not then swallow only out of politeness.

I am aware that in theory one *can* eat well in such places as France and Italy. The anecdotal evidence is overwhelming. It's just that it doesn't seem to happen to me. I have spent years of my life in France, holidaying, working and, for some time, residing. And yet the only really memorable meal I have had there was in a villa near Marseilles in 1977, when my mum let me put Orangina on my Ricicles because you couldn't get fresh milk.

Paris claims to be the restaurant capital of the world, but all I have ever had there is arguments. It's because of the anticipation. I expect so much that I trawl from *vitrine* to *vitrine*, scouring the menus, squinting at the interiors, getting more and more anxious, searching hard for authenticity, for originality, for somewhere that looks like the sort of place people talk about when they talk about Paris. But I never quite find the ideal I'm yearning for, and then cannot commit to a compromise, so that I almost always end up weeping at a corner table in McDonald's, somewhere off the Champs-Élysées, stubbing fags into the remains of a Royale with Cheese, and dreaming of J Sheekey and the Anchor and Hope.

If I do sit down in a *vrai bistro*, it's always the same old crappy tinned snails and yesterday's smelly fish and greasy frisée, and possibly intentional purple plate smears and syphilitic service and no soap in the loos ... until I wonder if France and its gastronomy are just a monstrous joke played by history and geography on me, and me alone.

Italy's the same. Worse, even. I've read about the wonders of the Tuscan table (and the Piedmontese and the Umbrian and the Genovese ...) in countless gushing magazine articles and shiny coffee-table books by Kensington housewives whose husbands don't pay them enough attention, and I know that somewhere out there are marble-smooth, knotted pouches of creamy burrata and tomatoes as pink and sweet as mermaid's nipples, being served by raven-haired girls in peasant smocks, in a garden in the shadow of a ruined abbey, where they don't bring a bill because they feed you only for the love of doing it ... but I've never found them.

I've never even found a place that wasn't just about to close for the afternoon, unless you wanted to finish off the congealed bits and pieces welded to the cloth on the hors d'oeuvres table, with a jug of house wine, for a bill that could have your eye out.

My last trip to Italy was that country's last chance, and she muffed it. I am not going to fall for it again. All that rubbish about lovely fresh food, charming people, casual, tumbledown restaurants in the shadow of ancient ruins, bambini frolicking between the tables, linguine cooked so al dente you could pick a padlock with it, ooh, darling, the tomatoes, the tinkle of pinot grigio hitting a rustic old tumbledown tumbler, simple grilled meats, ooh, darling, the mozzarella, the very pepper-grinder that gave Shelley the idea for *Ozymandias*, ooh, darling, the zucchini flowers poached in the tears of a gryphon ...

It is all rubbish. I was in Rome for a week and then in the Tuscan countryside outside Lucca – the very model of the 21st-century bourgeois holiday idyll – and almost all the

Italians I encountered were cheap, tacky swindlers who couldn't cook.

I know you'll all want to tell me that the best Italian food is not to be found in restaurants, and that Italians eat best at home. Well, so do I. But I have to go on holiday sometimes. You will tell me that the best places are off the beaten track, little brown places with no sign which you wouldn't even know was a restaurant unless you were a local. Yes, well, I am not a bloody local. And I am not Marco frigging Polo either. I have to go to places with signs.

I stayed at a place called the Hotel de Russie. It was meant, according to at least two guidebooks, to be the best hotel in Rome. Ha!

I booked three months in advance and chose a 'view of the garden' as opposed to a 'view of the city'. But when we arrived (me and some random flopsy I was dating at the time), they put us in a room at the end of a dark corridor, fully three days' walk from reception, with a view only of a wall. A cellar of a room. A room so mean and dark and lifeless I think Gollum would have called in the decorators.

They had clearly seen an unfamiliar name in the book, grasped I was English (hawk, spit, flick my teeth at you), and told the chambermaid, 'Clean out the broom closet, Maria, the Corens are coming.'

I said it would not do. They said it was all they had. I said that they had specifically promised me a view of the garden. They said they had not. And then I said that, if they did not give me a room with at least some natural light, I would leave. And still they said that was all they had. So I told them to call me a taxi. And so they gave me a great room on the top floor, windows on two sides and beautiful views.

Goddam, that sort of thing makes me angry: to provide rubbish as a default until the difficult people hit the roof, and let the nice ones go screw themselves. It's how you fill the world with Michael Winners.

Next morning at breakfast, same thing. Lovely sun-dappled garden restaurant, *buongiorno, buongiorno*, ah, English, have a seat here at the cutlery station where the waiters stack all the old plates and the birds come and crap on your lap; after all, you're only paying 800 quid a night (a monstrous error – when I booked I honestly thought that was for the five nights).

Breakfast was included with the room unless you had hot food (yes, I know, who in the world would expect to get a hot breakfast for only 800 quid?). So the flopsy and I ordered scrambled eggs each and two pieces of bacon. Only when I went to pay the bill at the end (at reception, surrounded by dead-eyed staff, searching over my shoulder for fat *visconti* in pale jeans and sockless lizard loafers to slime up to) did I discover that eggs and bacon for two had cost me 87 euros. Seventy-five quid for two plates of bacon and eggs. And we'd done it every morning.

We sent some laundry to be done: two shirts, a pair of shorts, three pairs of pants, some socks. Two hundred and twenty euros. One hundred and eighty pounds. At least three times the value of the clothes themselves. The pants were not even badly soiled, as this was before I knew how much the room cost.

We went to some restaurants. Couple of decent pasta dishes but otherwise, rubbish. These people not only have never heard of vegetables, but have no idea how to cook meat – it was all so overdone, so brown, so whiffy? 'So dead,' grunted the flopsy, who doesn't usually talk with her mouth full.

We went to the famous Dal Bolognese because Britain's foremost restaurant critic had said it was pretty good, another had said it was 'Rome's answer to The Ivy', and one of my favourite chefs had specifically recommended it for the *fritto misto*. But what a craven bumhole of a place it turned out to be. We got, naturally, the worst seat in the house, right by the front door. While most arrivals were greeted like old friends, we got not a flicker of a smile. No help with the menu. No suggestions. No tap water. No charm. There was a shameless attempt to up-sell us by 300 per cent on the wine (which happened everywhere), and the food was rotten. The *fritto misto* was a horrific heap of garden clippings floured and deep fried, like some misbegotten thing from the very dawn of food.

And I wondered, is this what it's like for you lot in Britain, not being me? I do my best to be incognito, but it's getting harder these days, and I do my best to factor in how the experience might be for one who doesn't know the place, or isn't known by the staff. But if what happens to you when you go to a new restaurant is what happened to me in Rome – if real life is like Italy – then, Christ, sorry. How have you coped?

Travelling northwards, trying to escape, things only got worse. After wiggling along the coast for a while (in that briefly joyful phase of 'tootling along the scenic route' which always precedes a mad motorway dash to get back on track by nightfall), we found ourselves peckish in Portofino and staring up at a sign for the Splendido.

'Oho!' I exclaimed, in the Woosterish manner that comes upon me when the roof is down, the sun is shining, and a worthwhile scoff looms out of nowhere, 'It's the Splendido. Michael Winner says this is the best hotel in the world.'

'But you hate Michael Winner,' said the flopsy.

I was flabbergasted. 'Hate him?' I cried. 'The man's a genius. The daddy of us all. The alpha and omega of high-quality lifestyle journalism. I revere him as a God or sainted thing.'

'I suppose I must have formed the wrong impression, then,' she said, 'from the way you always throw the paper across the room before you get to the end of his first paragraph, and hurl yourself to the floor, banging your head on the ground and begging to be shot rather than live to see another morning in which Michael Winner lives and breathes.'

'Yes, well, my feelings about Winner are a little complex,' I said. 'But he knows a thing or two about flash hotels. Let's at least stop in for a beer. If it looks fun we'll maybe have lunch. We don't have to be in Nice till eight, we've got hours yet.'

And so, after winding up the spruce little ornamentally gardened hill on which the fabled hotel stands, growing slightly anxious due to that humbling effect that famous old establishments continue to have on me, I found a spot to park, hopped out, dusted myself down, put a couple of bits and pieces into the boot and . . . clunk!

The boot lid bounced on its bolt and popped open again. And again, clunk! And again. Now, this was no lovely old relatively rugged English sports car we were in (alas), but a rented Renault Megane in middle-management-metallic grey with an automatically retractable hard top. A hard top that opens or closes only when the boot is locked. And the boot wouldn't lock. And the roof was open. So we couldn't drive anywhere (because rain was always possible and it's nasty on the motorway), and if we did, we couldn't then leave it on the street.

Furthermore, the boot was locked open so that all our bags were easily reachable to passers-by. But not so reachable that we could get them out, for the roof was folded down into the unlockable boot in such a way as to trap them there, in sight and stealable from, but unremovable. And thus, because I do not take setbacks well, my world began gradually to fall apart.

After first attempting to make myself more presentable in the hotel loos, which resulted only in the sweat being moved around my face and neck and my hair reverting to the default 'sick dog' look that doormen tend to read as 'beggar or hoodlum', I tipped a bellboy to keep an eye on the car (I think it was the first vehicle of its kind – that is, affordable and dirty – that he had ever seen) and phoned the emergency number on the back of the key-fob.

In the 45 minutes it took to get through, get redirected, make someone understand the crippling nature of the car's apparently minor problem and secure the monstrous lie that a mechanic would arrive in two hours, I was warned away from the main restaurant by a waiter in a white tux who clearly didn't think such a smart spot would be my sort of thing (perhaps because of the giant tap-accident splash in my lap, which I had to endure since my other clothes were all 'locked' in the technically unlockable boot), shown to a table at the poolside restaurant and handed the most staggeringly wonderful bellini – fresh and pink and gleaming like babies – that I have ever known.

'It's all right, this, isn't it?' said the flopsy, buoyed, perhaps, by the brief thrill that the world's favourite depressant offers as a tease before doing its real work, or perhaps genuinely able to meet with triumph and disaster and treat those two impostors just the same. 'We could be stranded in worse places.'

And one could. But one could be stranded there with better people than me.

'I've never seen a view so beautiful,' she said.

'What if they can't mend it?' I replied.

'See that little island over there, and the boats like white splashes on a blue painting?'

'It's been nearly an hour already, they're never coming.'

The flopsy went and tried the water in the pool. 'It's warm like paddling pools in the garden when you're little,' she said. 'And the water laps the edge so it's hardly detached from the seascape.'

'If it's really busted, they'll have to give us another car,' I said. 'But that means getting some tinpot hatchback, driving all night through those bloody tunnels and missing dinner in Nice. It's a total, total nightmare.'

The head waiter, a suave old Romeo about whom I'd read before, came over to tell the flopsy her eyes were limpid pools or cornflowers or something, and me that mobile phones were frowned upon here.

'But it's an emergency!' I yelled, leaping to my feet, drawing no more attention than a man in stained trousers shouting at a waiter in the world's best (and quietest) poolside restaurant should expect to draw.

The fellow shrugged. And then they brought a bowl of *trocchi al pesto* with little boiled potatoes and green beans nestling among the pasta and a bowl of wide noodles, possibly pappardelle, with a rich tomato sauce and clams and cuttlefish and mussels, and the flopsy said, 'This looks wonderful', and I said, 'It's been two hours now, I'm phoning them again from over there.'

The flopsy told me, when I finally returned to the table, that both dishes were wonderful, and beautifully washed down by the local gavi di gavi recommended by the old boy who liked her eyes. Hertz told me the mechanic would be two more hours.

'This is unbelievably good,' said the flopsy, when she tried a slice of the thin, crispy pizza layered with pale prosciutto we had planned to share.

'Two more hours!' I said. 'We could die here!'

'But look at the view,' said the flopsy. 'Smell the jasmine. Look at the lawns and the trees and the sky.'

'Look at the nonagenarian American millionaires in shorts with taupe Tod's loafers and their polymerised wives with dinky boutique bags and boron tits, bored with Rome and Siena. Look at the fat brat kids and the way the waiters stare at me. Look at the bill! Two bowls of pasta, a pizza and a bottle of the house white for a hundred and fifty quid! Look at the signed photo of

Michael Winner, who likes this place so much only because he is unable to appreciate anything that is not refined down to absolute bloody perfection.'

'At least he can appreciate it,' said the flopsy.

And it wasn't just two more hours. It was four. Six in all. I could tell you how we spent the afternoon dodging waiters who kept trying to trick us into accepting cool, frosty beers that would have cost more than the car itself; I could tell you how, when he finally came, the witless, chortling fool of a mechanic unscrewed the safety plugs on the boot's underside, slammed it down and smashed the sun roof to a million pieces; I could tell you how he left us stranded later on the motorway, claiming he had a serious accident to go to ('It's them I pity, not us,' said the flopsy); how we finally crawled into Genoa's no-frills, concrete, semi-military airport around midnight, where the Hertz guy only half-believed our story and gave us a tiny Fiat food-mixer which got us to Nice only as fast as if we'd kept the other car and pushed it all the way, and how we missed dinner at Tetou, with the famous bouillabaisse, where I'd always wanted to go; and how the whole holiday, my whole life, was ruined.

The flopsy, I suppose, could tell you, if you really wanted to know, about lunch at the best hotel in the world.

INDIAN

W hen I was little we didn't tend to eat Indian food as a family. In fact we did it only once, in the New Forest, when we drove into Fordingbridge for a curry in the sort of place I have since seen all over England but did not understand at the time: the small-town curry house run by the only Indian family for miles around, and serving that hybrid, not-Indian, not-British, not-really-anything food that the English wanted to eat in Indian restaurants for so, so long. Stews of barnyard gristle and tinned vegetables, essentially, with curry powder stirred in late in the process to make it taste a bit like curry day at school.

Driving home through the dark forest, feeling woozy and bloated (for I am sure he tackled Indian in much the same way as he did Chinese – hard, fast and without let-up), my father said, 'Darling, kids, I want you to do something for me.'

'Anything, anything,' we didn't quite say, but thought, leaning forwards and squishing into the gap between the two front seats to get into our parents' space as much as we could before being elbowed back because it was dangerous.

'What I want you to do is this: Next time I say that I fancy a curry, remind me that I don't.'

Oh, how boring.

And we never got the chance anyway, because as far as I know, he never ate a curry again. (He did go to the Cinnamon

Club in London a couple of times, I remember, and loved it. But that was top-end, new-wave, 21st-century, Michelin-starred, post-imperial, sub-continental super food – grilled venison chop with a brinjal chutney, seared sea bass with coconut, fillet of wagyu beef with stir-fried morels and saffron sauce – and no more a 'curry' than whatever the hell dark brown lancing of hell's own bum boil they were serving up at the Old Fat Memsahib in Fordingbridge, Hants. in the 1970s.)

So at university the curries were quite an eye-opener (as for some people, I guess, were the libraries, ancient buildings and brilliant scholars). It was only what everyone else had eaten for exotic with their own families back home instead of Chinese, but I never had. And so while other kids from smaller towns than London (smaller even than Oxford) smoked their first joints, went to their first nightclubs, and lost their virginity, I fell upon the bright new world of miscellaneous protein chunks in fiery brown goo.

Except not that fiery, because I usually had a biryani in the end, because it came with its own rice. I still don't know what a biryani actually is (is it like chicken tikka masala and chop suey and doesn't really exist at all?), but you could get it at The Taj Mahal on Turl Street for £4.95 the lot, plus beer at a pound a pint, or lassi for those who had actually spent the previous year in India, knew a thing or two about its cuisine, and needed the calories to make up the four stone they had lost to amoebic dysentery.

And there was a curry place on Cowley Road with curtains you could close around your table, which was handy when you had changed girlfriends without either of the previously attached parties yet being aware. So it was just the two of you, hiding your love from the town in a fart- and curry-powder-scented wigwam, drinking beer and burping into each other's mouths. 'Romantic' doesn't even begin to capture it. The chapter of *Brideshead Revisited* that Evelyn Waugh set in The Bengal Tiger up Cowley must have somehow fallen foul of his editors.

These days, I get the odd takeaway from Kentish Town high street, and if everyone else has reviewed a big new Michelin-touted Pakistani grill in Knightsbridge where the food has been whittled down to tiny roundels of rare protein punctuated with scratches of curry 'jus' and dustings of unusual orange powders, laid out narratively on a parallelogrammatic porcelain Petri dish so that a single portion of high-street rogan josh can be served to people at £35 a plate, then I'll mooch down there and be mean about it, but in general I don't much bother with the sub-continent.

The fact that I don't is a bit of a bone of contention with my more complainy readers, especially the fact that I seem to them to ignore entirely the many excellent restaurants in areas of concentrated Indian population in Britain.

They tell me I should come to Birmingham to write about 'the balti scene'. They scream for my attendance in Leicester, where, I gather, there are more Indian restaurants than in the whole of Liechtenstein. 'It is all very well going to Le Gavroche,' they cry, 'but what about Hackney's Curry Mile?'

And my answer to all of them is this: if you are an Indian or a Pakistani or a Bangladeshi living in Bradford or Leicester or Hackney then you already know that you are surrounded by good, cheap Asian restaurants, and you do not need a patronising whitey git like me coming down there to judge the 'scene' on the basis of a single fleeting visit to a random restaurant. And if you are a patronising whitey git yourself then you are probably happy with the poisonous curry house at the end of your road.

I hate people who witter on about how different Indian food is from what we think it is, and make a huge thing out of eating with their fingers to show what folksy bloody flatulent world music fans they are. I hate them, the bargain-hunting, just-back-from-Goa bastards with their sandals and henna tattoos and well-thumbed 'Southern Asia on 7p a Week' handbooks, who pronounce everything in a semi-correct patois full of high seriousness, and so extenuate the internal sounds of monosyllabic dishes that you think words like 'dhal' and 'naan' are never going to end. They sing 'biryani' like it was an onomatopoeic representation of birdsong. They think a meal for four should cost no more than 12p, that yoghurt tastes better when it's salted, and that authenticity is more important than flavour and is always brown. I hate them. I really do.

I don't have any colonial guilt. I am a Hungaro-Pole. The Raj was not the fault of any Coren. So I am not going to turn vegetarian and pretend I like Bollywood movies just because you lot wanted a continent to shoot tigers in.

But then I happened to open an email from a *Times* reader called Manpreet Bhullar which began: 'I don't suppose you have ever thought about venturing towards Hounslow [correct, Manpreet] but if you fancy coming into our neck of the woods we can show you the delights of Southall – a little piece of England that is forever Punjab: you can sample *jalebis* on the Broadway, go to the zillion-pound new gurdwara, etc.' How could I resist?

At 4 p.m. I pulled into one of the long, straight rows of two-storey Twenties houses that spray off Southall Broadway and rang Manpreet's doorbell. I was shown briefly into a front room with lots of gurus on the wall and a shy grandmother who retreated wordlessly to the kitchen.

As we left the house, cowering under brollies, Manpreet whispered: 'Look at the twitching curtains – it's because I'm leaving the house with a man who is not only not my husband but is not a Sikh. Although your beard helps. It's like living in a soap opera round here.'

Our first stop was the newly built Sri Guru Singh Sabha

Gurdwara on Havelock Road, the largest Sikh temple in Europe. Entering the vast gurdwara, we took off our shoes and covered our heads and then traversed a hall as big as a country on a narrow strip of red carpet to bow before the Sri Guru Granth Sahib, a holy text. Except my bow was rubbish. I did not put my hands together. I just sort of nodded like it was a bloke I vaguely recognised across a crowded pub. My bow was so poor it made Manpreet laugh. But not the fancily dressed guy sitting with the book. He eyeballed me and tightened his grip on his ceremonial sword. At least, I hoped it was ceremonial.

Outside the hall an old man with a long beard was sitting in front of a football-sized chunk of orange dough and kneading a smaller lump of it in his hands. 'Now you can have *kara prashad*,' said Manpreet. The old man raised his hand and from it I took the orange lump. It was exactly 98.4 degrees Fahrenheit. It tasted of flour and sugar and old Punjabi hand. Chestnutty, if you want to know. Not unpleasant. But requiring for its proper description adjectives as yet uncoined.

Thence to the kitchen (*langar*) where we approached a canteen down long strips of carpet again (me still shoeless and mock-turbaned) to have our compartmented trays filled with a dhal, a vegetable curry, two rotis, yoghurt with long pieces of something purple in, and sweetened yellow rice tasting of cloves. We squatted on the floor and scoffed and then washed it down with sweet milky tea. It was pretty good, and it was free. It is a sacrament of Sikhism (laid down by the third Guru of the Sikhs, Sri Guru Amar Das Ji) that in every gurdwara a *langar* should be open and providing food for anyone at any time.

You hear that? Anyone, at any time. And you Christians think you're civilised because 15p from your text-message votes to *I'm a Celebrity ... Get Me Out of Here!* gets passed on to some unspecified charity.

As we ate, Manpreet told me that she had been married to

Aran for two years – the marriage was arranged by their parents
and they are very happy. Marriage meant that she had to move
to Southall from her beloved Hounslow, but they are doing up a
place in Norwood Green and hope to move in soon. Aran, who
picked us up later, drives a brown Vauxhall Astra and reckons
he is two cars away from a Mercedes.

We went to get *jalebis* from Jalebi Junction, which Aran had
to order because Manpreet is shy about speaking Punjabi with
her strong English accent. A *jalebi*, by the way, is molten sugar
charmed by a fakir into the shape of a Curly Wurly and served
in a paper bag. Again, extant coinage is inadequate.

From there we strolled through prefabricated mazes of sari
shops run by Afghan Sikhs who fled the Taliban and freak Aran
and Manpreet out because they speak Pashtun and not Punjabi.
Then we looked at gold shops. The gold is very yellow and there
is lots of it. 'Basically, you buy loads of it for the wedding, your
wife wears it once and then it goes in a safe-deposit box until
you die,' Aran explains. Manpreet objects that they visited their
gold as recently as last year. Aran says he'd rather have a Porsche
Boxster.

We went to Memories of India in Osterley: newish refurb,
antique carved wood from India, lots of linen and etched glass.
Nice. Among the diners were a couple of turbaned boys with
jewellery and trendy beards who gave each other a ragamuffin
hand punch and were described by Aran as 'not the ideal Sikhs
to introduce to your sister'. He does not know my sister.

We ate good *papri chaat* and excellent little black *hara* kebabs
made of spinach and green bananas and split peas and a good
big tandoori pomfret, but Manpreet was unimpressed by the
lifeless paneer pakora and found the chicken drab, too.

Then Aran and I went to Glassy Junction, formerly the
Railway Tavern, now a Punjabi pub named after a slang word
for 'a glass of something – usually whisky'. Inside, it's 1964 with

Sikhs. You expect to see the Likely Lads grumbling in a corner in grubby turbans. Alas, we had to leave Manpreet at the gurdwara as women do not go into the Glassy. So we had a swift half of Lal Toofan, picked her up again, and headed to Madhu's for the best meal of the night.

Madhu's provided the catering for Manpreet and Aran's wedding at the Radisson Edwardian at Heathrow to which 380 guests were invited, some of whom M&A even knew. It is a lovely split-level restaurant with glamorous, immaculate service and brilliant food. I cannot adequately praise the Masai-style spare ribs (*nyamah choma*) or the deep-fried tiny vegetables with garlic and ginger (*pilli pilli boga*) or *mahkni* (butter) chicken or the exquisite *keema*-stuffed green peppers. I may know nothing about Indian cooking, but this is the very best example of it that I have eaten anywhere (and costs only what high-street curries cost everywhere). And if it is good enough for Manpreet and Aran then, by whichever god you pray to, it is good enough for you.

I did close an Indian restaurant down once. In fact, I closed an entire chain of them. And it was all Shilpa Shetty's fault.

You remember Shilpa, the woman who became famous in this country when Jade Goody, a poor, thick girl from the very bottom of the ladder, called her 'Shilpa Poppadum' live on telly because she knew no better.

Poor, thick, sad, fat Jade. Exploited in the time-honoured manner of the bearded lady or two-headed child by her bourgeois puppet masters on a primetime socioeconomic freak show. Well, it turns out that she was quite right to distrust Shilpa Shetty. Even Jade's use of the p-word was spookily prescient, because not very long after that the great Bollywood star (and wife of some rich bloke whose name escapes me) bought up my local curry house The Bombay Bicycle Club and by the time she'd finished with it the only thing worth eating there was the poppadums.

It used to be quite good, did The Bombay Bicycle Club. Good enough to lure me away from my favourites in Kentish Town to drive all the way to Hampstead, up past the gorgeous 200-year-old Italianate villas, to the spot that was once a restaurant called Keats's and then called Byron's and then, when they ran out of Romantic Poets (presumably because Shelley's was a shoe shop and Wordsworth's sounded too much like Woolworths), became The Bombay Bicycle Club, part of a small chain (I later found out) of two or three restaurants.

The onion pakora were light and zippy, the *machli* tandoori were meaty monkfish brochettes, the dhansak was good, the bhunas (we're only talking high-street standards here, not Cyrus Todiwala or Atul Kochhar stuff) were fine and spicy, the dhoti prawns, the must-have Calicut fish curry . . . And then there were always endless vegetable possibilities: the *shahi bagyan* (aubergine with onion and garlic), Bombay mushrooms, *aloo chat*, the best *bindi sabzi* around, *daal sag* made with the *daal* of the day . . .

You know? Not rocket science. Not posh. Not regional. Not top-class Indian home cooking for natives. But right at the top end of the stuff that is perfectly good enough for you and me. Most importantly, one could eat healthily there. I could eat a meal of mostly vegetables with maybe a bit of fish, a skewer of lamb, like God meant it to be. And, more importantly, girls could eat there.

It was bright and light with not too many Raj-era photos, and only the one penny farthing mounted on the wall (oh, the ludicrous cash offers I made for just one ride on it down the High Street). The staff were a nice big ethnic mix from around Europe and Asia, the clientele were a collection of local Hampstead Jewish oldies, young bankers, dating couples enjoying the late summer evening light through the big windows and students picking up takeaways. I loved it. I became a Bombay Bicyclist overnight.

And so one Sunday night, Esther and I popped out for a curry, as people do. We walked in, sat down. Everything looked the same. There was no telling. A familiar waitress brought us menus, and we asked for a couple of beers.

The first sign was the writing on the menu. Suddenly there were words in pink and green shouting from among the black ones. There was superfluous capitalisation. Dishes were apostrophised with daft phrases such as 'A BEAUTIFUL beginning to an INDIAN FEAST' and 'CRUSHED BLACK PEPPER. SPICY PERFECTION. Less than 10 per cent fat!'

Hmm, so they had got a mad person in to write the menus. Fine, fine. It happens. Or perhaps we had accidentally been given the children's menu, designed for little heads that get bored in the middle of sentences unless the words CONSTANTLY CHANGE COLOUR!!!! And have loads of POINTLESS exclamation MARKS!!!!!!! and the words get bigger and SMALLER all the time!!!

But who gives a damn how much fat there is in a tandoori king prawn? And anyway, wouldn't you imagine it would be much less than 10 per cent? And what is BEAUTIFUL about an onion bhaji and WAIT A MINUTE! What's onion bhaji doing on this menu at all? This place doesn't have onion bhajis. I'm just having a pakora and . . .

. . . aaaaaaaaargh! No pakora! No EFFING pakora!

And no Calicut fish curry, no monkfish brochettes, no lovely rogan josh, no dhansak. None of my lovely vegetable dishes. All gone! All blasted, all wasted! Just a list of bog-arse Seventies slophouse standards: lamb madras, biryanis, chicken korma, sag aloo and chicken tikka ma-bloody-sala.

And there was certainly no *barra chana shahi*, the knuckle

whole and slow-cooked. All the lamb dishes were just TENDER cubed meat chunks in gravy. Oh woe.

I called the waitress over.

'What happened?' I said.

'I'm so sorry,' she said.

'No, but who did it? Who did this terrible thing?'

'It was her,' she said, turning over my menu and pointing at an over-made-up, poodle-haired trollop in some Bollywood publicity shot who, on closer inspection, turned out to be none other than Shilpa Poppa . . . I mean Shilpa Shetty.

'She bought it,' said the waitress. 'She bought the whole chain. The old menus are gone. Just these dishes now. They said it would be popular. But everyone hates it.'

We ordered. It came. It was terrible. Don't want to talk about it. Six or seven bowls of brown cloacal waste, containing amorphous protein chunks. The sick of an infant who lives on Dairylea Lunchables. Why cubed? The meat here was always slices of chicken, big pieces on the bone, skin, fat, all that. Now it's all rhomboids from giant rectangular chickens reared on Mars and cut by machines undreamt of in Bernard Matthews's most foetid nightmares.

Got home, checked Internet, all true: 33 per cent stake in V8 catering group (owners of Bicycle Club) bought by this fat dancer (who is 'Co-Chairperson' and 'Brand Ambassador') and her millionaire husband, with a plan, clearly, to cut costs, level down to the LOWEST common denominator, and bang out the cheapest crap imaginable with a lot of smoke and mirrors to throw people off the (rancid) scent.

Okay. So a few weeks later I'm coming home from work late and I call 'curry' on speed-dial, not thinking. Get through to Bicycle Club. Curse my days. But hungry. Order up some harmless-sounding old-fashioned student curries. But also need vegetables. Can I get some saag?

'Saag aloo?'

'No, just plain saag. I don't want potatoes. I just want spinach.'

'Not possible. We don't have that.'

'But you have spinach, just ask the cook not to add the potatoes.'

'Can't. There's no kitchen here. This is centralised booking line in Wandsworth.'

'But I've dialled Hampstead.'

'All calls rerouted now.'

'Well, what vegetables do you have without potatoes in?'

'None.'

'I know that. You don't have okra any more and you don't have aubergine. You don't have anything. May I speak to the manager?'

The call-centre manager, after a long harangue from me, said she would call the restaurant to sort me some vegetables. But she was lying out of her invisible arse. When I got to the restaurant they said no attempt had been made to contact them. No off-menu request for just some simple vegetables, without a pile of cheap, bloaty potatoes designed to bulk out the dish and strip me of a fiver for slop of minimal nutritional value, had been made.

The lovely guy who handed over my food offered to have my vegetable dishes made on the spot. But I had a cab waiting. I said I had to go. He said he was so, so sorry. Head office had done this with the phones and he was no longer allowed to talk to his customers directly. He looked furtively around and then whispered an offer of his mobile number, for next time. Under-the-counter half-decent service that Shilpa, cackling in the counting house, need never know about.

But I looked down into my bags containing the grey food silt that The Bicycle Club now peddles, boxed into its new all-plastic, polythene-lidded microwave containers, cooked up, no doubt, in some off-site factory and shipped out at a cost of less than nothing to whichever mugs don't notice how terrible it is, and said, 'That's kind of you, but there isn't going to be a next time.'

I left the bags on the counter, got back in my cab and went home via McDonald's.

I wrote about it all, of course. What else was I going to do, bomb the place? And within months people started tweeting me photos of local branches of Bombay Bicycle Club being boarded up. I'm sad that I wasn't able to bring the place back to its glory days, but closing it down altogether was surely the next best thing.

Always Order the Fish

REALLY GOOD FRESH
(ENVIRONMENTALLY SUSTAIN-
ABLE) fish is very hard to come by, very
hard to store and keep fresh (you've got to really
cook it as soon as you buy it or there's no point), often
fiddly to work with, and very smelly to cook. It's
what restaurants are FOR!
It so happens that I eat out a lot, so it's a good way of not
exploding into an impossibly fat bastard, too, and getting the various
good things one gets from fish in terms of lean proteins, special
mysterious don't-actually-exist anti-cancer minerals and fatty acids,
without having to argue for hours about the glassy-eyed bastard on the
slab, wrap it in a billion bags so it doesn't bend everything in the fridge to
its own particular pong (mackerel butter is one of my least favourite things),
cook it almost immediately at the wrong temperature for the wrong time
so that it's either gloopy along the bone or all stuck to the foil/pan/oven/
wall/side of my head, and then spend a week living in a house that
smells like the command centre of some marine animal-oriented Nazi
death camp, some fish Treblinka. Auschfishtz, if you will.
It just amazes me that people will go into a restaurant and
order the steak. A thing you can buy almost anywhere,
keep for weeks, and cook however you like without
doing anything to it and it'll always basically be
okay. You're letting these chefs off lightly,
like that. At least make them work
for a living.

I WAS A WAITER ONCE TOO, YOU KNOW

I was. Of course I was. But then who wasn't?

In my case it was at The Dome. The Dome 'café-bar' (woooo . . .) in Hampstead, in the early 1990s. The chain is long gone now, but in its time represented the very height of faux-Parisian chic on the high streets of Chelsea, Chiswick, Hampstead, Oxford . . . until it over-reached itself and got gobbled up by the Café Rouge.

The Dome. Where I earned £2/hour serving frozen cassoulet, microwaved by 'The Captain', the illegal Russian in the kitchen, who smoked cigarettes while he worked so that the ash fell like salamander droppings into the steaming pots, and wiped steaks on the floor before he fried them for customers who thought this was really a French restaurant, maybe because of the red '*tabac*' symbol outside the door and the circumflex over the 'o'.

We all dressed as French waiters, with white shirts and black aprons, and stole in whatever way we could. The really bad ones stole from the customers, adding a tenner to the bill and hoping they wouldn't notice (everyone paid by cash in those days) or charging them for a bottle they hadn't drunk and then stealing the bottle. But mostly we just stole from the house. With wages this low (it reckoned out at 58 pounds a week after the deduction of emergency tax and national insurance), we had to assume that a certain amount of burgling the till was factored into the business plan.

I never once cheated a punter myself, because the poor fuckers were being robbed badly enough just paying for the food we served. I swear, the bacon for the 'classic English breakfast' came in already fried and got warmed up, if you were lucky, on demand. There was a smoked salmon omelette on the menu but when someone asked for scrambled eggs and smoked salmon you had to say no, because the omelettes came in already made. Like plane food. It was the most popular restaurant in Hampstead for many years. But one of those places where the staff always seem to be having a better time than the customers. I hate those places.

And I was shit at waiting. Always forgot everything. Couldn't get my head round it. Always taking the wrong food to the wrong tables, at the wrong time, dripping sweat into the soup and sneezing into the tiramisu so that aerosol Chantilly leapt up out of the bowl and spattered people's faces. Never got any tips at all.

I was soon demoted to barwork, where you were paid £2.50/ hour on the basis that you wouldn't get so many tips. The floor staff were supposed to put ten per cent of theirs into a tronc each night, to go to the bar staff and kitchen. But they never did. Mean fuckers.

So we, the barmen, found our own ways to make money. Which meant bypassing the till on cappuccinos, and keeping a box of five pees under the bar to give people change for their pounds without having to pop the register. You needed a lot of five pees, though, because nobody ever, ever invited you to keep the change. Not five fucking pence on a 95p cup of coffee. The mean, mean bastards. I am hating them all over again for it now, like I used to then. The spoilt, rich, arrogant Hampstead fuckfaces, parking their Porsches on the zigzag outside and mincing in to sip mimsy little milky coffees at the zinc bar and act all continental in their crappy local ersatz French *tabac*, but then greedily grasping back their change – playing the consumer role marked out for them by the group (Trusthouse Forte it was, I think, and then Grand Metropolitan) right up to the point where they flip the barman a *sous* and say 'ciao, boss', but stopping short, from pure meanness.

So, yes, we took each pound we fancied, maybe one in three, because it could not be checked (nobody except a fool ever fiddled the stock-taken stuff like bottled beers, wine and spirits), and when our pockets were laden down with oners, positively busting with brassy nuggets, we went for a fag break, crossed the road to the Post Office and turned them into notes. (Grand Met later put up coffee prices to £1.05 to discourage this little scam – they wised up when a barman at the Chelsea branch was promoted to deputy manager, the whistleblowing shit – so we moved to robbing on the draft beer instead, still round-numbered at £1 a half-pint, which was more lucrative anyway. We didn't sell whole pints, by the way, because we were so fucking French.)

God but we hated most of the customers. With their sunglasses on their heads and their jacket sleeves rolled up and their endless demands that the beer be colder or the service quicker. It was no wonder The Captain wiped their steaks on the floor. All we could do at the bar, by way of guerrilla war, was serve them last. Make them think we were coming to them and go to the little old lady lost in the crush and serve her instead, and give it to her on the house. Keep ignoring them and ignoring them and ignoring them . . .

Because you can on a bar. That's what makes it so wonderful. When you're waiting tables you are going into the customer's space, making yourself useful on his terms, and he is the boss and you have to stand there and take whatever he dishes out, be helpful, do your best, enable him to be the man, to boss you and make things work for his table, and you must scamper off, quickety-quick, to do his bidding and serve his whim. And then, at the end, if you have pleased him, he may throw you some coppers. This was before the days of 'service included' and it was left optional. On average, when you counted up, the punters at the Dome tipped nine per cent. For me it was closer to four.

But at the bar, they come to you. The bar is your space, there is a wall between you and your mark and you have what he wants, booze, lined up in bottles behind you and dispensed from taps in front of you, and if he wants some he has to get your attention. Especially on a Thursday or Friday or Saturday night when every half-decent bar, and even the Dome, which was not even quarter-decent, is rammed to damnation.

So first of all you never, ever serve a bloke if a girl is waiting. You're not going to get a blowie from a bloke just by making him feel special at the bar. Well, maybe you are, which is another good reason not to serve him. And never serve the ones holding a note in their hand as if you're doing this for the goddam money, as if you are some uniformed bellboy bum who can be bought by the smell of a tenner. Never serve the ones in sunglasses, because it's all about eye contact. Never serve the ones with expensive watches. Or ones who click their fingers or wave (as a waiter, if ever a customer waved at you across the room, the thing was to wave back and then carry on with whatever you were doing). Go to girls first, then mates, then tramps if there are any (there was one at the Dome called Bruno, who wore a beige coat and a hat and shook a lot and later died, of course), and never charge any of them more than a gestural, smokescreen amount. Then the poorer, shabbier-looking men, and then, finally, the glossy-haired, well-dressed ones with their Porsches on the zebra outside – which by then should have been towed away.

But mostly the job was about when the customers had gone. It was before the days of late opening and when eleven came round we shouted, 'Time, Ladies and Gentlemen, Please,' with a joy that was unalloyed. Although I tried to avoid the job myself. Because I was as shy in front of a crowd then as I am now, and thought my voice sounded too posh and unthreatening for anyone to take it seriously and properly fuck off home.

So my pal, Mike, used to do it. He was from Devon, I think. But he had a sort of Australian accent. Everyone did in 1990. Something to do with *Neighbours*, I think. Or INXS. Mike had played cricket for the county and had Marilyn Monroe tattoo'd on his right bicep and when he said it the people properly left. And then around 11.20, when a good 30 or 40 were still straggling, and someone was ushering them out of the door, Mike would stand up on the bar and shout: 'YOU DON'T HAVE TO GO HOME . . . '

And they'd all turn and whisper and think they were going to be allowed to stay for a lock-in. And then Mike would shout: '. . . BUT YOU CAN'T STAY HERE!!!'

And I thought it was just about the funniest goddam thing I had ever heard. Every time. And when the last punter was out we'd lock the doors. And we'd put up the chairs on the tables, and while the waiters mopped the floors and cleaned the tables, we'd clean down the bar, throw out the old juices (the tomato smelling like blood, the grapefruit all fizzy and urinous, the pineapple thick and funky), and crack open a row of cold Budvars on the bar, and drink them, and The Captain would come out of the kitchen with a couple of big plates of fries, and gradually, as each waiter and waitress finished their personal count, checked it against their bills, and turned it over to the manageress, everyone would be sitting on high stools at the end of the bar, smoking fags and drinking beers, or rolling joints in the kitchen, and we'd put the music up nice and loud, blues-y stuff that fitted the mood, and in the dark street outside groups of people would stop, and peer in, and sometimes knock on the door and we'd all shout, 'WE'RE CLOSED!!' at the same time and then laugh, because the people outside knew, just as we knew, that the Dome was only really any good after closing.

In the end they got rid of Mike because he was screwing Belinda, who was supposed to be screwing Darian (I've changed the names there for those two, because I guess maybe if they cared so much then, perhaps they still do) and then after that you weren't allowed to even mention his name. And it started to be less fun.

I had a girlfriend called Paula. I got her off Jonny Barton. But then she screwed Nick. I said that thing about blowjobs, but I didn't mean it. Or, rather, I didn't personally get any blowjobs in return for beers, even though you could. We were like little local celebrities in a way. It was the best bar around for kids between 15 and 20 and we were picked to work there because we were young and pretty with floppy hair and suntans from long holidays and looked hot in a white shirt (which was mostly our old school shirt) and a black apron. And without being able to play a guitar or sing, and without any money to speak of, it was the next best thing to have going for you. You could get people into the Dome and you could get them drinks. And you could make their boyfriends look small and silly. And that's all that matters at that age. And you could get whatever you wanted in return. And I suppose I wish I had. But I wasn't like that then, and rarely have been since.

On about the second late shift I worked, this girl Paula came in, recently unhitched from Jonny Barton (who shagged every girl he ever met, especially foreign ones, because he spoke at least seven languages already, barely out of his teens) and sat down opposite me as I was wrapping cutlery in paper napkins at the small marble table in the back corner by the kitchen (it was called a 'wrap station', and every time I was ordered by the manager to 'set up a wrap station', I pretended I thought he had said, 'rap station', and made the suitable surprised noises about the evils of pirate radio, and he never, ever, laughed). This was the 17 year-old Spanish girl who was working as an au pair for an orthodox Jewish family in Palmers Green. She was wearing a blue and white sailor dress and little white pumps. She put the rattan cutlery tray on her lap and held out pairs of knives and forks for me to wrap in a napkin and line up on the metal tray on the table, and as I took them from her I tried not to look at her brown little knees, in case I gave myself away.

So then I walked her home, and we went by the canal, which was not on the way. And we didn't get home until morning. And so that was that. Always my stupid way. I get myself into a position when I can just spend the summer messing around and screwing whoever I want, every night, week after week after week, but then I go and fall in love with the first one. Always. Every damn time. It's why I've hardly ever screwed anybody at all.

So. That was in my middle summer of university. Four months. Seemed like a lifetime. And it's why I never give waiters any grief, and never identify individual ones in reviews, and always tip as much as I can afford regardless of how well or badly they do their job (as long as they are kind and helpful). Because they're not really waiters. They're just people. Usually young people. And they're only passing through. And it's the least I can do.

REMAINING ANONYMOUS

For a long time – at least until I was 17 or 18 – my favourite poem in all the world was 'Dooley Is a Traitor' by James Michie. Not much is known about Michie, at least not by me, except that in 1927 he published a poem – full of good gags and chunky rhymes – about a convicted murderer on trial for draft-dodging. What the judge in this unique courtroom drama(tic poem) cannot understand about Dooley, separated as the two men are by a great gulf in class and education, is why a man who has killed in hot blood for his own ends should refuse to kill in cold blood for his king and country.

'Now is it that you simply aren't willing,' the judge asks the shuffling Cockney in the dock, 'Or have you a fundamental moral objection to killing?'

Dooley is aghast:

'No objection at all, sir,' I said.
'There's a deal of the world I'd rather see dead –
Such as Johnny Stubbs or Fred Settle or my last landlord, Mr
    Syme.
Give me a gun and your blessing, your honour, and I'll be
    killing them all the time.
But my conscience says a clear No
To killing a crowd of gentlemen I don't know.'

As Dooley warms to his theme the very notion of 'bravery' is reconstructed and the murderer's refusal to kill men with whom he is not on personal terms begins to sound like the highest form of honour. Too high for me. I am quite the opposite of Dooley. I can only kill a man I have not met. Once I have shaken hands with him I just can't do it. And by 'kill', of course, I mean 'give a really stinking review to'.

If I can just get into a restaurant and get out again without them knowing it's me, I feel free to tell it how I found it. If I have to kill 'em I have to kill 'em – and balls to the collateral damage (firings, closures, suicides) that may come as a direct or indirect result of my murderous actions. But meet the chef, the owner, or the parents or children of either, and I'm hamstrung. Smiles, handshakes, imprecations to accept no bill (always declined), a desire expressed to see me again, an invitation to come and eat with the family, to share old recipes, chat about the Old Country, sleep with the wife, and then what should I do? Go home and turn the place over?

Perhaps, but what I do is go home and look for the positives because I can see in my mind's eye the little guy standing there at the door in the new suit he bought specially, and so I dodge the issue, and write a quiet little piece about other things (favourite poems, etc) with coded messages in it to warn regular readers away.

That is why I am rarely the first critic to review somewhere new: because in the first few weeks of a new restaurant operation the public relations consultant will be there at all times, hosting tables, making notes, or just endlessly repeating the news that 'it's basically a whole new concept in eating and drinking'.

You walk in at such times and it's, 'Mwah, mwah, this is Giles Coren, Giles, do you know Serge, the owner? He escaped from a Serbian death camp by pole-vaulting over the wall with a stick made from his own bogeys, and then hopped to London on his only leg. His whole family was executed, including the pets. His dream was always to open a restaurant and he has dedicated it to the memory of his baby triplets who drowned in a horrible accident last week. He's a huge fan of your column. Enjoy.'

So at the very least I'll go in a little later in the life of the restaurant to try and preserve some modicum of a normal eating experience, and book under a pseudonym, and dress down and kind of shuffle a bit on the way in and look at my shoes while my wife announces the arrival of the 'Shumley-Twerpps' or the 'Wazzocks' or whoever.

It's a long shot that I'll get out completely unrecognised in a newish urban restaurant which, if not staffed largely by people who have had many other jobs in many other restaurants before, will no doubt have a set of photographs of current critics at the reception desk, but it might at least delay their realisation that the mighty Giles Coren is in the house.

And it really is better for one and all if they don't realise. Because the moment they do, they start to tremble and quiver. Sommeliers crack glasses as they pour, timid waitresses spill soup in my lap, and at the far edge of my eyeline I am aware of waiters, unable to take their eyes off me, wheeling the flambé trolley straight out of the French windows and into the street four floors below.

The kitchen, when it gets wind of my arrival, goes all to pot as well. The chef can't bear to let a dish leave the pass, so that my food always, always, comes out an hour later than every other table's, all cold and covered with thumb-prints because of the chef's misguided notion that visual perfection is what will thrill me. And I am left begging – begging – for something hot, on a plate, now. Pleeeeease.

And then they send out other courses I haven't ordered. 'Ze chef inseest you try eez famous turbot in wat waaan . . .' And if

I don't eat it it's thrown away. And I hate to be rude. And then they send some vile bit of foe gras or something. And I am begging – again, begging – just for a cup of coffee and the bill.

But, no, they keep me there and keep me there, until some bald, stressed little man in a butcher's apron comes out of the kitchen, smelling of fag-smoke and pig-fat and his own sweat, and sits down at my table with a bottle of beer and all I can do is look at the other tables, long-vacated, and envy their former denizens with all my soul, who have got home now, kissed their sleeping children, and are snuggling down to sleep.

So, yes, it's a massive pain in the arse being recognised – or 'busted', as I tend to think of it ('Busss-Stedd!' shouts my wife, sotto-voce, when the head waiter returns from the kitchen to say that the chef has invited me to take sexual advantage of his eldest daughter at my earliest convenience) – and I do what I can to avoid it. But I will not stoop to disguises. In America, on the other hand, disguises are very much par for the course.

I think I have never read a book so vain, pompous, self-serving and silly as the former *New York Times* critic Ruth Reichl's 2005 memoir, *Garlic and Sapphires: the Secret Life of a Food Critic*, in which she details the years she spent dressing up in increasingly elaborate disguises to sneak into restaurants four, five, six, seven or more times before forming her final impression, boshing out 500 very ordinary words and attaching an arbitrary row of stars. (It was quite the hot topic when it came out over here, and caused a deal of a stir in gastro-bookish circles. If I had a pound for every literary editor who asked me to review it, I'd have three pounds.)

Each chapter of the book carries the name of the 'character' she adopted in order to 'work on' a particular restaurant (sometimes for as long as a month): Miriam, Chloe, Brenda, Molly, a great legion of wigged women with prosthetic noses and comedy spectacles behind which Ms Reichl hides for fear that she will otherwise be identified as the self-important fatty from the local blatt, and be treated to some sort of special and inauthentic experience which will make it impossible for her to arrive at her saintedly impartial and earth-shattering judgment.

It is the great fallacy at the heart of a certain kind of restaurant criticism that the most important thing is to pass for a nobody, to go to the Ritz in holey dungarees, besmear one's face with horse dung and walk with a limp to see if they treat you less well than the King of Norway. (I have seen the Queen of that country treated very well, and been invited to mop up her leftovers – as you will know already, if you are reading this book backwards.)

But to disguise oneself is to pander to the myth of the two-tier restaurant world. To obsess over the perceived class division is merely to perpetuate it – just like all the weary old Trots who bang on about the unfairness and elitism of the Establishment only to consolidate their lucrative positions as critics of it. The more of a fuss one makes of one's anonymity, the more one mythologises and exalts a business, the restaurant business, that ought to be approached breezily and without hauteur.

But in New York they just don't do 'breezy'. They do only clench-bummed mimsiness and snobbery. New Yorkers care only how fashionable a restaurant is, how sizzling its tables, how to-die-for its guest list and how grovelling its staff. They don't really care about the cooking. And so they create an atmosphere in which certain people will, indeed, have a better time than others. It's their own little new-made class system.

But if the food is all you care about, such a division is not a problem. For example, Nobu, if they recognise me, can only serve me the same food they serve to little old you. But they can kiss my arse more. Now, as long as we don't care about having our arses kissed (and we don't, you and I), then what is the difference? Indeed, if we positively do *not* want our arses kissed, then it's better to be you than me.

One of the more ridiculous chapters in the book features Reichl's multiple visits to Daniel – at the time, the newly opened restaurant of Daniel Boulud of Le Cirque. She goes as Brenda, a hippy in a red wig, and has a lovely time despite looking like an escaped lunatic. She comes more and more to inhabit this 'Brenda' she has created – though she is nothing more than a straggly polyester syrup and a swipe of cheap lipstick – and goes back five times to make sure he can 'sustain that level of cooking'. (Five times, what a loser!)

Finally, she bestows four stars on this joint, quotes for our delectation Boulud's thank you letter congratulating her on her 'innovative style', and concludes: 'Rereading the review, I saw what had happened: Ruth did not write the review. Brenda did.'

Waiter, bring me a sick bag.

To me, this approach only shows how hidebound, backward and snobby New York society is, and Reichl's descriptions of such theoretically hot destinations as Le Cirque and Lespinasse make them sound like the stuffiest bastions of classist priggery since the aristocratic *salles à manger* of pre-Revolutionary France.

But that's partly because in New York there really is a 'restaurant scene'. There really are hip dining rooms, hot tables and places you'd flay your mom to get a reservation. People can impress each other in New York simply by telling each other where they had their tea. But that isn't really so in London.

This is because New York takes itself so seriously. It is the core personality disorder of the modern American, and of the New Yorker in particular. New Yorkers are just so pleased with their city and with themselves and with their mutual co-identification. I think it dates from that tortured

Gershwin-themed opening to Woody Allen's *Manhattan*. Possibly a little earlier. Possibly it's Truman Capote's fault.

Even as you walk the streets you can see and hear how marvellous the locals think those streets are, with their delis and their transvestites and their poxy little park and their foetid river, and their Iroquois and the silly statue and the never-sleeping and the so-good-they-named-it-twice and Broadway and the Yankees and Studio 54 and *Cagney & Lacey* and *Across 110th Street* and the taxis and *Sex and the bloody City* and oo-wasn't-it-dangerous-before-Giuliani-cleaned-it-up-but-we-don't-like-him-anyway-because-we're-arty-farty-Democrats . . . without ever admitting that it's just a town. Just a lot of buildings with roads between them, bad traffic and shops where you can buy stuff.

We're not like that in Britain. We don't really give a crap where a chef is from or who brought him here or which orange-skinned celebrity weirdos go to his restaurant. We just want a smiley waitress, a hot plate of something nice, preferably chicken, and clean loos with a proper lock on them.

But the tragedy is that there are critics here who make a great song and dance about anonymity, too. Going beyond what the rest of us happily do (which in my case is to book with a fake name and phone number, to dress like crap, make my guest announce our arrival, and to sit facing the wall) to preserve the mystery of their identities, withholding photographs from their bylines (no doubt enjoying the same frisson the Lone Ranger felt each time he donned his mask), and even when contributing to dull features in trade mags insist on appearing as blacked-out silhouettes, as if they were embedded in an FBI witness-protection scheme, rather than just being dumpy hacks who differ from every other flabby ink-pisser on the Street only in that when they claim lunch on expenses they don't have to pretend they got a 'story' from a 'contact'.

But how grim to skulk in the shadows all one's life like some hooded urban phone-grabber. How can it be worth it? One's job has to fit into one's life.

Say I've got a meeting in town at six o'clock, followed by a colleague's book launch in Soho which I should drop in on for an hour, and want to have dinner with a hot chick who lives in South London so have to meet halfway (I'm imagining myself single and gagging for it here, so as to liven up the picture – truth is I never go anywhere unless I know I can be home by six to bath the baby). I wibble around on the Internet for a bit and find a new gaff that is ten minutes from the party by cab, and another 15 to her place, and early reports suggest it rocks.

What do I do? Do I book a table in her name, meet her at the party, then cab it down to Belgravia for a scoff and a bottle, and back to hers for Ovaltine and *Book at Bedtime*, planning to dash something off in the morning if she can remember what I ate?

Or do I spend nine hours in make-up, book as Rgthi the Klingon, feel damn silly at the party in my rubber mask with gills on the forehead, put a bag on the bird's head when I get to the restaurant because there's a chance they might recognise her, too, remain silent throughout the meal (they might recognise the world-famous voice), order nothing I actually like (because if I have the caramelised sweetbreads followed by the pork belly with a bottle of cheap pinot noir, no pudding, two espressos and a bottle of still, then there's frankly nobody it could be but me), pay with one of my walletful of fake ID credit cards (as Reichl does) and then come back twice more even if it's rubbish?

But don't go thinking that I don't know what it is to be treated like shit in a restaurant. Before my greed and vanity made a TV whore out of me I used to go unrecognised all the time, and often found myself treated in the scummiest way imaginable.

I remember my fury at being seated in the nasty little holding pen behind the till at J Sheekey, feeling the draught on my ankles every time the front door opened to let in another bloated D-lister, feeling their eyes on my plate and my cheap suit, witnessing the fawning banter from the staff, as they dithered over taking the fellow's coat until I wanted to get up from my table, throw down my soup spoon and cry, 'Look, if you're not going to take his fucking coat off him, I WILL!'

I remember being so displeased with my table that I scouted into the other rooms to see what was available and found the place half empty because at least a dozen pukka tables had to be kept free just in case, *just in case*, Stephen Fry or Mariella Frostrup came in. Knowing that my presence there was valued by the establishment much less than the vague possibility of somebody drifting in who was probably on holiday in Mustique anyway.

I remember the bum seats by the outer walls of The Wolseley, never getting a table outside the River Café, being openly laughed at by receptionists at Nobu and Zuma, and of writing about my desire to throw a Molotov cocktail through the 'smug little mullioned windows' of The Ivy. But that doesn't mean I need to endure such treatment every time I eat, just to get a job done. I'm there to write about a restaurant, a room with tables and a geezer in the kitchen heating things up, not to start a revolution.

That said, a revolution was exactly what I wanted to start the night I first went to Roka, in Charlotte Street, in what was probably its opening month, and had that unusual thing: a truly awful experience in a truly terrific restaurant.

And when I say 'awful', I mean that it was typical of the small-minded, brutal, ignorant, greedy, snobbish, ugly, filthy quagmire of moral excrement which is, on occasion, the London top-end restaurant scene. It was a night that exemplified everything which you, the people, the *demos*, *hoi polloi*, the rock and well-spring of all that is great about our nation, worry might happen to you when you go to a flashy new restaurant and encounter them, the oligarchs, the parasites, the pampered plutocrats, the crapulent kakistocracy that tramples on the decent, the modest, the good and the kind, the right and the proper, to satisfy its greed, its vanity, its vulgar, cupiditous, misplaced sense of superiority. And when I say 'terrific', I mean that when the food finally arrived at my table – by which time my evening had already been ruined – it was about as good as one could hope to be served in a restaurant.

I was always planning to go to Roka pretty soon after it opened. Everyone knew that Rainer Becker, the chef proprietor at Zuma in Knightsbridge, the big opening of 2002, had been planning a second project right from the start, and that it would be very much like Zuma, and would thus serve brilliant modern Japanese cooking to horrendous worldtrash people (it is not fair always to blame Europe), so that while eating the finest raw fish and little robata-grilled delicacies, you would find yourself vibrating deep inside to the sickening throb of Ferraris pulling up and parking on the pavement. There would be a roiling, bubbling, babbling Babel of those languages that are spoken only in the most severely moneyed little principalities and fiefdoms of the world, and you would be subjected to a level of service directly correlated to how much money the particular staff member thinks you have in your wallet, in your bedroom safe, in your numbered accounts at banks in countries where sex with children and trafficking in Nazi gold are not only accepted, but are conditions of habitation. It is one of those restaurants – like Nobu, Hakkasan, Petrus, Zafferano, Le Caprice – of which one generally says, 'Great food, shit people.' Well, one does.

The restaurant critic I most admire in all the world loved

Roka. But she went to a 'soft' opening and asked the waiter to 'devise a meal of what he thought were the most interesting dishes'. The upshot was that the chef 'rose to the challenge magnificently' and she gave him four stars. It sounds like she had a lovely evening but it reveals nothing at all, I am afraid, about what it is to go as an unknown punter.

So I'll tell you. I strolled down jolly old Charlotte Street with its ageless palimpsest of great, average and terrible restaurants, and as I crossed towards Roka, I saw a man in a dark suit standing in front of the door with his hands clasped in front of his genitals. 'Oh darling, I'm sorry,' I muttered to my girlfriend. 'I have a feeling this place might turn out to be horrible.'

Sure enough, the man in the suit looked me up and down. Head to toe.

Evening ruined. I said, 'Good evening.' At this point, had he merely said, 'Good evening, sir,' and opened the door for me, I might have been prepared to forget the up-and-down thing. But he said: 'Are you here for the restaurant?' Rather than make a smart-arse remark, which would have come out wrong as I was already pretty irritated, I said: 'Yes.' And what do you think he said?

He said, 'Sorry, the restaurant is completely full. Reservations only.'

So I stabbed him in the eye, cut out his heart while he was still breathing and posted it to his mother. And then I said: 'How do you know I haven't got a reservation?' Eventually, sick to my stomach, I was allowed through to the front desk. I took in the large, airy, All Bar One-style room and gave them the daft name I had used to book the table. I was told to go down to the bar and wait to be called. Fair enough. It was 8.50 and my booking was for nine. I always arrive ten minutes before my booking because it gives them time to prepare the table.

The bar itself is a dimly lit subterranean room full of decorative barrels.

It looks like the *Pirates of the Caribbean* ride at Disneyworld, except that these particular bloodthirsty losers from around the world were wearing sunglasses on their heads instead of eye-patches. And it was more a case of 'yo ho ho and a rose petal martini' than a bottle of rum. Oh, and they wouldn't give us our rose petal martinis until we had handed over a credit card for security. Classy.

At 21.15 I went up to ask if my table was ready and was told that it was being cleaned and prepared (although not, as it turned out, for me). When I tried to return to the bar, however, the doorman barred my way and told me, 'Sorry, the bar's full.' I told him my girlfriend was down there, and my credit card, and my rose petal martini. Still he barred my way. So I barged past and went downstairs. Steaming. At 21.30 nobody had come to get us, we'd had two cocktails already and had started a bottle of wine (what else do you do in a bar for three-quarters of an hour?) and I was tense, a bit squiffy, and no longer hungry.

I went upstairs and shouted. They seated us, finally, just before ten. At the bloody noodle bar round the grill (boiling hot, sweaty) on stools, next to each other. Just rubbish. I grumbled to the 25-year-old Italian banker sitting next to me, him with the orange skin and the baseball cap on backwards and the snakeskin shoes. Oh, he said, they hadn't had to wait, they'd just walked in. No reservations needed for the noodle bar.

Imagine my delight. I broke things. I screamed like Violet Elizabeth Bott.

They gave us a table. And then it took 20 minutes to get my bottle of wine brought up from the bar. And then I asked for my credit card back now that I was seated where they could keep an eye on me in case I tried to do a runner. And the maitre d' went and got it and he handed it to me saying, 'Your card, Mr . . .' and he looked down for the name. And he looked up at me.

And down at the card. And then he said, 'Good evening, Mr Coren.'

Thereafter, I had the experience I had read about in the review by my favourite critic. The service became incredibly efficient. Instead of no attention at all, I had three waiters to myself. Everyone was incredibly polite and solicitous. The food was brilliant: fresh, excitingly prepared, imaginatively presented and not at all overpriced.

But I was buggered if I was going to say so in the review.

How to Complain

NICELY,
POLITELY, APOLOGETICALLY.
But firmly, and at the very moment of
disappointment. You must think of yourself as
a kind but rather strict parent, and the restaurant
(in an abstract ontological sense, not the individuals
working in it) as your child. Appreciate it and applaud it for
what it does well, and tell it very clearly and firmly, but not
hysterically and not pompously, when it has erred.

'I'm awfully sorry to make a fuss,' you might say, 'but this fish really
isn't as fresh as I'd hoped. You smell that faint whiff of ammonia? That's
never a good sign with a skate – although I do appreciate the hell of
keeping skate fresh for more than a couple of hours. I really can't eat this.
What else might I have as a replacement that can come quickly? I don't
want my guest to be kept waiting, or for her food to get cold.'

There's simply no way you can lose with that. If they try and tell you that
the skate is perfectly fine (as happened to me once at the Oxo Tower in
London), then you can invite them to taste it (as I did) and watch in glee as
they go green in the attempt.

The end result is likely to be free main courses, a jolly time and an
amicable departure. You have to think about what your goals are (and
the above is presumably about right). It may be insanely satisfying to
shout, 'Jesus H. Christ, Pedro, you expect me to eat this? It might be all
right where you come from, but in this country we wouldn't feed shit
like this to our CATS!' But it gets you nowhere. I know. I have
done it many, many times.

You can complain about more subjective matters
than rotten fish, such as the cuisson of meat, for
example, but you have to be even more
polite: 'Look, I know that "medium-rare"
is in the eye of the beholder,'

you might

say. 'But come on, I can

hardly chew this. I'm sure the chef got

momentarily distracted. Do you think you can

persuade him to do me one with a bit of pink in it?'

Again, at the end of a long hard day you might feel
more like saying, 'Excuse me but I ordered a steak, NOT A
FUCKING GYM SHOE!!!' But nobody is going to come out of
the evening well like that.

Remember, it's just a shop. You are not insulting anybody
personally by pointing out that the wares are not as you'd hoped, and
you are well within your rights to ask what can be done about it. You're
not in your mum's kitchen now, staring down at a plate of boiled gristle,
knowing that she's been slaving all day over a hot stove to make your
dinner because she sacrificed her promising career as a cabaret singer to
have children with your monosyllabic father (silent at the head of the table in
his shirt and braces), and there are starving children in Africa, and have you
got any idea what they had to eat in the war, and anyway you can finish
what's on your plate, and like it, and say thank you, and ask for seconds, or
you're getting it for breakfast tomorrow, and the next day, and the next . . .

You are the parent, remember. Not the child. The restaurant is the
child, and it needs to be told how to improve. It wants to learn. It will
respect you if you treat it firmly but kindly. And it simply won't
understand, or give a damn, if you leave your complaint to the
end of the meal or, God forbid, a letter some days later. You
must strike while the iron is hot, or the soup is cold, or
whatever.

If you do not, you are just a mug Englishman and
deserve to sit there while the Frenchies get all the
best food, the Spanish get all the freshest
fish, and the Germans get all the
money.

MY FRENCH YOUTH

I went to Paris because my girlfriend got locked out of her flat. She was called Katie, and we were together for seven years. But in October 1991 it was barely seven weeks. I was done with education but she had still to do a year out in France, then back to Oxford to do her final year. I was going to stay in London, get a massive job of some sort, write a novel, and potter out maybe six months later, when I was rich and famous, to say hi.

But ten hours after I kissed her goodbye at Victoria Station she called me up in tears to say that the keys to the flat she had rented didn't work, or the people weren't there or something, she wasn't very clear, but she was in a phone box at the end of the road in some terrifying corner of night-time Paris, and she only had thirty francs and she had all these suitcases and what on earth was she going to do? So I told her to go and get a strong drink at the *tabac* on the corner (I knew there'd be one, there is always a *tabac* on the corner in Paris, and it's always open, and you can get fags and strong drink and a shitty look from an actual French person) and to come back in an hour to the phone box and phone me again with her last coin, and I'd call her back with a plan.

An hour of phone calls just about got me a plan in time. Jonny Barton was in Paris. Obviously. There were still one or two girls he hadn't shagged in France, so he had enrolled at the

École des Beaux-Arts to do a course in sculpture and cunnilingus under some famous tutor or other. He was staying in a friend's flat very near the Eiffel Tower (where he was no doubt humping a different girl against the windowsill each night as they marvelled at the rigidity of Gustav Eiffel's extraordinary spot-lit strut work). He was in. I got his address. I gave it to Katie. She crossed Paris in a cab, which Jonny would pay at the other end, and she called me from there. Sorted. I was her hero.

I went to bed in North London very pleased with myself, for once. Katie had called from another country in her hour of need, and with a couple of phone calls I had saved her life. She was now all warm and safe in Jonny Barton's flat. She'd have showered by now and changed, and be drinking a glass of . . .

. . . oh shit. Jonny Barton. The King of Cock. The Sultan of Shag. The Pharaoh of Fuck. I had played right into his hands. What was I thinking of?

I leapt from my bed, grabbed my passport, threw some things into a rucksack, left a note for my parents (who were still hoping I might go back to Oxford for some post-graduate work, or get a job in some lame-arse publishing house, or whatever you are supposed to do with an English degree) and set off up my road at a run. It was the middle of the night. But I reckoned a night bus could have me at Victoria by three. I could be on a train to Folkestone or Dover or wherever the fuck by four. A ferry would take hours but I couldn't afford a hovercraft so probably Calais by tennish. Then a train, and maybe Paris by the middle of the afternoon.

Luckily, Jonny liked to move slow. I guess that's why the girls fell for him (that and the whole blond-haired, blue-eyed, I speak 14 languages and study sculpture at the Beaux-Arts thing). He would never nail her that first night. That wouldn't be classy. The thing was to get them hooked. And you did that by not fucking them. Not immediately. They'd have stayed up late chatting and drinking a wine Jonny knew all about, I reckoned (as the train finally pulled out of London around six), from his sophisticated sojourns in the South. There'd probably be some cool people hanging out in the flat, listening to jazz, and wearing suede, possibly tasselled suede. Katie would get an early night. In the morning they'd have breakfast. He'd show her the Île de la Cité and the top floor at Shakespeare & Co. They'd stroll the Left Bank, have lunch, then back to his in the late afternoon for . . .

. . . God. You know, I actually feel bad about the idyll I'm about to spoil there, by rushing in all sweaty and possessive, having sprinted from the Métro to reclaim my woman, who wasn't remotely interested in Jonny Barton anyway, I don't think (except in so far as he was, no doubt is, an extremely nice, funny, gentle man). How much more fun she might have had, being whisked around the glittering city by multilingual Jonny and his cosmopolitan mates, instead of being whisked away by me and all my endless sexual jealousies and paranoia, and shacking up on the fifth floor of a rickety old Napoleonic apartment block behind République, looking out over the weird, green Canal St-Martin, with no money, living off one battery chicken a week (roasted meat, then stew, then pasta dishes, then soups of the bones lengthened with couscous, then thinner soup, then grey water with a little fat on the top like the ninth boiling of a stoat), and burning furniture in the stove, which we smuggled up ten flights of stairs from the cellar, one chair leg at a time.

She was working in a school a couple of hours a day for a thousand francs a week and I was failing to get work as anything at all, writing stories that I didn't finish (or even start) for English magazines that didn't want them anyway, and being rejected by every media outlet, publishing house and school that I tried to impress with my stonking educational record. (Never let anyone tell you that an education counts for anything, when you don't know anybody, because it doesn't. And it doesn't even count for much if you do.)

I began training as a Berlitz teacher, but gave up halfway through the course because I could no longer afford the RER fare out to La Défense, where the offices were. And also because I had landed a job in a shop, thanks to the boyfriend of the only person I knew in Paris, the daughter of a friend of my parents. The shop was the Polo Ralph Lauren boutique at the Place de la Madeleine, where this chap worked himself, and he said they would hire any English public school boy who walked in the door, to help them sell their bogus Americanised vision of England to dribbling Japanese and Texan tourists who wanted to buy clothes in France but were afraid (quite rightly) of talking to French people.

And so my public school education got me a job. Lucky fucking me. I got to work 12 hours a day in the basement of a giant clothes shop, as a *vendeur* in the 'roughwear' department, selling giant tennis jumpers to fat plutocrats and pretending they looked good in them, and telling the phalanxes of Japs that, no, sorry, that is as '*shoshi*' as it comes, they're just made for big fat Americans, not diddy little guys like you, but '*mata doso*' just the same.

We were on commission though, and so I soon learned how to flatter the money out of a Frenchman's wallet.

'*Oh Monsieur, ça vous va très très bien. Vous avez vraiment l'air d'un Con, excusez moi, d'un Le Conte, ou d'un Jimmy Connors.*'

'*Oh Madame, c'est super chouette, ça. Ça ira parfaitement avec un jean. C'est vachement sexy. C'est hyper-beau. C'est tout à fait cool Raoul.*'

It made me sick. But it made me fluent in French. A combination of necessity and greed always will. And although I never saw daylight, but set off along the luminous, snot-coloured canal to the Métro station at seven every morning, returning around supper time each night, while above my foetid basement the world's greatest city disported itself in the last great days before the Channel Tunnel came and spoiled it all, I did begin to hit my sales targets (scribbling my *numéro de vendeur* on each tag even as I ripped it from the customer, flung it at the till and dived on another poor sod who only wanted to look around and maybe buy some aftershave, but could be bullied, with the right combination of snootiness and flattery, into buying a hand-painted leather jacket he would never wear for 20,000 francs, of which two per cent were mine) and I did eventually start to make money.

It was about 20,000 francs a month, I think. Or 2,000 pounds. Around 25 grand over the year I spent there (Christ, a year), which was a shitload to a fellow who was used to 60 quid a week working in a bar, or 12 hundred quid a term maintenance allowance at university. And, of course, I didn't have to pay tax. I don't think. Fuck. Maybe I was supposed to. What's the statute of limitations on that?

And so, when the money started to come in, sometime in the spring (have you ever tried to set up a bank account in France, provide the relevant documents from your landlord, employer and eight local professionals, six relatives and a chief of police then link them to the account of your American-owned employer in such a way that a piece of plastic poked in the wall of your own *arrondissement* will elicit cash money? You have? Well then you'll know that five months was pretty good going), I was actually rich.

And so we started to eat. Every night somewhere new, starting with the shonky little joints around the 10th and 11th where we lived, some of them dirty and mean but serving quite authentic stuff in their feckless way (roughly chopped *rognons de veau* with too much blood and piss, gamey steaks in

Roquefort sauce that trod the fine line between vomitous and fascinating) and then also the tragic *tabacs* that saved money by not bothering with a cook and serving microwaved croque monsieur

There were the cheapo Arab couscous shacks in the 19th (I think it was the 19th, Belleville sort of area), where we went weekly with my more-or-less Syrian friend Robin Yassin Kassab, the writer, who came to escape his dastardly step-father at Christmas and ended up staying on our floor for three months. He only had a pound or two a day to spend on food and found that by connecting with his Arab roots he could do that quite comfortably in restaurants. I went with him, mostly on Fridays, when they served the couscous with *méchoui* – slow-roasted lamb, all black and sticky at the edges and melty like butter inside.

There was a Chinatown out that way too, one of the two in Paris, and we went there hunting for Chinese that was a bit like home, but found only Vietnamese and Laotian and Cambodian and 'Indo-Chine' (even when the signs said 'spécialités Chinoises') and the best of these was a giant 600-seater place called Niouaville, with different kitchens for each of four or five South-East Asian cuisines, and trolleys that wheeled the food round to baying oriental punters.

And then there were the funky disco places and drinking dens and Tex-Mex hangouts around Bastille, when we had enough money to up sticks and move to a flat over that way, and then the bistros of Le Marais where we moved next, for a month, for big money, 5,000 francs, renting from a guy called Marcel, who was gay and had gone to Brazil. There I ate with relish the trotters and faces and bollocks and spleens of beasts and fowls, and swallowed frogs and snails with gusto and gallons of wine, laughing to think of the things I would leave on the side of my plate at home when I was little, because they were 'blooky' and grim.

And we ate in famous places too, the big brasseries that were having a real resurgence at the time, like Flo and Julien and that one by the Gare du Nord whose name I forget, and Bofinger, where you tried to get a seat under the *coupole* (it was usually my parents or Katie's coming over and taking us to these – and envying us our young lives in Paris because from middle-age you can't see how mundane youth truly is), where we sat in front of mounds of shellfish, great black lobsters and copper-coloured crabs, and little nutty oysters like skimming stones and then the bogey-like snails and slugs and whelks which I still can never see the point of, and then usually a whole goose's liver, the size of a rump steak, sautéed and served with chips, and eaten slower and slower as the evening wears on in the golden glow, and the armies of men dressed as René from *'Allo 'Allo*, marching around with pewter trays held high, and the clatter and bustle and fag smoke and drinking until well into the small hours, and my mum and dad all happy, and us too, and always getting a great table because as long as she kept her mouth shut the places always thought Katie was Emmanuelle Béart (who was a big-deal actress at that time, having starred in *Manon des Sources* or *Jean de Florette*, I forget which), and it was all a little bit, in its own exotic Froggy way, like a night at the Gourmet Rendezvous.

And when our folks weren't around there were cheaper versions of all that, like Charlot, where you got it all – the moustachioed waiters, high ceilings, bustle and yabber – for about 40 francs a head (except without the lobsters and foie gras) and the Café de la Cité where I heard my favourite restaurant joke ever.

Most of the people we knew in Paris were gay, because of my job. And the Café de la Cité was a gay restaurant (I finally grasped, after about 12 visits) where you got a starter, bavette and crème caramel for 50 francs, and all the wine you could drink for another 20 and there was a key on a string behind the bar which you asked for if you wanted to go to the loo, which was across the alley at the back, but also if you wanted to go outside in the alley and wait to be rogered by whichever lucky fellow saw you pick up the key first. Which meant that if you really did want to go to the loo you had to be fucking quick about darting across to the bog or you'd end up having to take one for the team, right there on the cold cobbles, so as not to be rude.

So we were in there one night with my mate James from the shop, who was a beautiful six foot six English public schoolboy on the run from the dreary heterosexuality of late 1980s Leicester, and seven or eight of his/our French gay pals (Katie was stoical about these evenings, which usually ended with a trip to Boy, the huge gay club at La Bastille, and only once took me aside and whispered very quietly, 'You know, Giles, it would be nice if once, just once, we could go somewhere where everybody wants to fuck ME!'), and we were whooping and squealing and drinking pastis and generally carrying on (it is staggering just how gay a large group of drunk gay French men can be) when the waiter came to take orders.

'Qu'est-ce qu'il y a comme hors d'oeuvres?' asked someone, although it was always the same, and never changed.

'On a des oeufs mayonnaise,' said the guy. 'On a du fromage de tête, et je pense qu'il me reste un melon.' (You must forgive my attempts to render the language here. I spoke lovely French in those days, like a little culotted tosser. But I don't use it much anymore, and it has shrivelled like an old plum.)

'Et a part de ça?' asked our friend.

'A part de ça,' said the waiter. 'Il y a des moules.'

'Ah, non,' said our friend sadly, and glanced around the table at his friends before adding, 'J'aime pas les moules.'

And the table fell about. Fell to pieces. Laughed until it was sick. Laughed so loudly that eyes popped out of heads and hands went red raw from slapping on the table.

'J'aime pas les moules! J'AIME PAS LES M-M-M-MOULES!! Oh la la la la la la la la la . . . J'aime pas les moules!!!'

I think they went through this every time they ate here. I certainly saw it four or five times. And I do honestly think it got funnier every time. Though I'm not sure it comes across on the page.

Wait. Sorry. You're missing a piece here, aren't you? I should have said. *Moule*, which is obviously French for 'mussel', also has a secondary, quite anatomically obvious meaning, to the liberated, and especially gay young Frenchman.

It means, not to put too fine a point on it, 'cunt'.

Sometime after that, gay Marcel came back from Brazil and we had to move out of his gorgeous flat in the Marais (it had a jungle theme in the living room, achieved by the cramming together of dozens of indoor tropical trees with myriad painted parrots suspended from the leaves and branches and a crazy cat that looked like a tiger, but shat with the terrifying abandon of a deranged house pet that has never been outdoors in its life) to a much cheaper one at Nation, in the burbs, where we lived in a crumbling apartment full of sunlight and flaking plaster, where there was not a fridge but a meat safe in the outside wall, and the shower was in the kitchen, right next to the sink, so that if you left the washing up piled high on the draining board without putting it away and then had a shower, and turned round sharply while soaping your goolies, you would be sure to knock the whole damn lot off through the shower curtain so that everything smashed on the floor and you couldn't get out without cutting your feet on broken crockery.

Ever since that time I have been assiduous about putting the washing up away when it is dry, even though I am now so super-rich that I live in a house where the shower is in a whole different room from the kitchen sink.

We hung out with Marcel a lot when he got back, and introduced him to James, hoping they'd fall in love. But they didn't. There was at least a foot of height between them, apart from anything else, and anyway Marcel was far too dainty and little and, well, gay, for James.

When James and I first met, folding jumpers together endlessly in the roughwear department (the very word 'roughwear' was simply the gayest thing I had ever heard), I used to elbow him in the ribs every time a really beautiful young boy with luminous, suntanned skin and glossy hair and bracelets and expensive clothes came onto the floor, and say, 'What about this one, James? Eh? What about him? Do you fancy him?' Until eventually James stooped down and shook me by the shoulders and said, 'Look, Giles, being gay means that I fancy MEN! Big, strong, hairy, smelly MEN!'

And then he'd turn and point at a huge fat Italian tourist with a beard, looking like a cheap Pavarotti, and say, 'Like HIM! I want to have sex with HIM!'

And eventually I left it alone.

But while they didn't fall in love, James and Marcel did get on. And that summer we all went down to Marcel's grandmother's house in Bordeaux in a rented Cinquecento, James folded up in the front seat like a stork in a shoebox.

On the way, we took a detour to the docks to buy fish.

'Il faut voir ça,' explained Marcel. 'C'est traditionelle.'

So we pulled up on the hot, salty quay and engaged some of the fishermen in conversation, and they brought out of their dark sheds wooden crates of big blue barnacled mussels and oysters, crates of shrimp and langoustine and crabs, cockles and clams, whelks, scallops, and giant ray, cod, hake and even,

I think I remember, great eels that writhed and squirted in dustbins of water.

'So how big is the kitchen at this place of your grandmother's?' I said to Marcel. 'What shall we get? Shall we get a sack of oysters for tonight and then maybe that massive cod. What about eel, do you know how to cook an eel? I've seen one skinned on TV, maybe if we—'

But Katie interrupted me with a tug on the elbow and nodded towards James and Marcel, who were away on another planet, as the filthy-haired young fishermen in their greasy jeans, shirtless and streaked with seaweed and fish guts, long-muscled and covered in scars and burns and misspelt, ugly tattoos, heaved and sweated and schlepped.

'I don't think we're here for the fish,' she said.

And, indeed, we left without any fish at all. And for the last half-hour of the journey the two boys in front didn't say a word. Just giggled. Giggled and giggled and giggled like schoolgirls.

Schoolgirls with massive erections.

It got worse. Or better, depending on your perspective. As we pulled into *centre ville* we passed a troop carrier parked up by the war memorial.

'*Oh, c'est comme un rêve!*' squealed Marcel. '*L'armée est arrivé.*'

So we got to his flat, put down our stuff, and as I went to put the kettle on (some habits you don't lose after a year in France), Marcel said '*Je sors. Dix minutes. James, tu viens?*'

But James laughed and said no. So Marcel went off on his own to get fucked by a soldier in the municipal car park, and really was back in ten minutes. Maybe fifteen. Time enough for his peppermint tea to be still quite drinkable.

The thing about Marcel was that his parents didn't know. And nor did any of his friends. The only people in the world who knew were James, Katie and me (in fact, you know, I'm just going to go back over these last couple of pages and change his name to Marcel, because, who knows, his parents might still be alive and reading this, and maybe he has a wife and family and everything). So this was the first time in his life he had been free to carry on like this. And it was terrifying.

The next day we went to the beach. Yomped through the woods and over a huge dune to the edge of the Atlantic. The next beach along was a nudist beach, and while Marcel thought that was our natural destination, we were having none of it. So we set up our little camp – Katie and me all English about it, making a windbreak with parasols, and laying out towels very carefully so as not to get sand on them, covering ourselves with suncream, while Marcel stripped to his tiny red Speedos in a second, slipped a little red Durex foil into the waistband (so French, I thought at the time, that it should be of a matching colour) and said, '*Bon, mes enfants. Je reviens toute de suite!*' and disappeared off over the dunes.

Ten minutes later, he was back. The condom still stuck in his pants.

'*Pas de chance?*'

'*Si,*' he said. '*Il s'agit pas de la chance.*'

'*Mais . . .*' I said, pointing at the still unused Durex.

'*Bof,*' he said, pulling it out and pinging it into his beach bag. '*La route d'enfer est pavée de bonnes intentions.*'

Half an hour later he was ready to go again (these Frenchies, I don't know). And this time he wanted me to go with him.

'*Juste pour voir, Gilles,*' he said. 'You are 'oping to be writeur, non? So you most see zees.'

'Marcel,' I said. 'Whether or not I ever end up being a writer is not going to depend on whether or not I have watched you getting bumfucked by a soldier.'

'Not bumfuck!' said Marcel. 'Ben, not necessarilee. And not soldier. Zey are gone now from Bordeaux. Ffft! Come. I am promise I do nossink. Look, I not take weez me Durex.'

'Very reassuring,' I said. But I went. And I told Katie if I wasn't back in fifteen minutes to come and find me.

'Not a chance,' she said.

And so I went with Marcel back over the dune towards the forest, and he pointed to where a chap was walking along butt naked, with a rucksack on his back and gigantic stiffy on his front, stroking it as he walked as if . . . I don't know what as if, there is simply nothing that such a sight resembles, except a man wanking while he walks along a sand dune.

'So, you can follow eem to where zey fock,' said Marcel.

'What an excellent reason not to follow him,' I said.

But we did. And when we got there we found a dozen or so naked fellows all standing round in a circle, jerking away like madmen, and in the middle of the circle a middle-aged bald man screwing a middle aged grey-haired woman in the missionary position.

'*Ça, je ne comprends pas du tout,*' I said.

'*Moi non plus,*' said Marcel.

And that was about it for buggery on that particular mini-break. In the evening we went for a dinner at a place with a sign outside that read, '*Foie gras à volonté.*'

'*On va manger QUE du foie gras!*' said Marcel, and marched in.

James didn't like foie gras and Katie objected on moral grounds (good for her) but Marcel and I tucked in hard. After the third helping of foie gras, as Katie and James were putting down their ice-cream spoons and thinking about bed, Marcel cried for more.

The waiter said he could not bring any more.

'*Mais il est marquée là, "à volonté",*' said Marcel.

'*Oui,*' said the waiter. '*Mais . . .* '

'*Il n'est pas question de "mais",*' said Marcel. '*Je veux du foie gras!*'

'Come on Marcel,' I said. 'It's not really the spirit. I've had enough anyway.'

'Spirit?' said Marcel. 'Zey put on ze sign ow you ave as moch foie gras as you want, so zat ze people zey come in ere and not over zere in ze ozzer place, and zen zey tell you 'enough!'. Zees can not be, Gilles. *Il faut râlé, Gilles. Il faut toujours râlé!*'

It was always the same with Marcel: '*Il faut râlé.*' If the starters came too slow, or the bread was not fresh enough, or the portions were too small, or the *cuisson* was not perfect, then as Marcel began to steam with indignation (for this was his city, his country, and he would not stand by and see his English friend shortchanged), I would always say under my breath, 'It's fine, Marcel, really, it's fine.'

'*Ah non, Gilles,*' he would say, with a sigh. '*Ça va pas! Il faut râlé. Toujours râlé.*'

I don't even know what it means. I guess just 'complain'. But there seemed to be something more to it when it was about Marcel getting what he felt he was entitled to in a restaurant. (If things pleased him then he would admit they were '*correct*' – but nothing more, never anything more than that.)

As Marcel rose to demand an audience with the manager on this matter of the hiatus in the foie gras supply, I stilled him with a hand on his arm and said, 'Come on now, Marcel. It's silly. In front of all these people. Aren't you embarrassed?'

'Embarrassed?' he said, truly baffled. 'Last night I have fucked two soldier over a motorcycle in a parking publique under my grandmozzer's 'ouse – what is to be embarrassed demanding from zis conard anozzer plate of foie gras?'

FRANCE TODAY

Umpteen times though I have done it in my life, I can never land at Calais and spread a map of France across the bonnet of my car without thinking of *Asterix and the Banquet*, which tells of a journey made across Roman-occupied Gaul by Asterix and Obelix in defiance of the ambitious and toadying General Overanxious, who has built a stockade around their village and declared that all Gaul is now conquered.

'Gaul is our country, O Roman,' Asterix cries out from beneath the walls, 'and we'll go where we like in it!' And he bets him that he and Obelix can break out, travel the whole country, collecting the food specialities of each region, and throw a banquet on their return at which he, Overanxious, will be the guest of honour.

With the fortifications breached, the pair head to Lutetia (Paris) for ham, then on to Durocortorum (Reims) for champagne, Lugdunum (Lyons) for sausage, Bordeaux for oysters and wine (glossing over how the oysters are going to taste when they have travelled 600 miles back to the village by Iron Age transport methods), and so on and so on . . . until they return in triumph, biff Overanxious on the nose (I always feel a bit sorry for him, not getting to enjoy the promised meal) and chow down.

But the odd thing is this: though published in France in 1965 (as *Le Tour de Gaule d'Astérix*), and a truly seminal work in the sequence, providing a bridge between the jerky cartoon treatment of the first four books and the smoother, more mellowed style of such masterpieces as *Asterix and Cleopatra* and *Asterix in Britain*, *Asterix and the Banquet* was not published in Britain until 1979.

It lay untranslated for 14 years because it was reckoned too French. The theme was too parochial. The jokes too foreign. English readers simply wouldn't get it.

And that's because it was all about food. The notion of a patriotism defined by regional delicacies was simply incomprehensible in that dark hour for British gastronomy, after the end of rationing but before Delia, Marco and Jamie. British publishers just could not see any future for a book in which something as dull as regional French food played a significant part.

But for the French in the mid-Sixties, emasculated by the humiliations of occupation, drummed out of Algeria and all but irrelevant on the world stage, food was all they had. And *Banquet* simply thrums with a national pride that puts cookery at the centre of the geopolitical scheme.

Cut to last summer, and there I am with my map of Gaul, sorry France, spread across the bonnet of a German car (significant in some way I am sure), looking to plan a route south that will let me eat as well as Asterix. I've tried before and always failed. Always eaten rubbish.

The plan is to head down towards Épernay for black-leg chicken in champagne at a beautiful little B&B I've booked. But experience tells me that we will in fact be breaking down somewhere between St-Omer and St-Quentin, where we'll stand by the side of the road in the first serious rain since April, being drenched every 15 seconds by giant Belgian lorries full of crated veal calves, waiting for a tow-truck that's meant to come as part of my holiday insurance, but won't, so leaving the car there to be burgled, and checking into a vile motel on the outskirts of

Arras which won't have a restaurant but will give us the number of a pizza place that can deliver to the room, where I'll remember Sassoon's First World War poem, 'The General' ('He's a cheery old card,' grunted Harry to Jack/As they slogged up to Arras with rifle and pack./But he did for them both by his plan of attack.'), and get even more miserable than the situation merits.

By the time the car is fixed, towards lunch the following day, it'll be far too late to make the gorgeous little spot I've booked in the Rhône valley (which would have been a lovely, day-long, roof-down toddle on the D-roads if we had indeed overnighted south of Reims, with maybe a lunch stop around Dijon), but I'll go for it anyway and after seven miserable hours of lunchless 100 mph bombing down the autoroute with the roof on, we'll finally give up, forfeit another hotel deposit, eat at McDonald's in Mâcon (I believe it gets three toilet bowls and a giant vomit in the new Michelin) and sleep in the car.

The day after that, we'll try to be brave. We'll tell ourselves there's still time to take a nice drive through the South and enjoy some old-fashioned motoring. But then outside Lyon I'll accidentally follow signs for Grenoble, because I've got it confused with Orange, and before we know it we'll be in the Alps, snaking up and down terrifying mountain roads at 17 mph in a huge queue of caravans behind an oil truck, and it'll be four hours before we eventually get our chance to overtake. When there's finally nothing between us and the truck, Esther will say, 'Okay, you can go . . . ' (because on roads like that in a right-hand drive car you just can't see for yourself) and I'll pull out to overtake just as she's saying, ' . . . after this enormous fire engine.' There'll be a great flash of headlights, a howling klaxon, a screech of tyres and . . .

Next time we'll fly.

But, as it happens, we did make it to Épernay. And from

there, with one or two small sat-nav hitches, to the very B&B in the guidebook, the one run by a lovely young couple with a very friendly dog, who would serve chickens from their own barn-yard cooked in the local champagne.

Except that in the six months since the guide was published, the couple had split up (poor things) and the wife was left with a three-year-old kid to bring up, a big cereal farm to run and a B&B to cater. So it was Ritz crackers, supermarket ham and melon, and desiccated cod in tinfoil (300 miles from the sea) with a giant bowl of terrifying string beans cooked to buggery and served in a sour soup of their own urinous juice. Oh, and a bottle of awful minervois, two-thirds empty.

Grim, grim, grim, and a fairly typical induction into the nation's gastronomic health. The friendly dog, of course, had left with the husband.

So in Beaune, where we arrived around lunchtime the next day after an early getaway, we thought we'd treat ourselves with a bit of Michelin. Not stars, by God. Nobody wants that palaver in a quickish roadstop, but three black knives and forks – which you'd have thought would mean a safe, representative plateful.

Le Jardin des Remparts was a five-minute walk from a town centre cloaked in dust and roadworks, and occupied a very pretty garden on a roundabout. Everything in France is on a roundabout, and the cars all honk as they go round, so as to be heard above the screech of the mopeds. They had a table for two; we sat. And then we saw a rectangular plate of diddy little things going by: luminous cubes of ham terrine, minuscule savoury ice-cream cones, nano-profiteroles filled with Époisses. And our hearts sank. In rural France is it really just a straight choice between frozen cod in tinfoil and this wankerish non-artistry of the nutritionally damned?

It would have been rude simply to leave. So there followed three grim hours of flaccid *amuse-bouches*, biblical wine lists, awful meat, some quite nice *pommes mousseline* in a champagne glass, soapy madeleines in boxes, a bill for two hundred-odd quid and an eighth of a day I will not get back at the end of my life. Turns out it used to have a star, but lost it in January. Husbands, stars, nothing lasts in this country.

We ate very well that night at a B&B in the Rhône valley: chicken stew in an earthenware pot, carafes of red and rosé, nice cheese, shots of frozen Cointreau. But our hosts were Anglo-Irish, so that doesn't count. We all know the Irish can cook.

In Orange, a dull town in Provence where we stopped for lunch the next day, we seriously thought about McDonald's. But we couldn't find one. And after half an hour of squinting at the *Michelin Guide*'s titchy and under-labelled map we found we'd walked to the opposite end of town from the only place they thought wouldn't necessarily kill you.

Down an alley I spotted a lovely looking garden, with parasols and a water feature and pizza menu. Pizza is always the safest thing to eat in the southern half of France. We walked in. A middle-aged man eating with a child glanced up at us. Then carried on eating. Then sighed and got up and came over. He pointed us to a table. A pretty young girl, his mistress I think, slouched over to us with a menu then left us for 20 minutes. When she came back we ordered pizzas.

'*Pas de pizza*,' she said. '*Seulement les soirs.*'

So we had spaghetti carbonara. The very worst of its kind ever made. And it took an age to come, no doubt because the chef had to wait for the town's cat sanctuary to sick up all those half-digested shoelaces.

But we got there in the end, to the old Coren homestead in the Alpes-Maritimes, where we do the cooking ourselves, and when friends fly out we take them to La Colombe d'Or, where I can't for the life of me get a decent table, and the turbot is 60 quid, but at least the view is pretty.

A couple of days later we went for lunch at the quite famous Auberge du Vieux Château in Cabris. But they wouldn't give us starters, or a side salad with our mains, because it was already nearly two and the chef wanted to go home.

And then there was Le Cheiron, high in the mountains at Gréolières, where it is safe to have pizza, and a cold, strong Leffe and maybe a marc de Provence for the road. Or was until Michael Winner went there, by some freak of chance, a couple of years ago. And now there is a sort of Winner cult in that remote region: faded photos of him pasted to the ancient, furtive walls, his name muttered disbelievingly by gawping Anglophones. It makes one think of those pygmy tribes one hears of occasionally, discovered in the Congo's dark interior, who turn out to worship a Fanta bottle, or speak perfect Forties English from endless rewatching of a single VHS tape of *Brief Encounter*.

Still, I'd have given my right arm for a cold beer with Winner in the faraway mountains a couple of days later when I found myself in the heart of Nice, staring down into a bowl of frogs' legs and thinking to myself:

'How? How did I come to be here, in this awful place, in front of this awful food? How can it have happened again? Why does it always happen? Why bloody always, always, ALWAYS?'

It wasn't a bowl of frogs' legs as such. More of a skillet. A black iron skillet secured on a wooden tray shaped like a turtle. In it were, perhaps, 18 limbs. I was about to say 17 (I am visualising the dish in my head as I write, counting over the legs in my mind once more, doing my best vividly to remember a dish that any normal man would by now have joined the Foreign Legion to forget), but one wants to tell oneself that the number is even, does one not? One wants to believe that what one has on one's plate are, at the very least, the lower appendages of 9 specific semi-aquatic animals, rather than some grubby under-chef's hasty grab from a plastic freezer bag containing, say, 250.

And when I say, 'legs', I really mean legs. I've eaten them many times before, but always gussied up, with the meat forced up to one end of the femur and bunched, so that it stands like a chickenny lollipop with some other seafood and a suitable sauce. But these were not like that. These were whole, great, bloody legs, about as long as my middle finger, with the plumpish thigh (a little ragged where it was torn from the living hip), the knee, the elongated calf muscle of a distance runner (as opposed to the bulging muscle of a sprinter), the ankle and then the foot.

The foot, of course, is more of a flipper. The fins one uses for snorkelling are modelled on it. And indeed they do a sterling job of propelling one through water with minimal effort. But they do not look great on a plate, still attached to the leg.

Nor had they been artfully arranged. They appeared to lie where they had fallen, as if in the aftermath of some terrible amphibious Agincourt, the corpses having been looted, the chain mail stripped off, the heads and arms and torsos devoured by vultures, and only the scattered legs left behind on the battlefield as evidence of the carnage.

On the plus side, they had been covered with crushed peanuts, which I picked at bravely with my chopsticks. There was a faint smell of lemon grass. These, then, were the famous *cuisses de grenouille à la citronnelle* at Nice's celebrated China Park.

Joke. Thin, defeated, mock-heroic joke. China Park is not celebrated and nothing it does is famous. It's a horrible little Chinese/Vietnamese/Hades place on a lurid Niçoise street, and I can only think that I had ordered this dish, unconsciously, as a punishment for being such a bloody useless bastard failure of a restaurant critic, and of a man.

I wasn't supposed to be there. I was supposed to be at Keisuke Matsushima, a trendy little Michelin-starred canteen where a young Franco-Japanese chef whips up his famous *mille-feuille de boeuf 'Simmenthal' saisi au wasabi*, sitting with my wife at the end of our holiday, finally having a decent restaurant meal in France.

But we couldn't find it. We couldn't bloody find it. I'd booked using the *Michelin Guide*, I took the guide with me in the car, I put the restaurant's address into the sat-nav, I drove the half-hour down to the coast from our house, all in my nicely ironed shirt and trousers and Esther ('Is it posh? What shall I wear?') all floaty and sexy and wearing serious shoes, and I found the restaurant, but there was nowhere to park.

There just isn't in that godforsaken town. Not for miles and miles and miles. It's all pedestrianised and tram-lined, and the pavements are all fenced off. By the time we eventually found a car park, nine storeys beneath the street, and our urinous lift had surfaced in the bowels of some deserted shopping centre, and we had found our way out into the fresh air (I say, 'fresh'), we had no idea where we were.

I had brought a map. Torn the page out of the guide so as not to have to carry the stupid great book around with me (you might as well paint 'I am a gluttonous English fool, please kick me in the balls' on your forehead). But the streets on the map were not all named. And although our restaurant was marked with an 'e', there were at least two other 'e's in the grid it was meant to be in. And the map's so bloody tiny and printed so feebly that at night, with their crappy French fizzing bloody pale orange streetlights, you can't see a thing. And you can't ask where it is because nobody in Nice is from Nice.

We surfaced from our car at exactly 8 p.m., the time of the reservation, and at 9.15 we were walking for the fourth time down the street the place was supposed to be on when Esther, in her pretty clothes and complicated shoes and four months pregnant, said, 'I think if I don't eat in a minute I'll die.'

So we went into China Park and sat down, defeated by the accursed Whore of Michelin just as we had been in Beaune a few weeks before, driven to chancing our arm and taking pot luck on a French street, which never, ever works.

And it's not like we were even meant to be at Keisuke Matsushima. We were meant to be at a hotel called Sezz Saint-Tropez, opened that very week, eating at Colette, the new restaurant of Pierre Gagnaire, possibly the greatest French chef in the world. St-Trop is a two-hour haul from us, but I was prepared to do it for the sake of a serious meal. We were warned that the traffic into town was very bad, so we booked a room at Sezz for the night and set off early.

We got up, drove two hours, came off the A8, wended towards the bay, traffic not looking that bad, down to one lane and then, pow! Solid traffic. Solid, solid, solid. I'm sorry, but when the sat-nav says you are 10.8 miles from your destination, and you move not a car's length in half an hour (sat-nav giving an optimistic estimated journey time of nine hours), you do not just sit there. You grasp that St-Tropez is for Russians with helicopters and boats, and you operate an embarrassing three-pointer, and drive home. Five hours of the day ruined, but at least, because you allowed (or so you thought) for the traffic, you are back in Cagnes-sur-Mer by lunchtime.

There, we stopped for a consolation lunch at a place called Charlot, which my parents always liked. Plate of squid and a small piece of bass, a green salad, two glasses of rosé and a coffee: €90. Ninety earth euros.

'You wouldn't pay that at Scott's,' I shouted to Esther.

'No,' shouted Esther. 'But then at Scott's the road outside isn't nearly so noisy.'

Well, I couldn't review that, now could I? I was looking to

end my French gastrodyssey on an up note. Which meant I couldn't review Paloma Beach at St-Jean Cap-Ferrat, either. Because although the setting was beautiful and the sea lapped at our toes as we ate, the bill for two courses, with some whiffy squid and one fish between four, came to – I hope you're sitting down – 400 (four hundred) euros.

On the plus side, we did encounter the only smiling waiter in the whole of France. But that was spoilt when we realised he was smiling only because the John Dory he had persuaded us to buy cost £200. Twice the price of my first car. No doubt the fishermen were down at St-Trop on the back of that, landing their helicopter at Gagnaire's place for the night.

I can't blame France for all this. I love France and I love its food: the greengrocers who sniff the melon and ask what time you want it for, the butchers with the beautiful cuts of lamb and the home-made *merguez* and dangling Corsican *figatelli*. I can only blame myself.

As a restaurant critic, France is my Krypton (along with Italy). My powers do not work here.

How to Get the Most from Your Local

THE BEST RESTAURANT in the world (I reply boringly, when boringly asked) is the nearest restaurant to your home/office/hotel/prison where they serve at least one dish you look forward to eating, are quite nice to you when you walk in, and have at least one bottle of wine that won't kill you. It's all about walking there and walking back. All about focussing on the time in the restaurant, not the time on the bus/train/plane/horse or in the car.

And if there isn't one, make one. This is easier than it sounds. Most people who run restaurants (the exception may be greasy spoons and certain ethnic takeaways) know how to cook, but don't bother doing it for their customers, only for friends and family. So become their friend.

Find any nearby Italian/Spanish/French/Polish/Brazilian restaurant and go once a week for a bit, even twice (a weeknight followed quickly by a Sunday lunch). Tip. Not stupidly high, but above the included service amount. Tread the fine line between generous pal and flash wanker.

The next time, ask them what they had for staff lunch or what the chef had for lunch. Ask for that. Ask what the best thing is the chef cooks, and if it isn't on the menu today, can they let you know when it's next on? Give them your phone number. (The last few times you've been introducing yourself by name and repeating theirs back to them so that you remember it.)

Always ask after their children. Buy them a drink. All of this may sound weird and pervy and sick and needy, but it is only in Britain that this behaviour is not normal. In Europe, staff and customers (outside of the haughtiest Michelin hellholes) go as equals. And chefs and owners are your special friends. In Japan, for heaven's sake, it is normal to take gifts

for the chef
three or four times a year
(nodding porcelain cats are popular, also pornographic manga). And for his
children. In return, he'll call you when they've
had in a particularly good fish, so endangered that
four or five Greenpeace activists had to be tragically
accidentally slaughtered in the landing of it, and prepare it
the special way you like it.

The point is that you are becoming a friend. Friends don't give
you the old whiffy bit of fish from the fridge. They don't leave you
waiting an hour for your dinner. They don't overcharge you. They don't
give you the shite table by the loos. They don't get huffy when you tell
them their wine buyer has sent them an iffy case . . . What they do is they
smile when you come in, give you a great table, make you feel needed,
tell you what's good, bring you a drink quickly and a free bit of something
they've been scoffing on backstage, and they flip you the odd bottle of
free wine, all the while leaning down conspiratorially to make rude
personal remarks about the arses at the next table to whom they will be
feeding last month's mackerel.

And what else could you possibly ask from a restaurant? That is what
a great restaurant is. That is what I get in most restaurants just because
of my silly job and being on the telly sometimes. I get people pretending to be my friend and trying to give me the best possible
night out – which is a bit revolting and sad, but better than
nothing.

But when I am old and jobless and nobody gives a
fuck what I think about restaurants or anything else,
I will do all of what I've just described, to
create a few little places here and there
that I can call home.

BOOKING

Have you noticed how when you phone to book a restaurant these days, they always ask for your first name as well as your last? It's only started happening in the last couple of years, and it's really very strange. It seems so intrusive. And so irritatingly faux-friendly.

'And the name?'

'Coren. C-o-r-e-n.'

'Cohen, thank you. And your first name, Mr Cohen?'

'Er, Giles.'

'Thank you Jules. And were you happy at school, Jules?'

'Eh?'

'Are you having regular sex?'

'Depends on what you mean by . . . '

'Tell me, how old are you?'

'Um, 42.'

'And are you comfortable with your, ahem, size?'

And so on. Just take the damn booking. The name's Coren, I'll be there at 8 p.m. And if you have to call me back, you can call me 'Mr Coren'. I don't want strangers calling me by my first name. I'm not Australian.

Apart from anything else, it can lead to especial difficulties for those of us – restaurant critics, international fraudsters, paranoid schizophrenics – who tend to use false names when booking restaurants. I called a flash new brasserie in Mayfair the other day and booked a table in the name of 'Foskett'.

'And your first name, Mr Focksit?'

'Oh, um, ah,' and suddenly I felt all devious and guilty, as when you see a plod car in the rear-view and you're not even pissed. I can make up one name, say it in the mirror and do my best to look like a Foskett when I arrive. But to have to think of a first name as well, on the spur of the moment, is a real task. It always feels like a trick question designed to root out my lie.

'Oh, um, yes, my first name, of course, no problem, my first name is, ah, my Christian name if you like, is, er, Bob.'

'Bob?'

'No. That's ridiculous, isn't it? Not Bob. Who's called Bob Foskett? Nobody. It's Erasmus.'

'Erasmus?'

'Yes. Erasmus P. Foskett. The third.'

'Really?'

'No. It's Sam. I'm called Sam Foskett.'

And then what happened was that the nice French lady said, 'Ah, hello Mr Foskett. We have your number down as 020 7167 9795, is that still correct?'

'No. I mean, yes. Probably for that Sam Foskett. But I'm a different one.'

'So your number is . . . ?'

'Wait, are you expecting the real Sam Fosk . . . I mean, the other Sam Foskett tonight?'

Fortunately, they weren't. Because if there's one thing we Sam Fosketts cannot abide, it is being seated next to another man called Sam Foskett who wants to talk all night about how he thought he was the only one. And am I one of the Marylebone Fosketts? And why has he never seen me at the Foskett ball in June . . .

*   *   *

But then even when you do get through the trauma of delivering your name to these nincompoops, they so often come back at you with, 'Brasserie or fine dining?'

It is one of the most baffling trends to afflict new restaurant construction in the past ten years, this insistence, wherever space permits (and often where it simply does not), on offering two different 'eating experiences' in the same building. Almost every new restaurant you care to mention nowadays offers both a 'relaxed brasserie' and a 'fine dining restaurant', and I just don't know why.

Well, I do know why. Money. That's all. Some people want to go out and be fussed over by a supercilious gauleiter in morning dress, have their wine poured for them drop by drop in a noiseless morgue of a room, and, if they choose, their main course chewed for them by a flunky and dribbled into their mouths, followed by a bill of more than a hundred quid a head, while others want to neck three beers listening to dance music and have a six-quid burger thrown at them from the bar by a pierced-nippled stripper on roller skates – and restaurateurs just cannot bear to turn either customer away. So they cravenly attempt to accommodate both.

More recently still, a habit has developed of offering a delicatessen and grocery store inside or alongside your restaurant/bar/brasserie, for punters who don't want to go out for dinner at all but whose money you nonetheless covet. Lots of good, exciting new places do this. Quite often you're sitting in the posh quiet restaurant, listening to the thump of the bass from the brasserie while watching people queue-jump for premium pasta in the grocery section. I don't know why they don't go further – open up a milliner's and mobile-phone shop next to the kitchen, why don't they? Or a Halfords, now that would be useful.

Ten years ago, this cupiditous multitasking would have been

unthinkable. If you wanted a long, slow, tightly organised and serious meal with event wine you went to Le Gavroche, Gordon Ramsay, Pied à Terre, wherever. You wanted a cheeseburger and a drive-by shooting, you went to Mickey D's. You didn't go into the Gavva and say, 'Tell you what, Michel, I'm not really up for this posh stuff today, could you grab us a pizza and a couple of frozen cheesecakes to take away?'

The problem for me with these restaurants of multiple possibility is the option paralysis they engender. I phone to book a table and they say, 'Brasserie or fine dining?' and I freeze in the headlights of their enquiry, wondering whether or not I want a limp, truffly *amuse-bouche* before my double-priced soup. And do I want it enough to iron a shirt specially?

'Brasserie' to me sounds all half-arsed and clattery with giant plates and clumsy provincial waitresses and soggy fishcakes and giant glasses of soave. And fine dining (pronounced 'fane daning') is just so impossibly Hyacinth Bucket.

So usually I say, 'Hmm, brasserie or fine dining? Good question. Let me call you back.' And then I just stay home and order pizza.

HAVING 'FUN'

I don't mind friends phoning me up for restaurant advice, I really don't. I'm flattered they think I have the sort of wide-ranging knowledge and instant recall that could be of use to a person frantically hunting for a great meal at short notice. But I haven't.

'I just want somewhere low-key for lunch,' they say. 'Good fresh produce, Mittel Europa fusion ideally, with maybe a Mongolian barbecue, live music (not too loud!), good skiing and a view of palm trees, no more than eight minutes' walk from Snaresbrook station.'

Or they want somewhere incredibly fashionable and up-to-the-minute where you can get a table for 12 this Saturday night at 8 o'clock, or a place that will impress the boss without looking too try-hard and the wife can have fish, or a good atmosphere but no Russians, or an authentic Balinese in Wembley with disabled access and a bowling alley. And I just don't know what they think is inside my head – some alphabetical Rolodex of impossible dining joints? I just eat, file and forget. Asked for a recommendation off the cuff, the only place I can ever think of is the one I've just been to. And even then I have trouble.

'That place you reviewed last week sounded nice,' they say.

'Which one?' I reply.

'Last week.'

'You'll have to help me.'

'French. You didn't like the pelmets. The fish was off.'

'Sorry, nothing.' .

'Inadequate veggie options. The beetroot was too soft.'

'You're sure it was me?'

'Cracking waitresses. You said there was one in a black skirt who looked a bit like Suzanne Mizzi in her mid-Eighties prime.'

'Oh, that place.'

But, asked for anything more specific, the best I can do is to stall them with a lot of 'mm's and 'er's and dumb questions like, 'Do you care whether the waiters wear shoes?' until I can get downstairs to the bookshelves in the loo and flip open the guides – *Time Out, Michelin, Harden's, Good Food* – and find something that fits their preposterous requirements. Which anybody could do. Except then they wouldn't have someone on the other end of a phone to blame afterwards.

'You said the cooking would be traditional, but they served crème fraîche with the treacle pudding!'

'You call some old pianist and his rancid dollybird "live music"?'

'I said, "Notting Hill", but it was in W8!'

A thankless life, it truly is. And the worst of all is when people ask me to recommend somewhere 'fun'.

What do they mean? Whoever said restaurants were meant to be fun? Playing football in the park on a Sunday afternoon in May is fun. Throwing tangerine segments at people out of the window and then ducking down below the sill is fun. Ironing all your pants and t-shirts on a rainy Wednesday afternoon while listening to Radio 2 is fun. But restaurants?

Surely fun is something you bring with you. They just do the food. And if they try to do the fun for you, like at, say, TGI Friday – where 'fun' means a fat girl with a lot of badges telling you in a baby voice to save room for the scrumptious banoffee meringue paving stone – it damn near kills you. With the right people, or enough people, you can have fun in any restaurant. But if you have a row with your wife in the car on the way there, then you can have no fun at all by the bucketload, regardless of the fizz and spectacle of the venue.

I suppose by 'fun' people mean dancing (shudder). I suppose they mean loud music and loads of people and huge bar areas to stand around in ogling birds in short skirts and then some kind of performance food and cocktails named after sexual positions. I remember such places. Mezzo, Quaglino's, Harvey Nichols Fifth Floor in its pomp. Dismal, they were. As unfun as someone sneaking into the operating theatre during a transplant operation and hilariously switching your replacement heart for a lemon when the surgeon isn't looking.

Sure, go somewhere to drink, smoke, dance, do drugs in the bogs and pull a Lithuanian grandmother with the names of nine different Chelsea players tattooed on her arse. But you want to eat there as well? You must be mad.

These days 'fun' places are done a bit better, admittedly. Certainly in London, where people are now thoroughly bored with great cooking and would rather just have a good time. Nobody in London gives a damn about the annual Michelin results any more, and the arrival of a world-famous chef to a Central London hotel outlet near you is met with little more than a yawn. What we want in London, I suppose, is indeed this thing you call 'fun'. Maybe it's the economic downturn. Maybe it's a reaction to the grimness and the misery and the poverty and the grind. Like Prohibition speakeasies in the Depression, Rick's bar in *Casablanca*, and East End pubs during the Blitz ('Another pint of mild for you sir, and, whoops missus, there goes the billiard room! Pesky doodlebugs!').

We want to hang out. We want a vibe. We want London to be like New York, where people fight for tables in the hottest restaurants but nobody really mentions the food because, let's face it, eating is for fatties, for bridge-and-tunnel rubberneckers, for the fans of TV chefs who bus in hoping for a glimpse. Eating, and making a fuss about what you eat, is – there is no other word for it – common.

I'd say The Wolseley started it, bringing the concept out of The Ivy: fantastic building, A-list crowd, smart service, perfectly okay food – great night out. And then Nick Jones of the Soho House Group took it on a bit to create places like the Dean Street Townhouse that one calls restaurants, and where there is nothing wrong with the food at all, but really they are night-clubs, bars, dives, rolling party joints . . . there is no actual word for them. Yes, you can eat, and eat fine. But that's not the point. I'd say the same is true of Mark Hix's restaurants, too. Mark is an absolute master of British ingredients, no question, and has come up with some genius dishes in his time. But the point of his restaurants is the art, the people, the noise, the getting wrecked and falling over.

It's about restaurateurs, not chefs. I think it is what dear old Marco Pierre White grasped before anybody else, when he tossed in his stars and started opening bistros. And as operations like poor old Gordon Ramsay's go publicly down the pan, people are wondering why they ever gave a damn about the cooks at all.

King of the new restaurateurs is probably Russell Norman, yet another Ivy/Caprice old boy, whose Polpo, Polpetto, da Polpo, Spuntino (and others whose names I forget – it would be so much easier if he went the McDonald's route and just gave them all the same name) have in the space of a couple of years made half-decent food, excellent booze, tattooed staff, tin ceilings, reclaimed furniture, and bustling queues the markers for on-message munching in London's West End that they have long been in Greenwich Village.

The problem with them, and the secret (I suspect) of their success, is that you can't book. It's a whopping pain in the arse. But also, apparently, great fun. So much fun that as the brand developed he went so far as to start doing away with signs over the doors, telephone numbers, anything that smacked of such dreary bourgeois things as convenience or ease of access. Spuntino, for example, doesn't even have tables. It's just a bare wall in Soho that really cool people know to stand in front of.

The first time I tried to go to Polpo, I thought they were kidding when they wouldn't take my booking.

'We decided that we've done our bit, opening a restaurant that people like,' said the chap on the phone, after telling me that, no, it wouldn't be possible for me to book a table. 'And we just want to say to people, "We're here, come if you like, and we'll get you seated as soon as we can."'

In principle, it was a great response from a new and jam-packed restaurant, simply to throw open its doors to the passing world, instead of booking itself to the hilt for three months to come. It's democratic and folksy and honest, and Polpo does not in any way set itself up to be a Michelin-type destination joint. It's just a Soho squat-and-gobble and it would be ludicrous, they are well aware, for people to book two months ahead and get dressed up all fancy-like and head 'up west' to throw down a couple of beers and a saucer of meatballs in a small, noisy room. (If you book months ahead, it's because you want to be certain of a huge, silent room full of sanctimonious waiters ripping the shirt from your back for a piece of foie gras that has been poked and prodded until it tastes of warm thumbs by some half-educated sociopath who dreams of getting his own television show.)

But the trouble with the 'no-booking' thing is that it asks you – or, more importantly, it asks me – to muffle up on a wet winter's night and skulk into town on public transport on the off-chance of getting something to eat.

'Nobody has yet had to wait more than 20 minutes for a table,' said the man on the phone – really nice, helpful and well-spoken. 'What time were you thinking of coming?'

Oho, I thought. Here we go.

'About eight p.m.,' I said. 'Certainly between eight and nine.'

'Ah, that's usually not the best time,' he said.

Best time for what, one wonders? It's certainly the best time for supper. Indeed, there are those of us who, literally, call that time 'supper time'.

'If you come a bit earlier then you'll wait less,' he said. 'Before seven thirty is even better.'

Before 7.30? Who in the world eats before 7.30? Children, soldiers, people under house arrest? Who else? If I eat before 7.30 I'm going to have to eat again later. Honestly, by 11.30 p.m. I'll be down the Bengal Lancer with a pint of Stella, ordering up a fat korma and a stack of naan breads.

So I rather sheepishly told my impatient friend Max (who, whenever we meet up, texts me 30 seconds after I'm supposed to have arrived to ask, 'Was it today we were meeting?') that we would be aiming for 7.30 p.m. at Polpo, and hoping not to wait too long. But he didn't seem to mind at all. He'd read about it online and was of the opinion that 'it sounds off the clock, on fire, sailing at eight bells?' and other epithets of the kind that masters of industry sometimes accidentally bring out of the boardroom and into the real world, where they baffle and stagger us with their butchness and opacity.

My cab turned into Brewer Street at 7.28 and I saw Max outside the restaurant, on the phone. Then my phone rang.

'I'm here, I'm here!' I gasped. 'And I've still got two minutes.'

'He says at least an hour for a table,' said Max, and then rang off, and I got out of the cab, and we shook hands. And did a little hug.

But, you see, 'at least an hour' isn't really okay. It's the whole problem with these places where you are supposed to be all cool and relaxed and just take your chance. You can do this in a Southern European town where it never rains and everyone lives nearby and strolls around from six in the evening till dawn, with a pastel-coloured V-neck draped over their shoulders, grazing on bits and pieces, dropping in for a prawn and a glass of prosecco here, a slice of ham and a Horlicks there, and kissing everyone they meet and generally being marvellous. If the place you fancy is a bit full, you can just stroll on to the next, kiss, kiss, glass here, glass there, no es problemo?

But in London you have spent an hour in a cab and paid 30 quid to get here. It's pouring with rain and freezing cold, so you can't stand about in the street wondering where to go instead. And if you do try to go somewhere else, they laugh at you for even thinking that they might have a table, because this is London, and didn't you know you have to book?

It would be great if everyone went over to walk-ins only (assuming the weather changed and we all moved into the centre of town), because then there would be an ebb and flow of table availability. But lone system-buckers rather screw you.

It's like the Italo Calvino story about the village populated exclusively by thieves (it's in Italy, so it could be anywhere): each night the thieves go out burgling, and when they get home they find they've been burgled. Which is fine, because they've got all the new stuff they've just robbed, to make up for what they've lost. But then one day one chap decides to go straight. He stays in. The bloke who comes to burgle him finds him there, so bottles it and goes home empty-handed to find that he has, as usual, been burgled. He is destitute. Very quickly the whole economy of the village breaks down – ruined by the lone honest man.

And Polpo is a bit like that man: by being all democratic and progressive, but acting alone, Polpo is in danger of destroying the whole fabric of our society.

But it's a jolly nice place. Max and I stood around for maybe 40 minutes by the bar, drinking a bit more than one would normally want to on an empty stomach, but eventually securing the odd plate of nibbles and only a couple of times being shoulder-slammed by a bustling waitress and spilling our drinks on our shoes.

My wife appeared at one point – just like if this had been Valladolid or Siena or something – and then suddenly we were at a lovely table, deep in the warm hustle of the place, which has the fizzing, exuberant atmosphere that is generated by the gratitude of diners who have spent the last hour worrying that they were going to have to go home hungry and eat a kebab at the bus stop.

From the warmth and comfort of the table, you first of all forget your long wait, and then begin to look back on it fondly as having been the very best of times (standing there, nattering, winking at girls, slugging back cocktails when the night was young), much as a married man looks back fondly on single days which were, in truth, full of nothing but the fear that they would never end.

The food was nothing to get over-excited about. It's like old-fashioned Soho trattoria stuff served in fashionably small portions for sharing. We had neat little greaseless *arancini* (fried rice balls), some fine *polpette* (meatballs), a plate of excellent fried calf's liver and two good little pizzettas, but none of the fish dishes really sung (the mackerel just wasn't morning-fresh and virgin-sweet enough for a tartare) and many of the dishes were blurred, indistinct and erratically seasoned. But I had a lovely time. Max got it bang on with a text the following morning that read: 'Great dinner, despite the food.'

And perhaps that is the point of a Venetian restaurant. The only meal I have ever had in Venice was at Harry's Bar, possibly the most famous, and famously fun, restaurant in the world. The place was rammed, the staff were lovely, the maitre d' (as at Polpo) a real gent, the atmosphere terrific, and the food quite, quite awful.

And then we had to get home from Venice.

Book a Table, Not a Restaurant

IT'S AN OLD Michael Winner line, but it holds good for us humbler mortals too. Don't just phone up and book a time and a date. Because it is the first law of restaurant filling that they will put you, when you arrive, in the shittest table they have – the one all on its own in the basement, next to the broken, smelly loo, under a dripping soil pipe, with a feral hunting dog tied to the leg of your wobbly chair.

Because the chances are, seeing as you're British, that you'll take it and say 'thank you'. And sit there in silence for a bit, internalising your disappointment, and then say 'this is nice, isn't it?' as your wife wipes her finger across the table and makes an inch-deep trough in the ancient layers of hog fat, dust and rodent droppings.

And then that's that table dealt with, and they can breathe a sigh of relief and not worry about having to give it to someone else. And gradually they give the next worse table away, and the next worse, all so that the nicest of the tables – the ones with a nice view, the best light, comfiest seating, most cover space, most discretion from neighbouring tables, a good eyeline to the most senior member of staff – can be given to regulars/friends/rich people/celebs/Russian gangsters who just happen to drop by. But those good tables should be being held for YOU. You're waaaaay more important than some Russian crook

and his
anorexic teenage smack-
addicted mistress.

All you have to do is ask. If you don't know the restaurant already then drop in beforehand if you can to make the booking in person and walk round the room, checking for the best table. In the flesh, they can't refuse you any of them.

And if you've never seen the room before and are doing it on the phone, you can still ask for 'a nice table', 'maybe by the window' (as those are generally the best) or 'not by the loos or the till', you can make a little joke of it on the phone, and then make sure you get the guy's/girl's name, write it down, check it before you set off for the meal and ask 'are you Blank/Blankita?' when you arrive, and then if the table is not good, you can remind them of your little phone chat and, I swear, they will move you to a better table.

You must learn to do this. You must remember that somebody will be getting the best table that night (and the same goes for someone getting the best portions, quickest food, friendliest service . . .) and the only reason for that person not to be you is that you didn't make it clear enough that that is what you expect, and what a wonderful fellow you are, and how you thoroughly deserve it.

Remember if it's not you that gets the table, it'll be Michael Winner.

LEGALLY

C an there be anything more counter-intuitive than choosing to pay a visit to a restaurant the day after it has lost a court case?

I don't consider myself a fussy eater. But expecting a joint to keep itself off the wrong end of an historic verdict in Her Majesty's Court of Appeal is surely not too much to ask – especially a verdict upholding a critic's right to describe the atmosphere as 'joyless', the ingredients as 'the cheapest . . . on the market' and the food as 'inedible'.

When, in the spring of 2008, I read in the newspapers about the victory of *The Irish News* over a Belfast restaurant called Goodfellas, where 'the chips were pale, greasy and under-cooked' and 'the cola was flat, warm and watery', I tittered quietly to myself, thanked God for Jamie, Gordon and Hugh and peeled myself another organic carrot.

And then *The Times* rang and said there was an easyJet flight leaving Gatwick for Belfast at 7.45 that evening. Obviously, in the light of this historic judgment for freedom of speech, I would be wanting to review the place myself.

Obviously?

Well, obviously I was not excited about eating there. Despite what some people think, I do not enjoy ripping restaurants to pieces. It makes me feel sad. For them, and for myself, who had to swallow the meal. I go out of my way to find nice restaurants.

I never go to ones that I suspect will be bad, for the fun of mocking them. Life is too brief and fleeting to go deliberately to bad restaurants. In general, my method of restaurant selection is to read the other reviewers I admire (both of them), and go wherever they say is good.

But it doesn't always work. And sometimes I do eat poorly. And I say so. In terms as florid and surprising as possible, because otherwise one is just grumbling. And for years and years, from the very dawn of my reviewing life in the middle Nineties, my copy had come back to me every week covered in the hysterical red ink of the in-house libel lawyers, striking out anything remotely negative or interesting.

If I wrote, for example, that something 'tasted disgusting', some snivelling legal bean-counter would insist that I change it to 'in my opinion it tasted disgusting' because it is not a fact, it's an opinion.

And I would shout back, 'But, you moron! You brainless, stuffed-shirt, pink-faced, witless gibbon, OF COURSE IT IS MY FUCKING OPINION! It's a review. The whole damn thing is my opinion. I am paid to give my opinion. To write or say that something is disgusting is ALWAYS an opinion. There is no objective version of it.'

But they always changed it anyway. A really nice bit of writing (if I do say so myself) would often be rendered, in my opinion, disgusting, by the addition of up to a dozen 'in my opinion's, added in by some tin-eared bumhole of a failed barrister.

And if I wrote something more interesting than merely 'it tasted disgusting', it was worse. If I wrote, 'the soup was a verminous radioactive slime possibly derived from the cold-pressing of toads', I would be told that not only was this merely my opinion, but that it was too emphatic, and I would have no defence of 'fair comment' or 'truth' in law, because the wording of it so clearly revealed malice.

Whereas all it revealed was an imagination more fruity than a lawyer's.

I'll digress for a moment. I'll tell you what happened when I sat in a three-day libel meeting prior to the publication of my first book, the ghosted autobiography of James Dyson, the vacuum cleaner tycoon (go buy it on Amazon, it's a riot, still in print, available in Japanese, Korean, French, Norwegian and even American, and is the only book from which I have ever made any serious money).

James's manner of self-expression tends to be plain and direct, as befits a master of industry. But I felt it was important to liven the language up a bit just to keep people bobbing along in the boring bits. I was 25. I was naïve like that.

James had vented at length to me about how the designers always descend on his engineering products and ruin them with their unnecessary fiddling. So I wrote randomly, of one product: ' . . . and then the designers came in and made an aardvark's lunch of everything'.

Two and a half days into this libel meeting, we came round to this sentence.

'I don't understand,' said the lawyer.

'Well,' I said. 'You know the expression, "a dog's dinner"?'

'Yes,' he said.

'And you know the expression, "a pig's breakfast"?'

'Yes,' he said.

'Well,' I said. 'It's like that. Just another way of saying "a mess".'

'But the other two are expressions,' said the lawyer.

'So is "aardvark's lunch",' I said.

'But I've never heard it before,' he said.

'That's because it's a new expression,' I said. 'I made it up.'

This flummoxed the lawyer. He muttered to himself a bit. I wondered if smoke would start to rise from his head and there'd be the smell of circuits shorting.

'I just want to be sure what we're saying about these design-ers,' he said. 'I don't want to jeopardise a defence of "fair comment".'

He thought a little more and then said (and I'm not making this up): 'What does an aardvark have for lunch?'

I laughed. James Dyson laughed. The publishers laughed. The lawyer didn't laugh.

'Seriously?' I asked.

'Seriously,' said the lawyer.

'Well,' I said. 'As far as I know, an aardvark is a sort of anteater. So I guess he eats ants. Although I doubt he breaks them down into specific meals as you or I might do, but eats them more or less whenever he can.'

'I see,' said the lawyer. 'And did the product in question, after tampering by these designers, in any way come to resemble, er, ants?'

I looked at him for a flicker of humour. Of humanity even. But saw none.

'Shall we just put "dog's dinner"?' I asked.

'I really would rather,' said the lawyer.

And so we did. It's there in the book to this day.

And that is the sort of thing I encountered weekly with my reviews. So. While I had no interest especially in eating at Goodfellas, I was delighted that a newspaper had successfully defended its legal right to say publicly how bad the food was, and realised that it was my professional duty to attempt the same.

On the plane I read through the court papers, the complex arguments of the plaintiff (*The Irish News* was seeking to over-turn a previous libel decision against it in the High Court) and the summing up by three judges. The paperwork was, bizarrely, fascinating. And, for reviewers and critics, truly world-chang-ing.

Lord Lester of Herne Hill, QC – may his name be whispered as a blessing – won the appeal for *The Irish News* on the following basis (I'll have got this only more or less right, so don't quote me. Or sue me):

1. That anything written in an article flagged as a review is to be accepted as 'comment' (regardless of whether it is presented as opinion or fact);
2. That the bare substratum of fact required to sustain that comment is that the reviewer has had the experience he or she claims, in this case that he has ordered and been served the meal described;
3. That 'fair comment' is defined as any comment an honest person could have drawn from the 'facts' available;
4. That a comment may be called 'fair', 'however exaggerated, or even prejudiced, the language may be';
5. That malice has no power to mitigate a defence of fair comment, as long as the reviewer genuinely holds the views he expressed.

In short, as long as I ate the meal I claim that I ate, and as long as I truly believe what I write, I can say anything.

Goodfellas was in Kennedy Way, just off the Falls Road, a Catholic-owned joint on the edge of a loyalist enclave strong on militant murals, marching and, not so long ago, rifle-volley shows of strength. The windows were smoked dark and impenetrable. The patch of grass outside was littered with empty bottles of WKD Blue. There were two sets of entry doors, of which the outer one was formerly remote-controlled, testifying to times when the threat of a loyalist 'spraying' was very real. Times when the least of your worries was a dodgy restaurant review.

The Fat Duck this most certainly wasn't.

It was about three-quarters full inside, which was impressive on a wet weeknight in March, and almost everyone was fat. Obesity in West Belfast seems to be even worse than in the poorest areas of mainland Britain. There was what appears to be a hen party in the next room comprising 12 women seated around a large square table, each of whom, on her own, weighed as much as a whole hen night of women from Fulham. (I guess these were battery hens.)

The men had big square heads and little pink faces, short spiky hair, stud earrings and big appetites. It was like Westlife had got old and fat overnight. Which they sort of have, if you've seen them recently.

To be fair, the welcome was not, as *The Irish News* had it, 'daunting' or negligent. A very pretty and charming waitress sat me at a very small table next to some very large people. She brought me a glass of cola (Goodfellas has no licence) which was, indeed, pretty flat and not especially cold and (as *The Irish News* critic claimed) clearly not poured from a bottle but shot from a gun. So much for decommissioning.

The menu was terrifying. Hundreds of choices – 14 starters, 14 chicken dishes, 15 pizzas (including 'The Whop'), 13 pasta dishes as well as a do-it-yourself option, where six styles of pasta can be paired with a cream or tomato sauce and any permutation of 25 further ingredients to create millions of possibilities (if you've ever fancied rigatoni with smoked salmon, sweetcorn and barbecue sauce, Goodfellas is the place to get it).

Then there were ten beef dishes with ten sauce options (100 more possible combos there) including the alluring-sounding 'gravy'. Half a dozen pig dishes, some specials and 24 *contorni* (this is an Italian restaurant, don't forget), of which eight are potato.

Portions were massive. Waitresses struggled by with Brobdingnagian tureens of pasta and pizzas like dustbin lids (but smellier). I ordered a small *farfalle all'arrabiata*, and then the chicken marsala – the very dish that Caroline Workman, the *Irish News* critic, had described as being served in a sauce so revoltingly sweet as to render the dish inedible. I nipped to the loo. Two of the cubicle doors were locked but the third opened, straight into the kitchen. Most unusual. This does not happen at Le Gavroche. Perhaps I am spoilt.

My little pasta dish arrived. A huge disappointment: it was fine. Not fine in the sense of tasting like something an Italian would dream of eating. But fine in the sense of being the sort of thing I used to cook as a student when I was too stoned to dial a pizza. The chips I ordered were fine, too. Precut and frozen, yes, but that's normal even in a good gastropub, and these were nice and crispy. I was gutted. It looked like there would be no opportunity to test my rejuvenated confidence in a restaurant critic's right to freedom of expression.

Then my *pollo marsala* arrived: an oval dish containing a chocolate-coloured liquid and pale lumps of something. I ate a mouthful. The sweetness was, indeed, alarming. As was the consistency of the meat. Without the court papers to confirm what I had ordered, I'd have guessed I was eating thin strips of mole poached in Ovaltine.

It was revolting. It was ill-conceived, incompetent, indescribably awful. A dish so cruel I wept not only for the animal that died to make it, but also for the mushrooms. Ms Workman said it was inedible but, to be honest, as it sat before me, congealing quietly, I could not leave it alone, but returned to it every few minutes with the grim fascination of a toddler mesmerised by a pile of its own faeces, nibbling at it, gurning with revulsion, then nibbling some more. A note on the menu said: 'All of our meals are freshly prepared'. When I asked for parmesan cheese, they bring a pot of that powdery pre-grated grit that smells like desiccated dog vomit. I thought I'd better have a pudding, so I ordered the apple crumble. Alas, what they brought me resembled a mixture of budget muesli and aquarium gravel served in an old man's slipper. The accompanying custard was pleasant only in that it reminded me of a scented pencil eraser I used to enjoy sucking in the hot summer of 1976.

I came home, and I savaged the place, wielding my newly granted superpowers of self-expression on this poor, benighted little Irish craphole. And since then I have written up restaurants just as exactly as I find them.

And I haven't heard a peep out of the lawyers since.

BLOGGERS

It is my misfortune often to be in restaurants quite early in
their lives, when word is not yet out, and custom is slow. On
these occasions it is usual to be eating one's dinner in a room
that is quite empty, but for a few tables of flabby people taking
photographs of everything on their plates before eating it.

These people are bloggers. And all power to them. But I think
photographing one's food in a restaurant is easily as rude, disrespectful and brutish as making a phone call, scrolling a
BlackBerry or dropping one's trousers in the middle of the
room and taking a massive dump. And, really, if you see it
happening, you should complain to the waiter and see what
transpires. Just for larks.

I had a go at them for it once in my column and, ye Gods, the
Internet caved in on me.

I had no idea how many of my Twitter followers were food
bloggers (who else would they be, I guess?). I had no idea that
so many of them thought it so fundamental to the art of reviewing that photos of everything be attached to each piece of prose.
I had no idea that, at the merest hint of huffiness about the
practice from me, so many of them would go utterly m-m-m-
m-m-m-mental. Even *The Guardian* dropped an orchestra,
calling me 'the curmudgeon-in-chief of restaurant criticism'
and declaring food-snappers harmless.

Apparently, I am a snob. I am anti-democratic. I am jealous.

To the first two, well, maybe. It is only natural that an entrenched medium-sized cheese of the old media should fear the onrush of potent online pretenders to his position. But 'jealous' I don't get. If *The Times* wanted photos of the food that is reviewed on its pages, it would have them. Many newspapers and magazines do. But we've tended to rely on whoever's writing the review to describe what he's eaten more or less faithfully, in three dimensions, and with smells, tastes and sounds into the bargain.

A photo gives you almost nothing. Everything looks shiny and greasy in a photo (especially me). All food looks disgusting. Anything even vaguely tubular looks either phallic or turdulous. Blogs are a terrific resource for the lazier sort of restaurant bum, and I follow many of them. Some are written well, many are very informative, but almost all are illustrated with assorted photographs of todgers and bigjobs in various exotic contexts.

Just now, I was looking at a blog about Brasserie Joël, where I'm going tonight (and which I'm reviewing next week), by the estimable 'Dos Hermanos'. The brothers enjoyed their food, but the pictures almost had me cancelling my reservation. Praise for the stuffed courgette flower, for example, was illustrated by a slick, green, shiny penis with a terrible inflammation of the scrotum. Below that was a delicious slab of pork belly on which, so far as I could see, a dachshund or some small terrier had moments before left its little calling card – nor did the text offer any alternative interpretation of the glistening bronze tube uncoiled upon the meat. It was thus fortunate that the 'small roasted banana', served brown and whole with the dessert, had been captioned, because it looked most awfully like the dachshund had been back to finish what it had started.

Food photography is a largely fraudulent science. Much of the great food photographed in recipe books has been trixed up with all manner of adulterants to help it survive and show well under lights. It's not stuff you can eat, any more than you can have sex with one of those airbrushed, tinted and re-boobed fantasies of womanhood you see in magazines. But they are images to which we have grown used and, by comparison, a straight snap of a plate of grub looks revolting.

I have broadcast a photo of food only once, when, overexcited about eating Pierre Koffmann's cooking for the first time in years, I took a picture of my/his pig's trotters and tweeted the pic. I got a chorus of 'Yuk's in reply (for what I had tweeted looked like a poo with tusks), and it took acres of prose to correct the impression I had mistakenly given of M. Koffmann's savoury repertoire.

But it's not the existence of unpleasant food photographs on the web in itself that really bothers me. It is a mad new media world we live in and if that is how it is going to be, then that is how it is going to be. The gruesome thing is the act of taking the photos, there in the restaurant, when other people are trying to have a nice time. It's so vain, craven and self-important: 'Look at me, look at me, I'm taking pictures for my blog with my runty little camera-phone. I'm not some shlub spending his hard-earned money trying to have a nice time with his wife. I'm worrrrrking.'

Food-snappers turn what should be a place of pleasure into a place of work. One minute you're having a glass of wine with an old friend, the next you're in somebody's office. You're talking while they're trying to knuckle down.

And it puts unnecessary stress on the restaurant. The poor chef, informed by his staff that a flock of clicksters is in the house, will now spend hours trying to make their platefuls look like pretty pictures. Photo-blogging puts all the focus back on presentation, ahead of flavour and integrity – it throws us back to the bad old days of the early Eighties. The chef may well panic, he'll ignore other orders, the waiters will start to tremble and drop things.

Crucially, there is a version of the 'observer effect' (usually described in particle physics) at work when you carry a camera: by the very fact of its being there, the nature of the experience is changed, delaying things, cooling and spoiling the food, jittering the staff, irritating other diners, making the occasion you plan to write about far more of a lie than it needs to be.

How to Deal with Food-Poisoning

IT'S VERY HARD to pin food-poisoning on a restaurant. They will be reluctant to admit it because there would have to be an inspection and closures and people would lose their jobs and mortgages and the business, which is likely to be heavily leveraged, might well go to the wall.

But if you wake up in the night, say six hours after eating, and are puking or diarrhoearing then it may well be the restaurant. And the most likely thing is faecal-digital transmission. Pooey fingers, in other words. It's unlikely to be rotten food.

Staff work long hours and are very busy. They do not always have time to wash properly. They use their mobile phones in breaks while they are taking a dump and then in the kitchen afterwards with little flecks of grot possibly still on them, they scratch their balls, they pick their noses, they put their fingers in the pots to taste. They shouldn't but they do. The fashion for open kitchens means you can watch it going on any day of the week. It fair turns my stomach.

Personally, I think you have to lump it. Feeling rank from a bit of body grot out of a stranger's crevice is the price we pay for being too lazy to cook our own food. You wouldn't ask a stranger to bathe you, or kiss you or make love to you, would you? (Not if you were sober.) So why to touch your food? Just take an Imodium, try not to think about it, and

in 24 hours
it'll all be gone.

   If you must have satisfaction
then call up, ask to speak to the
manager and arrange to talk to her or him
in public. (There is no point doing it on the
phone.) Tell them what you experienced. Give
them exact timings. Say you are casting no aspersions.
Say you are sure their produce is good and their kitchens
are clean, but that you suspect they may have at least
one, probably only one, staff member who is not meeting
health and safety standards (use those words, very calmly
and quietly) and it is a shame that a little faecal-digital
transmission has ruined an otherwise lovely meal.

   Nine times out of ten, you will be apologised to and offered
a free meal. The other one out of ten times it is a place that will
not last long.

   But do not shout and rave about your rights and the law. As
with complaining to the waiter from the table, it is about what
you hope to achieve, not what you can get off your chest,
or how big your balls are. Legally, the chances are that
you can prove nothing. Nothing at all. You will look like
an idiot. The truth is probably that you have a feeble
stomach or, more embarrassingly, that you're just
not used to rich food. In a good week I'll eat out
ten or twelve times and I get the trots once
a year at the absolute most. I guess
I've just eaten so much shit my
stomach doesn't care
anymore.

MOCK DOG, SIR?

Today, we have naming of dishes. Yesterday, we had local sourcing. And tomorrow morning, we shall have what to do about farming. But today, today we have naming of dishes.

I don't usually think much about the names of dishes. I pay scant attention to menus. My friends order food in a burble of excitement and fun, wondering aloud what words mean, asking the waiter, making little jokes about what things sound like, giggling over words like 'faggot' or the many ways of misspelling 'Caesar', see-sawing backwards and forwards between the dishes they know they like and the things that are unfamiliar and exciting . . . and when they're done, I randomly order whatever has not already been spoken for, and sit back and wait for the kitchen to make a terrible hash of it so I can call for the bill and a taxi.

But I am sure we have all noticed that we are at the moment in a very 'unpretentious' period for dish-naming. In a reaction against some barely remembered epoch (was it the 1790s?) when everything one ate had a daft and fancy foreign name (*Lobster Pierre Choderlos de Laclos, sauce Antoine de Saint-Exupéry, sur son lit de pommes de terre façon, merde, je ne me rappelle plus le nom, tu sais, le mec qui etait le chef de Talleyrand, je voulais dire Antonin Worrall-Thompson mais ce n'est pas lui . . .*), dishes these days, from the humblest gastropub to the highest fallutin' Michelin-starred Chelsea clip-joint, tend to be called, with glorious, in-yer-face unpretentiousness, simply 'pork'. Or, 'sardines'. Or, if you scroll down to the lone, miserable vegetarian option, 'potato'.

Sure, there is usually a 30-word justificatory sous-script explaining how and why every element of the dish was constructed, because nobody can ever truly cork up the verbosity of chefs, but, in general, brevity has been identified as the soul of class. Brevity and the low vernacular: 'beef in crust', 'burnt cream', 'cock in wine'.

It is a weird, strangulated form of pretentious unpretentiousness. And it feels to me like the most pretentious sort of naming there could be.

An example of truly unpretentious naming, indeed of the wittiest and most expressive application of a name to something edible since our ancestor Adam came up with 'kangaroo', was a dish I had recently at a nice little Italian restaurant in Mayfair. It didn't have a name when I ordered it. It was the risotto of the day. I tend not to enquire further. If I fancy a bowl of rice I'll have a bowl of rice. There is nothing I don't eat so there is nothing they could put on it that could ruin it.

The dish itself was fair enough. It was made with new season grouse, the legs confit'd and stirred into the rice with Scottish girolles and chanterelles, fresh mint and a red wine reduction. On top was the breast of half a grouse, sliced, pan fried for a couple of minutes either side, a little blood running into the rice for yet more flavour and depth. As grouse dishes go, compared to the boring old roasted version with bread sauce and game chips, this was a revelation.

And it was invented on site. They don't have grouse in Italy, but they do something vaguely similar with teal, apparently. So a dish that was original, made wondrous use of bang-on-the-season wild British produce, and tasted wonderful. It hardly needed a good name too.

But then the bill came and I saw that, by God, it had one.

Risotto con grouse.

The perfect name.

'Risotto' exists only in Italian, 'grouse' only in English. So when an Italian chef puts the two together what else is he going to call it?

That's what poetry is. Giving something the only name it could possibly have.

And to get deeper into this issue let us go to a certain little Vietnamese restaurant in Hoxton, London's 'Little Hanoi', where I went with the great (well, famous) Malcolm Gluck, the *Superplonk* guy, to learn about pairing wine with Vietnamese food. (I don't really eat Vietnamese food, so to be honest it was probably a pretty pointless lesson. Much like the 700 maths lessons I had in the 1980s. But much more fun.)

Malcolm was good friends with Hieu, the owner, and so we were fed without recourse to the tedium of the menu. Thus, as with the famous grouse (did you see what I did there?), I ate the dishes first, and learned their names later. And learnt more about naming, too.

We began, for example, with an eel salad: grilled slivers of the unique, oily fish meat tossed with strips of carrot and mint, with a citrussy dressing. 'How you enjoy the Vietnamese long fish?' asked Hieu.

'You mean the eel?'

'Shh!' he said, only half-joking. 'English won't eat it if we call it "eel".'

What an odd lot the English are. What strange gastro-nomen-clatural finickiness to reject 'eel' on the grounds of squeam, and then dive headlong into a bowl of 'Vietnamese long fish'.

Next up was a very spicy bowl of what looked like dozens of baby squid, albeit brown squid, tossed with slices of what appeared to be some sort of marrow or gourd. But the squidlings tasted of chicken, rich like the oysters under a roasted bird. The whole was a rich, peppery meeting of flesh and vegetable, full of offal and zing.

Its name?

'Hasn't got a name,' said Hieu. 'Except for "chicken gizzard and muop".'

Like 'chicken gizzard and muop' isn't a hell of a name in its own right. A hell of a name. But they don't bother to put it on the menu because English people won't eat gizzards (and even I might ask what a 'muop' was before I ordered it), and the Vietnamese punters know, obviously, that it will be available. Obviously. Have you ever heard of a Vietnamese restaurant where you couldn't get gizzards and muop?

It was also nice to hear that Hieu gets his gizzards by the bagful from the farm which sends his chickens. One doesn't often hear Oriental restaurant proprietors in this country talking about farms.

Then came a big plate of galangal, rice paddy, lemongrass, Vietnamese basil and red chilli and a giant, piping tureen of pig's trotter marinated in yoghurt and turmeric and steamed in its own juices. You serve yourself a fat portion and then throw in the herbs and leaves to offset in each mouthful the richness and chilli fire with cool scents and exotic balm. A staggering meeting of fire and water, earth and air, pig and paddy.

Its name?

'Can't tell you. Can't say in front of English.'

'Really? Don't be silly.'

'OK. You want to know? "Mock dog".'

'You're kidding?'

'Not kidding. It's called mock dog. It's why it's not on the menu. English people are funny about dogs.'

'So it's a substitute for dog because you can't get dog in Britain?'

'Nooooo,' he says, like of course you can get dog in Britain. 'In Vietnam, it is bad luck to eat dog in first half of month. Bad luck for business. So until the fifteenth we eat this. And then afterwards, real dog.'

Sounds feasible. I don't know, he could have been winding me up. And he did say you couldn't get dog here, to be fair. Although apparently you're allowed to serve cat, 'as long as it is killed quickly'. (Don't you love the legislative assumption that there are people out there who might want to kill it slowly?)

Another great name was on the specials board: 'Saigon torch roast pork belly'. Saigon torch roast. Like some terrible euphemism out of *Apocalypse Now*.

'Pork belly has quickly been roasted by a torch,' explained Hieu. 'To get blacken, and a taste of dog.'

'Torching pork makes it taste like dog?'

'Yerrrrrs. Obvious. Vietnamese always torch a dog before cooking, to get rid of unpleasant flavour from its fur. Torch pig, everyone think it dog.'

On that basis I can tell you that dog tastes mighty fine. You could even try it at home (with that stupid crème brulée blowtorch you got for Christmas 13 years ago and have never used). But it would be more exciting to go to Hieu's place in the second half of a month some time. Something that I promised I would do, but don't seem to have managed yet.

Avoid Restaurants with a Waiter Posted Outside

HIS ENTHUSIASM FOR YOU TO come in is inversely proportional to how nice they will be to you when you are inside. This used to be a piece of advice you only needed for visiting foreign, generally third world, countries. But it is happening more and more in this country, outside the curry houses of East London's Brick Lane, for example, and it is as true here as it ever was abroad: treat that man who is being all smiley and nice as if he were a mugger and a rapist who is only interested in brutally separating you from your wallet, your dignity and very probably your life.

THE VEGGIE OPTION

I am a vegetarian. I imagine this comes as a surprise to you. What with me always writing things like: 'the carpaccio of slowly beaten weasel cubs was both lively and well-garnished' and 'I was particularly taken with the red pepper and songbird ragout that accompanied my fricasseed orphan.'

But it is true. After decades of laughing at the rabbit-food that goes into vegetarians and the terrible wind that comes out of them, I finally joined their number, some years ago now, because it is right and proper and decent, and because it is both environmentally and morally sustainable.

Most farming of animals is cruel to the animal, harmful to the environment, wasteful of resources and scandalously neglectful of the common gustatory decencies in the product it puts on your plate. Personally, I was always prepared to source properly farmed meat for my own table but eating away from home became embarrassing. I just wouldn't touch the dead things that friends and restaurants served up. So I did the politest thing, and turned veggie.

I love being part of the vegetarian community. We wink at each other in the vegetable aisle of organic supermarkets, have sexy fumbles under the bushes at pick-your-own plantations, and stick close to each other at dinner parties like Jews at a Chelsea match. We are close relatives of both the cycling and the dope-smoking communities, our sense of social responsibility having driven us paradoxically into the counter-culture; we cleave to ancient values while espousing futuristic ideals; we smell a bit funny and we're always knackered.

Though a committed vegetarian, I do lapse occasionally, like any abstemer.

I eat meat maybe four times a week. Obviously it's a bit more often than that in winter because of the weather. Say, six times. That's red meat, of course. A couple of times a week I also have a bit of chicken, as long as it's supplied by my local organic butcher in Kentish Town, which I think of not as a butcher but as a health-food store that is temporarily out of nuts.

That doesn't make me a carnivore, though. Any more than smoking the odd fag makes one a smoker. Personally, I don't smoke. Although I confess I'll snarf down maybe seven or eight of somebody else's fags when I'm pissed.

Which is rare, as I'm teetotal.

Thereafter, I'm 100 per cent meat-free. Unless you count bacon. And you can't. All veggies eat a bit of bacon. And, of course, fish. Otherwise it's tofu schnitzel and beancurd wieners all the way. And also 'Beanie Burger Insiders' with this great yicky fake cheese stuff inside, and all those fake sausages you find in Waitrose called 'Lincolnshire' and 'Cumberland', presumably in homage to the great beansprout breeds of the ancient North, such as the belted Hereford bean, and the fearsome longhorn sprout.

And as a vegetarian I think I am qualified to say that, as a rule, the best vegetarian food is cooked by meat-eating chefs with a grounding in essential culinary traditions, rather than beardy weeds who have been brought up on samphire and yams, who have removed all that is tasty and good and bred into our genes, and replaced it with, well, things that can fill you up well enough if you're not too fussed about pleasure.

And for this reason the best vegetarian food is usually to be found in omnivorous restaurants. Of course, there is seldom much choice in the way of veggie options – a state of affairs about which vegetarians will never let us hear the end – but in my opinion choice is an overrated thing and I would much rather restaurants focused on doing one or two dishes brilliantly than offered a whole load of stuff done only okay (to say nothing of the extent to which huge and varied menus depend on freezers and microwaves). Especially if I were vegetarian and all concerned with waste management and the future of the planet (like one assumes they all are because if they are not then, Christ, what on earth are they in it for?).

That said, I have had one or two decent evenings in vegetarian restaurants. No, wait, that isn't true. I have had one or two decent meals in vegetarian restaurants. Different thing.

One of these was a place that was not only vegetarian, but vegan. And not only vegan, but 'raw vegan'. Allowing almost no heat at all. (A sort of escalation of wrongs that reminds me of Nicholas Nickleby being told by the headmaster of Dotheboys Hall, 'Your mother is ill; in fact she is very ill; in fact, she is dead.')

I forget its name, but from the moment I saw its menu I was put in mind of a novel called *La Disparition* by Georges Perec, a book with a perfectly decent plot and a bubbly narrative character which ran to fully 300 pages without once employing the letter 'e', the commonest letter of all. It was damnedly, damnedly clever. But I couldn't finish it.

Nor could I finish the late Gilbert Adair's possibly even cleverer English translation of it, *A Void*.

I had a bash, later, at *Les Revenentes* (this was back in my early twenties, when I still thought literature mattered), in which Perec, in order, he said, to use up all the e's he had saved by not using any in *La Disparition*, allowed himself only that vowel, and no other.

And I tried Ian Monk's brave English translation (*The Exeter*

Text: Jewels, Secrets, Sex) too. And I finished neither. Indeed, I came out of them, as I had come out of the 'e'-less efforts, barely able to read at all.

That's the thing with lipogrammatic literature (in which the author imposes some sort of restraint or deprivation on himself, often to get the juices flowing when there is a creative blockage – a sort of creative sadomasochism): it can be incredibly impressive, but it can never have real soul. *La Disparition* was the best novel I have ever read which doesn't have any e's in it, but it isn't nearly as good as any of the novels I have read which do.

And just as Western literature is built on e's, so modern Western cooking is built on meat. You can take them away and try to do it without them. And it is sort of possible. And people will no doubt clap politely. But they will not drool. Their hearts will not race. They will not weep.

I am not in any way hostile to vegetarianism or veganism, as I've said. I am not one of those Shire Tory fatties who make jokes about 'people who knit their own yoghurt' and chortle till they choke on their pork chop. I accept (up to a point) the neo-Malthusian projection which says that past a certain population point only non-livestock farming can sustain life on earth, and I accept totally the health benefits of a (mostly, but not entirely) vegetable diet.

I even accept that vegetarians (and even vegans) can be (although usually are not) great lovers of food. But I reserve the right to observe that, with the exception of those religiously or medically constrained to the meat-free or meat-and-dairy-free diet, they usually do not love themselves very much.

Like any food fad, vegetarianism (and veganism especially) is so often a smoke screen adopted to disguise a body-dysmorphic eating disorder. It is simply an excuse not to eat. And, indeed, this raw vegan *haute cuisine* joint was positively rammed to the rafters, on a lazy Monday night in high summer, with very thin people, mostly women. (Don't get me wrong, it's not a complaint – better vegans than fat people.)

It was a funky, warehousey, Shoreditchy sort of place with clean lines, a long, sexy bar, hard-edged, boxy tables and stools, and a restrained, rather minimalist outside space, with white walls and stripling bamboo whistling in the breeze.

The staff were kind and solicitous, and were quick to say that we should notify them of any allergies. Although I could not see anything on the menu of twiddled-up crudités to which one could possibly be allergic. Nuts, I suppose (from which this place made its 'cheese'), and wheat, which it professed to use only sparingly.

There was apparently only one non-vegetarian waitress (by far the healthiest-looking staff member), who, while insisting that she loved the food, suggested that we ate four starters, two mains and a couple of sides if we wanted to be full. She also said that she relished the nightly staff meal but that (unlike her vegetarian colleagues) she was usually starving hungry by the second half of her shift.

Indeed, the staff here seemed an impossibly ascetic bunch – best exemplified by the wafer-thin, pale-faced young barman whom I spotted nipping outside at one point, for a crafty apple.

We had 'caviar' that was a sprinkle of chive pearls (made by a process borrowed from Ferran Adrià's molecular gastronomy) on little potato cakes with sour cream, in essence four minuscule canapés, then ravioli that was four more canapés made from folding raw slivers of beetroot around 'cashew herb ricotta', then four warmish dumplings of spinach and water chestnut and of shitake and tofu that were wholesome and crunchy but a long, long way from the life-affirming punch of common-or-garden dim sum served at full throttle.

'Farm salad' was a long row of small, boiled potato halves, with parallel rows of barely cooked tomatoes and double-shelled broad beans under a scatter of watercress. The 'linguine' in Linguine Alfredo were long shavings of raw courgette dressed with an ersatz pesto and truffle oil that was really hard to get down, with its cold, slimy texture and unpleasant faecal whiff (note to chefs: truffle oil does not work on cold green veg).

It is such a shame that the food most likely to help you live for ever manages simultaneously to deprive you of the will to live.

'Lasagne' was a tower of olives, mushrooms, courgettes and 'walnut bolognaise', which tasted only of familiar vegan horrors (as with so much vegan food, most of the dishes featured a clash of high, wheatgrassy chlorophyll notes with the rude, sweaty aggression of sesame oil).

The most complex flavour came from some smoked fresh tofu glazed with green tea in the 'Buddha bowl', which got closest to the taste of the meat-searing 'Maillard reaction' that stirs the atavistic yearnings, and gives actual pleasure.

Even as I (smugly) write 'atavistic', it occurs to me that defensive vegans (is there another kind?) will say that we humans were designed to eat like this. That we were originally foragers of berries and roots. But that was only when there was no fresh meat (or even carrion) available. And as I sat there with a feeling not of fullness exactly, but of having ploughed through a hundredweight of crudités, or of having drunk a gallon of tap water, it occurred to me that, yes, our ancestors must occasionally have felt like this after dinner a million years ago. But only on one of those rainy nights in the cave, when nobody had managed to bag a mammoth.

Indeed, scanning this super-trendy restaurant's pale denizens, it occurred to me what a vicious circle meatlessness can generate: for there was not a man among the weeds and waifs in there who looked physically up to the job of killing a mammoth. Or even a mouse.

* * *

One of the things I do envy vegetarians, however, is that they can never be fooled into eating raw donkey, which happened to me a couple of summers ago in a restaurant in Lombardy.

All I can say in Italian is 'Twenty Marlboro Lights, *s'il vous*, I mean, *per favore*', so when the menu said *Contrefileto di Asino con Salva e Peperoncini Lombardi*, I identified it as beef from 'Asino' and ordered it.

The rawness was a surprise, for a start. So was the greasiness, the graininess, the high metallic tang with notes of straw, musk and poo.

'*Esto es un vacho?*' I asked the waitress when the third mouthful just wouldn't go down. She didn't reply. '*C'est quoi? C'est du boeuf?*' I said. '*Che es? Es una mooooo, moooooo?*' She laughed and said, 'No, no, no', and put her hands above her head to form pointy ears.

Was I eating bat? Had I, perhaps, swallowed two thin strips of raw Leonard Nimoy?

And then she made a terrible noise, a noise that crosses linguistic boundaries like no other. She went, 'Hee-haw, hee-haw.'

Horse I'd eaten, and liked. But donkey? Donkeys were things I'd only seen in Spain, dead at the side of the road with their legs in the air, their gastric juices blowing them up into hilarious *It's a Knockout* obstacles until one morning you'd drive past and they'd have . . . well, anyway.

I chewed a bit more. It really wasn't nice. I like the bland full-bodied honesty of a horse steak, but this was just too potent – too rodenty, to be honest – and I wasn't sophisticated enough for it. I shouldn't have gone straight from horse to donkey. I should have got accustomed to a plate or two of mule and then worked my way up.

Cat I've done. Not a problem. They're not pets out there, they're farm animals (actually, I wouldn't call them 'farms', they're appalling places, similar to British hen batteries but not quite as smelly; well, differently smelly). People say cat tastes like very sweet, dark pork. Not true: pork tastes nice, cat does not. But it's hard to make comparisons when a flavour is so new to you. That is why people describe everything as tasting like chicken. Cat does not taste like chicken. More like rat, if anything.

A WEEKEND AWAY

L eaving London is confusing for me. It always makes me
feel very briefly excited – swinging out of town on a Friday
evening in summer, hitting the green belt, leaving the
neighbours to their weekend of dusty roof-terrace barbecues,
pub 'gardens' and dog-turdy parks, to plunge into the fresh
green avenues of this ancient land – but then very quickly I
become sad.

The countryside makes me sad, I think, because I am not entitled
to it. It is not part of me, nor I of it. I am not of the rural peasantry,
and never was, and I am not of the landed posh. Nor am I of
anything in-between. My people got off boats in London at various
different times over the course of the last century, and stayed in it.
They were not curious about what the countryside looked like, and
they did not go there. They would not have known what to do when
they arrived. And nor do I. Not in any truthful way.

Instinctively, I am of the party that says, 'The countryside
must not be treated as a playground for the urban middle
classes.' But that's a shame. Because I'd like to have a playground.

I suppose, in my heart, I think that the countryside ought to
be worked. That the people who live there have the right to
affordable housing. Certainly that they should be allowed to
hunt foxes, shoot whatever they like, course hares, fish for
otters, eat mink, go after sheep with beagles and set their ferrets
on the moles to stop badgers getting tuberculosis.

But I can't do any of those things myself, because I don't know how. And if I tried, I would embarrass myself horribly. I'd confuse everything. They'd shout, 'Pull', and I'd cast my line and take out the beagle's eye, then grab my rifle and shoot the horse, when everyone knows you're meant to use a shotgun.

So then it comes down to 'going for walks'. But that baffles me too. I go because I feel I should, not because I want to even slightly. I don't think I even have that part of the brain where Englishmen usually form the thought, 'I'd like to go for a walk.' The ancestral yearning isn't there. Corens go for a drink, they go for a bite to eat, they go for a wee. All these involve, to a greater or lesser degree, walking, but the walking is never advertised as the fun part.

All that said, I'd very much like one day to have a house there. In the country. Nowhere specific. It's all the same to me. But I don't want to upset anybody. I don't want to put up house prices for the locals (which I suppose means I will have to trick some old lady into selling me her home for practically nothing), or spread urbanisation with my sophisticated ways, or dilute great ancient languages like Cornish and Kentish and whatever it is they spoke in the Lake District before it went over to Japanese.

The problem is the getting there. Mostly, it's the thing where you down tools on a Friday afternoon and head off towards the M25, hoping, what with the traffic, to be on the motorway proper by 7 p.m. And then it's 73 miles to junction 19, turning off at about 8.30 on to the Awhatever, which briefly becomes the Asomethingelse (according to the map), before turning back into the Awhatever, which you rejoin in the wrong direction just after 9 (with the words 'kitchen closes at 9.30 sharp, chef is very strict about that' ringing in your ears), so that at 9.23 you are still racing away from your no-doubt grisly supper (and into the dark and the rain and the howling of wolves) in the hope of eventually coming upon a roundabout that will swing you back in the right direction and eventually off on to the B3000008 for 7 winding and badger-strewn miles and a just-before-midnight feast of 4 thin gingery biscuits (2 per cellophane packet) and a slurp each from the mini-carton of UHT milk on the tray next to the plastic kettle.

So the next time you head off on the Saturday morning instead, dreaming of fresh air, walks on the beach under salmon-skin skies, steaming fish and chips, frothing pints of Adnams and frantic sex in the four-minute window before *Match of the Day*.

Although, obviously, what always happens is that rain drives like all hell out of the salmon-skin sky and soaks your jeans so it's sore to walk, and the only beer is Foster's Ice, and the chips are frozen, and the fish stinks, and you get mugged by the spotty hoodlum who was jamming coppers in the chip shop fruitie and saw the glint of your shiny London coins, and then you get lost on the way home, and you huddle under a dolmen until the rescue helicopter comes, and then your bird goes home with the pilot, and the telly doesn't get BBC One, and you wonder why in the world you didn't stay home and roast a chicken and read a nice book.

And don't go saying that there is still always Sunday. Because when I check out of a hotel on a Sunday morning after a weekend in the country, I like to get on the road immediately. I hate all that palaver of leaving your bags at reception, then idling away the time till lunch stealing things from charity shops and throwing rocks at the old people coming out of church, eating and drinking too much, and then falling asleep at the wheel and killing nine people.

I like to set off straight after breakfast for a slow wibble home along the B-roads, which give you a much nicer sense of progress through the country and throw up far more diverse *objets de conversation* in the way of history, architecture and roadkill, stopping for lunch after a couple of hours as soon as I see a nice little pub at the right sort of time.

But a plan like that is fraught with problems. To begin with, what if you happen upon a perfect little thatched pub with a brief and enticing menu, using eggs from its own chickens and herbs from the garden, at quarter past eleven? You can't have lunch at quarter past eleven. You can have lunch from about 12.45. So you have to hope that until that time you do not see anywhere nice, for having passed it by you will then compare everywhere you come to later against it, and kill your Sunday with regret for the chance not taken. And then supposing you do happen upon a lovely little spot bang on lunch o'clock? How do you know there isn't an even lovelier place in the next village? I just can't enjoy a good local pie and a pint of Adnams if I'm worrying that two miles up the road there might be somewhere with a slightly better view. Or nicer plates.

And then you end up at the mercy of the 1.15 panic. Up until quarter past one, you can be reasonably fussy about where you stop. But as soon as you hit 1.16, every pub you pass could easily be the last one for 40 miles. And then it will be half past two and everything will be closed. At 1.12 p.m., you pass up a little place with a hog roast in the garden and beer from its own micro-brewery being poured at the table by resting Playboy models in Heidi outfits, just in case the next place has a duck pond; at 1.24, you're literally sprinting across the car park at Happy Eater, hoping they've still got a table.

And then there's the problem of the countryside running out, as can happen so quickly in the South: one minute it's all hedgerows, windmills and dormice in little hats punting along the Cam, next minute you're into the real England of endless mini-roundabouts and Morrisons car parks, and you might as well press on for a Big Mac at Shepherd's Bush.

It's a minefield, I tell you. A minefield.

And then, when you're really fretting, your wife says: 'Come on, we don't need anything flash. I'm happy with a ploughman's on a wooden picnic bench by a stream.'

Oh really? Just a ploughman's on a wooden picnic bench by a stream? You might as easily ask for a really good Chinese in Belfast with a fun wine list and views of Kilimanjaro.

So she points out of the window and says, 'That place looks nice!'

'Are you mad?' you cry. 'They've got a sign out offering Sunday lunch for six quid. It'll be Botulism Towers. And think of the sort of people who are attracted by a six quid Sunday lunch. Darts, football shirts, tattoos, lots of swearing and the smell of junk-food farts are all very well, but I prefer to eat among people whose hair is cut with scissors. Anyway, it's only 1.09. What's the panic? We've got six minutes yet before the world caves in.'

And so, gallantly, you pull over and take a look at the map, nosing around for a stream or a tumulus or a wood or any other cartographic code for 'nice spot' which you might get to by pulling off the main road and tootling along narrow tracks between hedgerows, and hope along the way to spy an inn or tavern of some sort, in the manner of travellers long ago . . .

Once, in just such a situation, I noticed on the map the village of Slad, childhood home of Laurie Lee.

I am a bit of a Laurie Lee nut. I am a huge sucker for that 'semi-peasant spirit of a thousand-years-old tradition' stuff. I know that *Cider with Rosie* is an overblown and purple depiction of a world that never was, but I just lap it up. At times I truly yearn, with a physical pain, for 'the England that was traded for the petrol engine'.

And so I considered for a moment pointing my own petrol engine in the direction of Slad. There's a pub there called the Woolpack, which is folkloric among us Lee-heads as the pub in

Cider with Rosie where a traveller told one too many tall tales, and was beaten to death for it (as any travel bore should be), and as Laurie's local when he returned to Slad in the Sixties, to live out his days there.

'Let's go there, then,' said Esther.

'Except it might be awful,' I said.

'We only want a bit of bread and cheese,' she said, with all the breathless, rustic innocence of Rosie herself.

'We might be too late,' I said. 'We don't know how long it will take to get there along these lanes. And you know country pubs: one minute past two and it's all over.'

'You're such a pessimist,' said Esther. 'These days it's probably open all day.'

'Maybe,' I said. 'But they'll probably be horrid to us because we're from London. They'll think we're tourists or Laurie Lee pilgrims or, worse still, rich folk who are going to buy a country cottage, drive up house prices and destroy the fabric of the community. They'll laugh at our accents and roll their eyes, and then they'll cut our throats and feed us to the pigs.'

But we pulled off the A419 Stroud to Cirencester road just the same, and headed out that way down leafy lanes, and almost immediately, at a small village called Sapperton, saw a little stone pub, perched on a grassy hillock above the level of the road, with a lawn in front of it, and herbaceous borders fat with colour in the June sunshine, and one or two trees, under which people were sitting with pints and plates of food.

'Wow,' I said.

'Gosh,' said Esther. 'I suppose this must be the place.'

'What place?'

'The place with the tree, and grass, and a ploughman's.'

'You don't think we should push on to Slad?'

'No,' said Esther. 'Definitely not.'

And so we parked on the lane, tucking in tight to the hedge, and got out. And, in my London way, I hurried up the road to the pub in case two dozen people suddenly appeared out of nowhere and ate all the food. And, even as I hurried, I worried that maybe a mile or two further on there might be another, better pub.

'Darling,' I said as we walked into the cool interior, 'do you think that maybe, a mile or two down the road, there might be?'

'No,' she said. 'I don't.'

I told her to go and 'bag a space' on the lawn, in case there was a sudden rush of customers, leaving us with two plates of food and nowhere to sit, and ordered a pint for me, water for her, a ploughman's (woohoo!) and the home-made corned beef, served with chips.

Choosing my beer, I told the landlord I had better have the lightest ale, as I was driving, and asked if it was okay to sit on the lawn (I worry that in the country they'll have special rules). Not only was it okay, he said, but there was a blanket out there we might like to sit on.

I took out the drinks and Esther spread the pretty blanket, lined on the underside for extra dryness. We sat, Esther all picturesque and Rosie-like in a summer dress with a straw sunhat. I nestled my pint in the soft folds of the blanket and leaned back on my elbows and was about to say that things could not be more perfect, when my pint, which was not quite as well nestled as I might have desired, teetered (oh, why do I never learn?) and fell.

'Move! Move!' I yelled as the stream of beer gushed towards my girlfriend, who rolled away from the flood and leapt to her feet. I leapt up too, grabbed up the blanket and, reckoning that wool is pretty resistant to water and, if shaken off in time, can dry out fairly well, flipped it hard, like a maid spreading sheets on a bed, and sprayed up a fine mist of beer which drenched Esther, and then blew back all over me.

Esther looked briefly downcast and said, mildly, 'Thanks for that.' And we went to the loos to wash.

My main worry now was that they'd find out what a klutz I was (do they have klutzes in Gloucestershire?) and discover that I'd laughed in the face of their hospitality and ruined their blanket to boot. Regret, which stalks me like a hungry dog at the best of times, now encircled me like a fog.

I wanted another delicious pint. But, oh no: the guy knows I'm driving. He'll think I've raced the first pint and am having a second. I could pretend that Esther's going to drive, but she hasn't got a licence. And if I do get stopped by the police, even though I'm well under the limit, I'll be arrested for sure as I stink of beer now from head to toe.

I went in and explained, and the man gave me another pint. Gave, do you hear me? For he refused payment. Esther was sitting on a bench when I came out and I stared mournfully at our blanket, inconsolable with having spoilt everything.

'Look,' I said, pointing at the blanket now steaming in the sun. 'It's nearly dry.' But just then, before the blanket had had time to become truly habitable, our food came. And it was delicious: the corned beef was served in two big triangles on a wooden board, and the ploughman's was a lovely big slab of mild single Gloucester, warm bread, and a little Kilner jar of home-made piccalilli. We ate on our laps, looking at the blanket.

'Sorry,' I said. Meaning for ruining lunch, but also for the semi-peasant spirit of a thousand-year-old tradition having been traded for the petrol engine.

'It doesn't matter,' said Esther. 'We can go to Slad now without having to worry about the food, and just put our heads round the door of the Woolpack and see what it's like inside. As long as you don't get beaten to death for telling traveller's tales.'

'Traveller's tales?' I said. 'I've never told one in my life.'

Tip!

YES,
YOU. YOU MEAN
BASTARD. Things have changed a bit
since including service on the bill became
common practice here. In theory, if you really, really,
give a damn, you should enquire whether the included
service charges are pulled into what is called a 'tronc' and then
divided between waiting (and kitchen) staff to be paid on top of a
salary, or if they are merely used to pay the salary. The latter is really not
on. And you are then perfectly entitled to refuse to pay it and then tip the
waiter cash. But in my experience you are only making trouble for the staff.
They accepted the conditions and salary of the job when they started working
here, like anyone else, and if you want to make a personal gesture then you're
going to have to make it out of your own pocket.
I think a tenner is fine as a tip on top of an included service charge. I make no
distinction between establishments. Indeed, even back in the days when service was
largely left to one's discretion, I never really understood the percentage system
whereby a young Polish kid in a local trattoria who runs her tits off all afternoon
serving pizzas to squealing kids and grumpy mums should get so much less than
some snooty, overbearing Frenchman in epaulettes at the Hotel de Posh. Appreciation is appreciation and a flat fee seems altogether more human: you go out for
a meal, you pay, they take 12.5% service, and if they were good, and kind,
and nice, you flip them a tenner. Maybe a twenty if you've dressed up. I
find it hard to hand over a measly browner when I'm wearing a tie.
Obviously if you were in a group and all got drunk and
stuck around and made life hell for the staff then you need
to drop a LOT of money on the table – much in the
way that vile tycoons make huge public
donations to charity.

EASYJET'S PORCINE
PLASMA 'SPECIAL'

I dined once upon a time on porcine plasma. Not wittingly, mind. I wasn't stunt dining for some terrible television show (although I'm sure I would if they asked), nor was I the intrepid guest of some lost Amazonian tribe, taking part in a holy pig-blood gargling ritual which to refuse would have grievously offended my hosts (would that my life had gone that way).

No, my ingestion of porcine plasma was unwitting until after the event and came in the form of a . . . wait, hang on, here's fun: I won't tell you what I was eating. I will merely transcribe the list of ingredients that I subsequently read on the side of the container in which it had been served, and I'll see if you can guess what it was that I ate.

Those ingredients were as follows: wheatflour, water, malted wheat flakes, muscovado sugar, wheat gluten, barley malt flour, wheat bran, yeast, salt, spirit vinegar, emulsifiers: E472(e), E481, E471, vegetable oil, flour treatment agent: E300, chicken breast, water, glucose syrup, thickener: E1422 (from maize), free-range pasteurised egg yolk, maltodextrin, acidity regulator: E260, stabiliser: E415, preservative: E202, black pepper, pork belly, porcine plasma, sugar, thickener: potato starch, natural smoke flavour, stabilisers: E451, E450, antioxidant: E316, preservative: E250, lettuce, inulin, whey powder (from milk), milk protein, stabilisers: E415, E407, flavouring, colour: E160(e).

Have you guessed what it is yet? Come on. It's easy. Glucose syrup, bran, porcine plasma and inulin? It can only be a chicken and bacon sandwich, can't it? More specifically, a 'Caf Culture' chicken and bacon sandwich served on an easyJet flight from Gibraltar to London Gatwick. It came in one of those triangular boxes with a tab on it that read: 'Pull here and enjoy!' An injunction more suited, frankly, to being written above the bar on a Club 18–30 holiday. I should have known better, really.

If I was going to be pulling any tabs, they should have been attached to the ripcord of the parachute I was wearing when I jumped at 35,000 feet and left the sandwiches to my fellow passengers.

How can you need 15 different E numbers in a sandwich? How the hell long does it have to keep? Was this food created with a crash in mind which would leave the surviving passengers having to live on the plane's store of chicken and bacon sandwiches for 30 YEARS?

And don't you love 'Caf Culture'? It is a name no doubt intended to conjure up images of Ernest Hemingway, Proust and Gertrude Stein at a pavement table outside Les Deux Magots, languorously puffing at cigarette holders between mouthfuls of maltodextrin and flour treatment agent: E300.

And what about '*natural* smoke flavour'? Is that the craziest, wrongest, dunderheadedest misappropriation of the word 'natural' you ever heard, or what?

And why 'free-range egg yolk' in the crappy mayonnaise but not free-range chicken or pork? Is this because they care a little bit about chickens and want some birds to have an okay time but aren't such crazy animal lovers that they want to extend this munificence to the entire animal kingdom? Or is it that 'free-range egg yolk' mayonnaise was the only kind they could find, and they're sort of apologising for it?

Which brings us to the porcine plasma, which features in the ingredients list as one of the constituents of their 'smoke flavour sweetcure bacon'. Just what in the world is it for? Porcine plasma? I mean, let's leave aside the current world squeamishness about pigs in the wake of a feared swine-flu epidemic and ask simply: what is it about the yellow liquid component of blood in which the blood cells are suspended that makes it so much more excellent for the creation of bacon than the blood itself?

You know how you make plasma? Course you do. You remember school biology lessons. You simply place a test tube of pig's blood in a centrifuge and spin it until the dark cells separate and collect at the bottom, then you pour off the translucent yellow liquid and MAKE IT INTO BACON!!!! And then MAKE SANDWICHES OUT OF IT!!!

It's the most bastard awful thing I ever heard. I looked up porcine plasma on the Internet to see if its use in food for humans is normal, and could find nothing.

On Madeinchina.com, for example, I found that, 'Porcine plasma powder is high quality protein feed, which is made of quarantined fresh blood of healthy animal and produced by special technology (patent application number: 0011539. 9). It retains the functional immunoglobulins which can defend piglet from intestinal infection, reduce immune irritation. It is the best protein source that prevent piglet from the growth stagnancy after weaning.'

And on the website of the *Journal of Nutrition* I found that, 'Spray-Dried Porcine Plasma Reduces the Effects of Staphylococcal Enterotoxin B on Glucose Transport in Rat Intestine.' Which is apparently terrific news because 'in rats challenged with SEB, SDAP supplementation can increase glucose absorption by 8–9% during the interdigestive periods'.

But it still doesn't explain what it was doing in my sandwich. Bacon, just normal bacon, is the most delicious thing in the world. The smell of it frying is famously the thing most likely to turn a wavering Jew or Muslim away from the kosher/halal path. But they sure as hell don't mean this stuff. Indeed, it had quite the opposite effect on me, and very nearly turned this life-long bacon scoffer to religion.

JAPAN

There is nothing worse than a fresh convert to a country, a cuisine or a religion suddenly telling you that everything you have ever done is laughable, clumsy and blasphemous. But that is exactly what I plan to do now.

If I had spent any longer than 59 hours in Japan, I think it might have blown my mind so irreparably that I would have been unable to talk about it at all. But my trip having been so short, I think I can probably just about convey the enormity of it. Although I cannot hope to weave a narrative whole. Not in such a way that your Western, your *geijin* ear could grasp it. Japan isn't like that. All is simplicity, all is brevity. The painting, the poetry, the music, the food.

So I will give it to you in little pieces. Like sushi.

A grey mountain
The whisper of cool fish
On your hot tongue

Only kidding. I haven't got it so bad that I think I can do haiku.

My hotel room has a smart loo. Seriously. It is more intelligent than at least half the people currently working in London as waiters. The seat is warm when you sit down. It oscillates after a period of inactivity. When you have finished, a control panel

203

offers 'front cleaning' and two different levels of 'rear cleaning'. After the probing jets of just-right water (Heston Blumenthal has not a finer feel for the perfection of temperature), warm air blows you dry. When you stand up, it flushes.

My bum has never been so clean. I have not yet eaten a morsel in Japan, but if they take this much care of your food on its way out, imagine what care they must take on its way in.

Tsukiji fish market is the biggest in the world and easily the size of a small town, like Rome. Just before five on the first morning I meet Mr Yamamoto, executive chef of the Mandarin Oriental, who has secured me a pass for the tuna auction.

He tells me to walk straight and never change direction unexpectedly because of the electric trolleys. They come from behind, rapid and silent, a driver standing upright at the wheel, and they do not stop. Once, once, I step sideways to avoid a puddle. There is a screeching behind me, and screaming, and boxes going over and loud cursing, and Yamamoto yanking me away from the aftermath.

The tuna auction hall is as big as a football stadium. On huge pallets, hundreds of tuna, big and smooth and shiny as blue-black motorcycle sidecars fresh off the line, heads removed, exposing the cavernous space of the collar (a ten-year-old could climb inside), tail chunk squatting by each body to provide indications of colour and fat content. A gash in the side for similar. Men in blue overalls and rubber boots (I am in Converse, and my feet are frozen), with a torch in one boot and a metal hook in the other. They roam among the fish, probing with their hook at the gashes, peering in to the fish's dark interior with their torches.

Then the clatter of a bell. A man standing on a box starts shouting. A cacophony of other men replying. The bell rings again. Two men spring into the picture with a cart, six men hoist the fish aboard and off the two men run. Thirty thousand pounds, maybe £40,000, has changed hands for this fish. By lunchtime it will be sashimi. Sooner, maybe.

Still at the fish market. Beyond the tuna stadium, acres of 'living' fish in blue plastic boxes full of water, pipes lead in and out of boxes, aerating: halibut stacked like pancakes, gently rippling; eels of all sizes writhing; the odd shark, tail-flicking in its tub; dog and catfish, cod, bass, bream, plaice, yellow tail, red snapper, scorpion fish, red and spiked and furious, ranks of them, gasping for oxygen, flipping and popping in boxes; and fish a metre long and spike-nosed that are gold and petrol-blue like a mackerel crossed with a javelin; and also fugu, the big-deal blowfish which is said to kill you if the sushi is not cut right (*geijin* journalists make a big deal of it), swimming sadly, big as cats, costing 60 quid a kilo.

The market is full of sushi bars, serving the freshest sushi in the world.

Mr Yamamoto likes Daiwa. I have never eaten better food anywhere. Wooden like the inside of a sauna but cool with the dawn air, it has two sushi masters and stools for ten people at the bar. The staff shout their greeting as we walk in. Green tea and a tall bottle of Asahi. Two small, frosted glasses. Pouring for each other, Mr Y and I, never for ourselves. The other eaters are fish-truck drivers in blue overalls, a couple of salary men, a lone student.

The fish pieces are giant, completely covering the rice, which is visible as a bump under the flesh blanket. The older of the two chefs (his son has a restaurant next door but Mr Y visits only the father) keeps it coming, one piece at a time, lifted over the counter and pressed on to the wood before me with a muffled '*hai!*'

A piece of pale, buttery *toro*, cold and firm on warm rice, the crucial juxtaposition, barely findable in London, where it is often reversed: room-warmed flesh on fridge-cold, gritty rice.

A pile of golden urchin piled on rice with a seaweed perimeter. The same treatment for cod sperm, thick and white and creamy, piled high. The truckers stare.

'They haven't seen a *geijin* eat this before,' says Yamamoto.

I'd have feared it was a dawn joke played on the white boy and they've never seen a Jap eat it either, if it hadn't tasted so fine.

Raw squid bound with seaweed; the same topped with urchin; raw prawn, barely dead, the head whipped off, pressed with the flat of a blade and tossed on a grill; the shell peeled off, I chew the translucent silver body and then the head, pink from the heat, is served, which I crunch down; mackerel; warm, yellow eel dressed with a dark slick of something humming with '*umi*'; octopus slivers with salmon eggs on top; squid, melting and slippery with a mild smoky body of flavour; scallop . . .

The raw fish is tongue-like, fleshly, so alive. Having it in your mouth is like kissing, not eating. It becomes part of me so effortlessly. It's like we're eating each other. And I just keep thinking, I could come and live here, give up everything just to eat this breakfast once in a while.

Later, looking for tempura at three in the afternoon, I spot a place called Ten-Ichi in the guidebook. An hour later I have not found it. Tokyo has no street signs. And what's more they're in Japanese. A neat Japanese woman in jeans and a jacket, about my age, carrying a portfolio asks, 'Can I help you?'

I tell her about the restaurant. She says she does not know it but will walk me to the right street. She says that even for the Japanese navigation is difficult, let alone for *geijin*. Then she puts her hand over her mouth and laughs.

When we fail to find the correct street, Setsuyo goes into a tailor's shop to ask the way. For five minutes I watch them discuss it, turning the map round and round. And then the guy comes out, puts a sign on the door which, I guess, says, 'Back in five minutes', and walks us there himself.

Ten-Ichi, original, 70-year-old restaurant of a small chain. Setsuyo won't eat, but sits with me to help me communicate with the chef. The place is a stone-floored, bamboo maze of paper-walled rooms. Waitresses are in traditional kimonos of the hardcore variety, with the big boxy things on the back, standing on the other side of the room's threshold, unstirring until beckoned.

It is just Setsuyo and I sitting opposite a chef with a huge sunken basin of boiling oil. A tiny, spidery shrimp with long feelers is dipped in batter then dropped into the oil with two-foot steel chopsticks; seconds later it is out, and I'm eating it. Then conger eel, spread little fillets given the same treatment and served with a dipping sauce and a sprinkling of curry powder; two asparagus spears; sliced lotus root; two small green peppers.

Eventually comes *kaki-agi*, the symbolic final dish, Setsuyo explains. It means something like 'last bits fried', and is a single beignet, a sort of tangly bubble and squeak of prawn and scallop. But then, meaning something else, a bowl of the darkest miso soup containing beautiful tiny clams, no bigger than the rivet on your jeans.

The chef approved of my eating habits (as the drivers did at Daiwa they like a glutton here, I guess) and said I was no '*neko-chita*', which is 'a person with a cat's tongue' and has to do with being finicky, I think.

In Asakusa, in the shadow of a major temple, I saw a restaurant that served only 'tonkatsu': I have no idea how to write it. Setsuyo (who, having little to do, has offered to guide me round town) pumped it into her translator calculator and got '*wiener schnitzel*'. But it is made from pork, not veal. It was all they served. Just a little place. Wood and paper walls, a man frying, his wife serving, one old man reading a paper and smoking while he drinks a beer, another reading pornographic manga while he eats.

In Tokyo, any restaurant that is any good serves only one thing.

Nearby, there is a tofu restaurant. Only tofu. We nip in for a taste. Suddenly, I get tofu. 'Must be eaten same day is made,' says Setsuyo. 'Like bread in UK.' And I should weep again, this time for the tragic gap between Setsuyo's imaginings of British eating traditions and the long-life, pre-sliced, refrigerated modern reality back home.

And yet, still, I don't think you're getting quite how seriously the Japanese take their cooking. So I'm going to have to tell you about the knife I bought when Setsuyo took me to the food utensil district. Yes, district. It's a wide main street with half a dozen tributaries on the edge of Asakusa, close to Tokyo's oldest temple, near to a damn good schnitzel shop with no name.

She wanted to show me the shops that make fake sushi for window displays. Yes, shops. Plural. Quite a lot of places exist in Tokyo by selling only those little plastic maki rolls, and bits of mackerel and prawns. There are also some that sell silk sushi. The Gucci outlets of the fake sushi world.

But my interest lay with knives. So she took me to the main knife street. I chose the knife shop that I liked the look of most. It had probably a million knives racked up on the walls. Maybe more. From tiny little knives for filleting winkles to giant blades so light and sharp a 90-year-old woman could use them for taking the legs off a hippo. And beneath the wall racks, drawers. Drawers containing things so dangerous Hans Blix would have a heart attack.

An old guy comes over. I won't bother to describe him. He's basically Mr Miyagi out of *The Karate Kid*. He bows. Setsuyo introduces herself as my translator.

I say I want a knife.

He asks what for.

I say just a general chef's knife. That's what they call them in England.

He looks puzzled.

He asks if it will be for vegetables or flesh.

I say flesh.

Meat or fish?

I say fish, just to say something.

Raw or cooked?

Raw.

For filleting?

As opposed to?

Scaling, gutting, chining . . .

Okay, filleting.

Not head or tail removal?

Um, why?

Need weight for bone cracking.

Okay, bone cracking.

Carbon or stainless?

Difference?

He tells me. For, like, twenty minutes.

He wants to know how I'll clean it, where I'll store it, how often I'll use it . . .

He lays out seven or eight suitables on the counter in front of me. The scene seems a cross between Q getting Bond tooled up for a big adventure, and the scene in *Kill Bill* when Uma goes to get her Samurai Sword (a scene which was filmed, interestingly, just around the corner from here, in a famous teahouse).

Eventually, we choose a knife. It has no brand name on it, just a

Japanese character from the old alphabet (I have been in this shop long enough now to grasp the three different kinds of Japanese character). It is a foot long, two inches deep, very thin, gently tapered to a heavy heel. The flat of the blade, when turned to catch the light, has a wavy look as a result of the tempering process.

He says it is a 68. This means that when brought down hard on a stack of newspapers it will cut to the 68th page. The best European knife, he says, a Henckel, will cut to 54.

He brings out the Tokyo equivalent of the *Sunday Times* (containing only slightly fewer articles by A.A. Gill) and, without screaming '*hai!*', disappointingly, brings the knife down hard. We count the cut pages: . . . 63, 64, 65, 66 . . . 66! He looks crestfallen. He throws the knife in the bin. It is a dud.

He pulls out another. He tries again: . . . 63, 64, 65, 66, 67, 68!

With the knife chosen, he disappears out back to get six or seven identical knives so that I can select the one that feels best in my hand. The one which, he says, I feel I can work with for the next 50 years.

While he does so, I think of the last time I bought a knife, in the Selfridges kitchen department, where the entire selection offered by that vast department store did not contain as many knives as Mr Miyagi had for filleting eel, and how, when I asked which was the best, the sales guy said, 'These are the most popular, but these are more expensive', and turned back to his conversation with a colleague about who was taking the first lunch break.

Mr Miyagi returns with the half-dozen identical knives and invites me to try each one.

I pick one up in my left hand, the hand with which I do almost everything, to feel its weight and heft, and I make a couple of swooshes at the air at I don't know what, flying tomatoes. As I do so, My Miyagi clutches his hands to his face and screeches.

Panicked, I look at Setsuyo. Have I breeched some ancient safety rule?

'He is devastated,' she says. 'You didn't tell him you are reft-handed!'

'It makes a difference?'

'Right-handed knife utterly useless for reft-handed man,' she translates. 'He is very, very sorry, for wasting your time.'

And truly, he looks on the verge of tears. (I have been cooking for 25 years, and have bought a lot of knives, and nobody has ever, ever mentioned the existence of left-handed knives. Gordon Ramsay is left-handed, and I have never seen him, on any of those shows, ever mention his using special knives.)

We go through it all again with his left-handed knives – the shadow of the Sensoji Temple lengthens across the street outside – until we arrive back at square one.

He asks how I will sharpen the knife. I tell him on a steel, like Gordon Ramsay showed us in *The F-Word*.

Hands to face again. Little screech.

'Mr Miyagi says might as well throw knife in river now!'

And so he brings out his whetstones. Various grades. The best is a white one, which, he says, must be soaked in water until seven minutes after the last bubble has risen. It weighs about six kilos. I shake my head and say I don't want to lug it to the airport and then bust my baggage allowance.

Misunderstanding, he offers it as a gift.

I refuse politely. He says he cannot bear to think of such a knife as I have bought being sharpened on a steel or knife-sharpener (as he has heard *geijin* infidel sometimes use), and says he will not let me take the knife unless I take the whet-stone.

And then he shows me how to sharpen it. Beginning with the point, then doing the bevel, then the heel of the blade. The effort and love he puts into the stroking and rubbing, you've got to assume he gives Mrs Miyagi a hell of a time in bed.

So I accepted his gift of the stone. And in return I gave him a small, porcelain 'good luck' cat that I had just bought for my girlfriend (our luck ran out soon after).

That evening, more sushi, somewhere else, no name I could read. A moody-looking Russian hooker sitting with a pasty-faced local takes a mouthful from a plate of plaice sushi featuring cuts from three different parts of the fish and suddenly cheers up immensely.

Still at the evening sushi, ten 'salary men' emerge from a room and put on their shoes. Leaving, each one bows to the sushi master behind the counter.

The last one hands him a huge present and says something long and formulaic-sounding. I ask Setsuyo what he said.

'He said, "I'm sorry this is such a humble present, it is all I could find." It is what we always say when giving a present.'

Pause for a minute. And try to imagine Alan Sugar, after a routine business dinner, giving a present to the chef. And apologising for it.

A random pub – or Izakaya – this one is a Yakitori pub. All the pubs specialise in a certain kind of food. A guy brings two of those dinky glasses for our crisp Asahi beer. I say how good it is to drink beer like this from such small glasses, so that it stays cool and lively. The guy asks Setsuyo what I said, and she tells him, and a couple of minutes later he comes back with two glasses, wrapped in tissue paper and hands them to me, and bows. The present is comfortably more expensive than the price of the beer I drink and the two skewers of duck's gizzard I eat.

*   *   *

On my third, and final, morning, eating breakfast in my hotel kimono in my room on the 38th floor of the Mandarin Oriental, I glanced out over the nightmarish twist and strain of traffic that tangled from horizon to horizon, and noticed that there was blue sky for the first time, instead of the grey veil that had hung over the city since my arrival.

And then I noticed the violet humps of hills in the distance, beneath white clouds. And then the clouds moved a little and I saw a higher mountain. The top of it flat and covered with snow. My jaw fell, literally, open. Food fell out. I could not have been more awestruck if I had been looking on the face of God.

Suddenly I was in Japan. Suddenly I was painted blue on a plate, by a stream, under a cherry tree in blossom. I glanced away to pick up a napkin, and when I looked back, Mount Fuji was gone, swallowed up again by the cloud.

Nobody else I spoke to had seen it for weeks. Some didn't believe me. One told me it was good luck.

Japan was once so exotic that Gulliver came here (Part III, 'A voyage to Laputa, Balnibarbi, Glubbdubdrib, Luggnagg, and Japan'). He stayed in Edo, which became Tokyo, and was gone several years. I got here in 12 hours, stayed for 59, and left. But by the time I got back to Heathrow, and was immersed again among the fat, track-suited, burger-eating, foul-mouthed, cultureless beasts that are my compatriots, I felt very much as Gulliver did, returning from the land of the Houyhnhnms – disinclined to retake my place among the Yahoos, or to admit that I was one of them.

In the long delay before the luggage arrived at the carousel I went to the loo and was appalled, when I'd finished, to note that it had neither the wit, nor the decency, to flush itself.

*   *   *

As soon as I got home, I unpacked my knife and ran for the kitchen. I rested its edge on an onion – I applied no pressure, none – and the onion parted for it. I threw an apple in the air and held the knife out, still. The apple split cleanly, simply falling through the knife. It is a very good knife.

But it is a knife of which I am not worthy. A reminder of a food culture so far in advance of our own, understanding and feeling so much that we will never know, that it makes me feel sad and small. Our lives are too fast, our attitudes too cheap, our relationship with our food too distant and sullied and dimly grasped, to get anywhere close to a Japanese way of eating. There is no point in trying.

So it sits in my kitchen in its long, black box, lined with red velvet, propped between the cookbooks, and occasionally, while tearing open a Thai takeaway bag to fill two plates and rush back to the telly, I look up at it.

And I bow, silently.

How to Get the Most from a Sushi Bar in Britain

OKAY, SO THIS isn't Japan. What we have here is 'Japanese restaurants', a thing that exists in Japan only for tourists. Essentially restaurants that serve a little bit of everything to people who don't really understand the eating culture, instead of concentrating on just one thing. And you're just not going to find the quality of fish that the Japanese demand, because the Japanese are prepared to pay more than we for fish, so, like, duh. But I still think you can replicate the Tokyo experience if you try.

Most Japanese restaurants will have a sushi bar. Sit there, not at a table. I'm going to assume the staff are Japanese. If they are not, all bets are off. This is a 'fun' place for a 'night out' and has nothing to do with Japanese food. You might as well just get pissed and order the fried stuff. I'm sure you'll have a very nice time.

The guy or guys at the counter will probably greet you in Japanese. If you're hardcore, you'll learn a couple of Japanese greetings and say them back, but there's no need, as long as you give a beaming smile and bow a little bit – you can pretend to yourself that it's a nod – and say 'hi'. 'Hi' is a very useful word in this context because as well as meaning 'Hello' to you, and making it possible for you to say without feeling a dick, it is also a Japanese homonym. So it sounds not entirely un-Japanese. And what it means in Japanese is 'yes' or 'okay', so it's not like you're saying 'pomegranate' or 'butt plug' or something.

What you can do at the counter, you see, is talk to them about the food, even though you have no language in common. Because you can point, and so can they, and even mime. At the table you're all at sea. If you say to a Japanese waitress, 'We'd like a seaweed salad to share, and do you have any scallops?' she will only stare at you in silence, and then possibly cry. She can do nothing but write down barked dishes. She can't answer questions and it is unfair to expect her to.

But the guys at the counter will be used to Japanese people asking, as soon as they come in, 'What's the best fish to have today?' So when you ask that in English, they'll know what it means. Context is everything. And it is a crucial question. It shows you understand about fish. It shows you care about the thing that is their job. It shows you have eaten sushi before. If you just say 'ten salmon sushis and some of them avocado rolls', it's fine, but it just means you're a big-nosed milk-smelling lard-arse who should have gone to Pret.

When the guy points out a fish in response to your question. You can reiterate, 'That's good, TODAY?' and as long as you're happy he's au fait with the time element in your question, order some of it, and nothing else, even if it is something you think you 'don't like'. You are not here to 'not like' things. If there is all sorts of food you 'don't like' then you should have gone to Pret.

When he puts it in front of you (possibly with a 'hi!'), eat it and tell him what you think of it. Honestly. He'll love a 'wow! That's fantastic' and if you make a slightly uncertain, 'meh' sort of

gesture, he will
try and give you something
better for the next thing.

The deal here is that he is your guy.
He's doing it for you. He'll be making sushi for
platters for waitresses to take to people who have
ordered from tables, but you're getting a relationship,
and an experience, and the best fish.

Use some Japanese fish names, you don't need that many,
learn the ones you like, ask for them by name. Always, though,
ask, 'Have you got any hamachi (yellowtail)?' – don't assume
they have it. It's not a supermarket. Give the chap the opportunity
to nod and affirm that he has it.

I think, and so do the Japanese, that it's best to eat some sashimi,
and then some sushi. But it's up to you. Sashimi is so pure and cool, it
seems like it ought to be the first thing.

Get some miso soup with it, for something warm. Unless you have
tea. If you're drinking sake then pour for each other, not for yourselves.
It's not the biggest deal in the world, but it's what the Japs do, and I
think it's fabulous. Quite sexy. Very sexy. I mean, frankly, wouldn't
you sleep with someone with whom you'd been exchanging
dribbles of warm spicy liquid all night?

Use chopsticks for sashimi but your fingers for sushi. Nobody
eats sushi with chopsticks. You need to be able to hold it
firmly enough to wipe it (fish side down and very briefly)
into the very small puddle of soy sauce you have
made by pouring it from the ceramic jug into the
little saucer and either seasoned or not
seasoned by mixing a nubbin of wasabi
into it.

Generally, English people
pick up a bit of

sushi with
their chopsticks, wobble
it over like someone carrying a
tray of snakes to the lake of soy sauce
they have poured for themselves, drop it in
rice-side down, so that it soaks it all up like a
Vileda floor sponge, then attempt to lift it up again
but pinch the fish too hard so that it comes off the rice,
which disintegrates into the bowl, and then hurriedly flip
the dripping flesh into their gobs so that brown sauce
dribbles down their chin onto the special 'pulling shirt' they've
worn for the occasion.

And even if they get the food intact to their mouths, they then
have to chuck it in whole which it is not designed for. So there is a
frantic, mouth-open, cement-mixer initial chewdown to make the
mouthful manageable (especially with women and their generally
slightly smaller mouths), which your Japanese guys will think is either
revolting or absolutely fucking hilarious, depending on their mood.
They won't show it though. Too sophisticated for that.

When you've had enough, pay and leave. Don't start eating fried
and steamed and boiled stuff off the menu at the counter. That's
monstrously uncool. You're playing sushi here.

As with when I was talking about developing a local
European restaurant, the thing to do is to go frequently until
they know you. It will take longer here because we do all
look the same to them. So find out their names, buy
them the odd beer, say things like, 'Do you have any
of that terrific unagi (eel) you gave us last time?'
And you're in downtown Tokyo before you
know it.

Or don't. I don't care.
Go to Pret.

SALT

Posh salt came under fire recently from a bunch of meddle-some scientists in a report published under the auspices of *Which?* I do not know which *Which?* it was which came up with the idea – *Which Cruet Set?*, perhaps, or *What Salt Pig?* ('incorporating *Whose Pepperpot?*'); indeed I was baffled to learn that *Which?* was still around. I thought it had faded away in the 1970s along with the Egg Marketing Board and *Listen With Mother*. But, ding dong, the *Which?* isn't dead after all, and its chief policy advisor, Sue Davis, took it upon herself on Thursday to declare that, 'Many of us are trying to reduce the amount of salt in our diet but our research shows people are needlessly spending more money on premium salt because they often believe it is healthier than traditional table salt.'

'Rubbish!' I cried at my newspaper, half choking on an unusually large but extremely tasty crystal of Halen Mon, the flavour-enhancer with which I generally season my morning egg, unless we have a spot of Pink Murray River about the place (we have an actual salt shelf in the larder at home, always with five or six varieties of salt on it in assorted delightful tins and boxes and dinky hessian sacklets). 'We don't spend more money on premium salt because we think it is healthy, we spend more money on it because it is PREMIUM!'

We spend money on it because it is pretty and fun and has slightly different flavours in it – especially the smoked Maldon

I sprinkle on my buttered baked potato of a winter's teatime. We spend money on it because life is short and you have to die of something and that vile powdery stuff full of 'anti-caking agents' you get in a drum from the supermarket throws up a choking dust that always makes me think of Wilfred Owen and 'beggars under sacks', and is barely fit for gritting roads.

'It is disgraceful that chefs still encourage people to use so much sea and rock salt,' chimed in Professor Graham MacGregor, chairman of Consensus Action on Salt and Health, or CASH, which is a hilariously clunky attempt to mimic the Action on Smoking and Health organisation's fantastically serendipitous 'ASH' acronym, without quite managing the same synchronicity ('Hi, I'm Professor MacGregor and I work for CASH!').

And it's not just the organisation's name that's off on a wonk, it's the whole campaign.

Firstly, the salt that is killing this nation with heart disease is not small pinches of white stuff added to home-cooked food to bring out the deft flavours of fresh vegetables, line-caught sustainable river fish and small portions of free-range organic chicken. It is the hidden and copious salts in fast and processed food, ready meals, cured meats, supposedly healthy breakfast cereals, biscuits, cakes, chocolate bars and even soft drinks that is doing all the damage, largely to poorer and less educated people, who are growing increasingly obese and whose life expectancy is lowering for the first time in six generations.

Upper-middle-class johnnies like you and me, on the other hand, who scatter a little Tidman's natural rock in our broccoli poaching water, are living longer and longer, and dying of practically nothing at all. To be honest, if you're any sort of democrat you should be wanting people like us to eat *more* salt, so that we die a bit younger and rebalance the statistics.

And secondly (or is it thirdly?, I forget), salt isn't bad for you anyway, unless you have a specific genetic predisposition to turn cholesterol in food into passage-narrowing arterial fur. It's bad for some people, but not everyone. One might say the same of peanuts, shellfish, soft cheese or pornography.

And thirdly/fourthly, here's where you people from *Which?* and WIPM and CASH are most grievously barking up the wrong saltlick: you rant about the Cornish Sea Salt Co. selling its product for 75p per 100 g where Saxa is only 8p, or Himalayan Crystal Salt luring people to their deaths with its 1 kg bag for £13.46, but, surely, if you want people to eat less salt then you should want its price to be as high as possible. It's cheap salt that is the enemy here, not the expensive stuff.

Because, believe me, in a world where salt costs as much, weight for weight, as fillet steak (as the Cornish stuff does), people are going to use an awful lot less of it. So you're just plain wrong. Expensive salt *is* healthier and *does* reduce heart disease, and for you to attack it is like anti-smoking campaigners calling for cheaper fags or the Pope campaigning for free condoms.

Froth all you want about the ponciness of it all, but you must expect us to take your pronouncements with a monstrous pinch of, I think, on this occasion, Fleur de Sel from Zauber der Gewürze. It's just under a hundred quid a kilo and quite divine over tomatoes.

WHO IS THIS AL FRESCO?

The arrival of spring, to many people a joyful thing, always brings me a glut of tedious enquiries from friends, readers and commissioning editors about where to eat al fresco. And, every time, because it never ceases to amuse me, I answer:

Who is this Al Fresco? And why do you want to eat him? If you mean 'outdoors' say 'outdoors'. This is England, we are English, we fought on the beaches and on the landing grounds, we fought in the fields and in the streets, we fought in the hills, we never surrendered. So do not come to me speaking the language of Musso·the Wop ('He's a Big-a-da-Flop') when you are looking for advice on a table outside an eating place.

And anyway, why on earth do you want to eat outside a restaurant? It is a thing I have never understood. You pay to go into a place and eat, not to get quite close and then be made to stay outside. Men spent thousands of years inventing the roof – millions died in the rubble of early prototypes – in order to protect himself from the elements, and now, the moment it isn't raining, you want to go and sit on the bit of land owned by the eating house that is not covered by the roof?

I suppose I can half see the appeal of it in a very hot country that is too primitive to have air-conditioning, such as France, where it might be nice to sit outside under the shade of a vine, overlooking the sea, and be brought things to soak up the booze. But on some suburban English high street, outside Café

Rouge in a grabbed hour's weekday lunchtime, in direct sun, turning your face to soak up the rays and hasten the moment when your face turns a deep mahogany and slides off like an old hat, being gawped at by every passing oaf, hassled by beggars and charity thugs, deafened by the bleepbleepbleep of reversing lorries, assailed by the stink of bin vans and diesel, peppered with particulates, plane-tree pollen and pigeon shit, dogs squatting by lamp posts in your line of sight as you swallow a lukewarm dusty sausage chunk . . . ? It's utterly mental.

When pushed, I tell people the River Café. You're by a river there, at least, and it's a courtyard so there's no traffic noise or smell, and the food is very good. But the whole experience always makes me sad I am not somewhere else. The smell of grilled squid, a drizzle of good green oil on fresh bread and a swirling glass of gavi di gavi consumed in May sunshine (all for only a few hundred pounds per person) might make some people feel glad to be in Hammersmith, but it only makes me feel sorry not to be in Southern Europe. Which is no good at all.

And anyway, even the sainted River Café is ruined by smokers. Not their fault. Like it is not paedophiles' fault or drink-drivers' fault. But they do love an outside table. They think it's OK if they're outside. They don't know what we're fussing about. But there was one at the table upwind of me outside the River Café last time I went, some desiccated old skank sucking on a cheroot and reminding me with its sick familiar scent, even as I slid a fillet off my whole roasted 45-quid Dover sole, of cancer, death, tramps, sadness, poverty, crime, death, sweat, muggers, desperation, vomit and death.

So, that's outside tables. If you want to eat in the fresh air, then go to the park. And if you have your pick of parks, then obviously go to Hampstead Heath. Because while Hyde and Richmond and Regent's are all perfectly decent outsized gardens for napping in on a warm evening, feeding the ducks and copping off with someone else's wife, the Heath is something special. It is real countryside, more real than what lies outside London for the most part. It is heath, it has never been anything else. It is a fragment of the stunning, humming mantle that surrounded London before London overspilled its edges.

Coming over Parliament Hill and looking down as the greenness rolls into the city, you see London nestling there, twinkling, as it did once for travellers who came in by stagecoach, on horseback and on foot, long ago, in the High and Far-Off Times. There are woods here, and plains, and streams and lakes and ancient dwellings and great houses. It is all you need. If you want to eat outside, eat here.

But, of course, picnics are a pain in the arse. You go to all that effort, roasting and jugging and pickling things, and fitting them into the wedding list hamper with the proper plates and cutlery and glasses, and then you get to your picnic spot and you just drink the wine and eat crisps that someone else has brought because you can't be bothered to unpack.

So next time you picnic you just take sandwiches in a plastic bag, and the hamper lies for ever on the floor of the coat cupboard, reproaching you every time you go in there for a scarf or a jacket, for being old and unadventurous and unromantic and ungrateful.

And the time after that you don't even bother to take sandwiches, you just pick up a can of Sprite and a stick of Peperami at Costcutter and consume them on a bench by the lake, watching the alcoholics fishing for that giant carp you see sometimes in the local paper.

So there you have it, eating outside is for tramps and fag smokers (two communities with a huge crossover section in the Venn diagram because if you stink of rubbish and old piss already you might as well smell of fags) and especially so when the weather is hot. I can just about get hip to a burnt sausage or a bit of hard baked potato scoffed in gloves on Bonfire Night, but when the weather warms up then, like the Southern Europeans whose food we turn to at such times, the sensible ladies and gentleman head straight for the cool indoors.

Except, of course, when we are at big outdoor events. And by 'big outdoor events', I really mean cricket. But also a bit of horse racing. And then maybe a low-key music, art or literary festival. But mostly cricket. And the scandal is not about dodgy outside catering from vans in general, because we know about that, and we plan accordingly: we can either be arsed to pack a quality picnic or we decide to go unencumbered, eat well before we leave, and accept that come mid-afternoon, if we've had a few drinks, we'll be eating something warm and shrivelled and smelling of socks from a plastic sheath, spilling ketchup down our shirt and throwing half of it in the bin.

But there is a thing afoot these days where temporary fast-food shacks at sports matches and concerts and the like are setting themselves up as 'quality' options. People are getting fussier, the caterers realise, and with chains like Leon and Hummus Bros and the Ultimate and Gourmet Burger companies doing so well, they are thinking that maybe there will be profit in providing this sort of fast-but-good food at public events.

I was at Lord's recently for a not especially gripping day of Test cricket (it's never gripping when I go; if I had been present at every game of international cricket ever played, the history of Test cricket would have ended in the early 1890s through sheer boredom) and, around teatime, went strolling for some scran. Round the back of the Grand Stand was the usual collection of vans, including one called the Fine Burger Co. Well, you can see what they are trying to do there, can't you? Ultimate Burger, Gourmet Burger? Fine Burger. And at £6.50 a pop (compared to, say, £2 for a big sausage roll from the van next door), it was clearly going to be quality.

So I handed over £13 for two cheeseburgers – one for me, one for Esther – and took delivery. Ah, what a joyful summer moment: a temperature in the middle 60s, a light breeze, blue sky, the whiff of newly mown grass in the air, watching cricket on a weekday while the Muggles are at work, England about to win the first Test of the summer, and a premium burger in my hand, fat, juicy, with that red, smoky flavour and the hot, cheesy mouth coat we crave.

Except, it felt strangely cold, and hard. I pushed away the napkin and pressed the bun. Stone-cold. Fridge cold. Who keeps burger buns in the fridge? And the cheese looked as cold as a dead mouse on a foggy morning too: utterly unmelted, a rigid yellow edge at the corner of the bun. The menu had said 'Cheddar', but this was as like unto the Kraft cheese slices of my youth as any piece of cheese I had ever seen (and nothing wrong with that, in itself, for a slice of hot, melting, yellow processed cheese is just what a burger needs, it's just the misleading description that is so irritating, and the inability to achieve even that meanest of culinary accomplishments, a bit of melting).

Still, I'd shelled out now, so I bit in. Inside the cold bun and cold cheese was a warmish beefburger of the frozen, 12-for-£2 variety you see advertised in the window of Iceland. The texture was stiff and mealy, the flavour grey, sad, doggy.

The sun was out, the sky was blue, with not a cloud to spoil the view, but it was raining. Raining in my burger.

How dare they? There was nothing 'fine' about it. It was totally not fine at all. It was not even mildly okay. And there was nothing to merit a £6.50 price tag either. This burger was identical, i-freakin-dentical, to every crap-awful turdburger I've ever had outside a football ground, except that those ones came in a floury white bap and were slathered in greasy onions, cost £2, exactly fulfilled my expectations of them and were thus totally delicious. This, on the other hand, had a theoretically interesting bun and a sliver of salad, but so failed to deliver on its promises as to constitute the most disappointing thing I have put in my mouth since Robin Stopford dared me to lick a science lab locust in 1979.

This is the excellent foppery of the modern food world, to spy a gap in the market for double-priced hamburgers with a positive adjective in front of them and seek to plug it with the same old traditional rubbish, adding only the posh word and the eye-watering price. It is very much the M&S marketing principle. You take the same old product and identify that words like 'organic' and 'free range' are playing well in the marketplace, but realise that legally you can't say that about your food so you just slide other, subjective and essentially meaningless words into the template and hope that nobody will notice. You know the sort of thing: 'These are not just tomatoes, these are red, round, bulbous, tomatoey tomatoes, with skins and a little green stalky bit on.'

By the same token, the people from 'Fine' had done nothing to their burger except describe it erroneously and double the normal price tag. This was not just a burger, this was a lavishly adjectived, preposterously over-described, linguistically inflated but nutritionally thoroughly bankrupt burger. It was an abomination, a horror, a downright summer food scandal.

Esther and I hoicked our burgers straight into the bin – £13 down the tube, which is the price of a two-course set lunch at any number of excellent restaurants – and bought, with our remaining two pound coins, a sausage roll from the sad old van next door. Excellent, it was. Flaky, greasy and hot, with a pink, fatty flavour. The same as we used to eat in the bad old days before the food revolution, and all the more delicious for not being ashamed of that.

As well as the Fine Burger Co, there also appeared to be other 'Fine' food vans in the area. There was definitely a 'Fine Fish and Chips' and also, I think, a 'Fine Pies', although I'm not certain of that. All I can say is that, as you head off into the great outdoors for your summer fun, and find yourself feeling a little peckish, just be wary of anything that describes itself as 'fine'. And, to be on the safe side, it's probably best not to take 'great', 'excellent' or 'tasty' too seriously either.

In these situations the safest thing to look for, sadly, is probably a 'Mc'.

Insist on Tap Water

MINERAL WATER IS a preposterous vanity. It is flown and shipped around the world, from France and Norway at best, from Japan and Fiji at worst. It is bottled in glass that is mostly thrown away and is stupidly heavy to freight, or in plastic which never, ever, decomposes and just goes to landfill or ends up in one of the 'plastic patches' the size of Texas currently gyring in our oceans.

Food snobs and restaurant critics make a big song and dance about mineral waters they like and don't like. New York's Ritz-Carlton even caters to the whim of abstemious punters with a dedicated water list and sommelier.

The vanity of it! While half the world dies of thirst or puts up with water you wouldn't piss in, or already have, we have invested years and years, and vast amounts of money, into an ingenious system which cleanses water of all the nasties that most other humans and animals have always had to put up with, and delivers it, dirt-cheap, to our homes and workplaces in pipes, which we can access at a tap.

And yet last year we bought three billion litres of bottled water. 3,000,000,000 litres! I have no idea how much that is. But it seems a lot. Especially when we were fooled into buying it because of labels that said 'pure as an alpine stream', 'bottled at the foot of a Mexican volcano' or 'cleansed for three million years beneath a Siberian glacier'. What morons we are.

We spent £2 billion on the stuff. And then we grumble about water metering and annual domestic bills of a couple of hundred quid for water that is just as good, and whose consumption by us is unlimited. Those two billion pounds could go some way to mending the odd leak, don't you think? Towards digging the odd reservoir?

From the restaurants' point of view it is just a clipping system. It's more free money. The mark-ups are bigger even than they are on wine. You'll pay four to five pounds in most posh London restaurants for stuff no different, no different at all, from what you brushed your teeth in that morning (not leaving the tap on while doing so, I hope). The result is billions of unnecessary food miles, non-biodegradable waste, millions of tonnes of greenhouse gases, more urban pollution, hell in a handcart.

The problem with asking for tap water is that you can feel a bit cheap. You're asking for something that is free. If you're insanely rich, you won't care. Because if you're insanely rich you won't care about anything. Least of all what some dribbling hired flunky in polyester trousers thinks of you. But if you're not. If you have self-worth

issues of
any sort that can
be heightened by a sense of
ill-belonging in a fancy restaurant,
then you will be afraid of looking like a
cheapskate, and may, as I did for years and
years, end up buying a bottle or two (pissing away
a crisp, useful ten-pound note) of water just so that
nobody thinks you're poor.

They play on that, these restaurants. Nudging you to more expensive wines, adding supplements to the tastiest things, charging the earth for a side saucer of manky potatoes . . .

You mustn't let them!

I made a big stink about this in 2007, started a campaign which got taken up all round the country, penalised any restaurant that did not make 'tap water' its first liquid offering when I sat down by docking points from its eventual score, absolutely hammering the (many) places that attempted to charge for tap water, and things began to change a bit. (It's probably the only good I have ever done in my piddling life.) And it is now the norm in more enlightened places to offer tap as a matter of course, usually iced (there is nothing more derisory and disrespectful than a glass of tepid, iceless tap water), often filtered, sometimes even carbonated.

But some still do not. And you need not stand for it. You must be proud of your insistence on tap water. You are not being cheap. You do not care how much it costs, you just give a damn about the environment, the fish, the lickle thirsty babies in Africa, the future of our planet. You must demand to be served iced tap water in a jug, not just a glass, and if they do not then you must stand on the table and shout, 'This restaurant is a fucking disgrace!'

And if they give you any trouble then just give me a call at *The Times*. And I'll take it from there. attempted to charge for tap water, and things began to change a bit. (It's probably the only good I have ever done in my piddling life.) And it is now the norm in more enlightened places to offer tap as a matter of course, usually iced (there is nothing more derisory and disrespectful than a glass of tepid, iceless tap water), often filtered, sometimes even carbonated.

But some still do not. And you need not stand for it. You must be proud of your insistence on tap water. You are not being cheap. You do not care how much it costs, you just give a damn about the environment, the fish, the lickle thirsty babies in Africa, the future of our planet. You must demand to be served iced tap water in a jug, not just a glass, and if they do not then you must stand on the table and shout, 'This restaurant is a fucking disgrace!'

And if they give you any trouble then just give me a call at *The Times*. And I'll take it from here.

IN HOGARTH'S FOOTSTEPS

As Friday May 26, 1732, slid rainily into Saturday May 27, and sober men, having put their wigs out to be powdered, were well into their fourth hour of sweet dreams about the next 250 years of Whig supremacy, William Hogarth, then 34 and chilling his boots after the completion of his *Harlot's Progress*, was getting hammered with four friends at The Bedford Arms in Covent Garden.

At about one o'clock they resolved, as one so often does in these situations, to embark immediately upon a road trip. The plan was to parody the Grand Tours of Europe, then in vogue among rich young fellows with nothing better to do. But Hogarth and his pals would eschew Paris, Vienna and Florence in favour of the far handier Medway estuary. They ran home to pick up fresh shirts and loose change, and then staggered and sang their way down to Billingsgate where they drank hard at the Dark House until a boat was made available to waft them wetly down to Kent.

What we know of the next five days is recorded in Ebenezer Forrest's 'AN ACCOUNT of what Seem'd most Remarkable in the Five Days' Peregrination of the Five Following Persons, Viz. Messieurs Tothall, Scott, Hogarth, Thornhill & Forrest. Begun on Saturday May the 27th. 1732 and Finish'd On the 31st. of the same Month'.

And what we know is that they walked and ate and walked

and drank and had pigdung-flinging fights and ate and drank, and that Scott was beside himself when, after passing out under a hedge, he found his greatcoat besmirched 'with an Ordural Moisture of a verdant Hue' that left him inconsolable for the rest of the trip. And they ate and drank and played hopscotch and looked at churches and drew pictures and ate and drank and listened to local folklore and laughed at it and laughed even more when Hogarth shat on a church porch to demonstrate his anti-clerical convictions, and they ate and drank . . .

And so it was that on a certain day, some 275 or thereabout years later, I met up with three gentleman at the Lamb and Flag in Covent Garden (because the Bedford Arms is no more) to plan a recreation of that Peregrination for our own time. I am still not sure why – except that Jonathan Myerson (the esteemed author) planned a novel about the young Hogarth, Martin Rowson (esteemed political cartoonist, author, &c.) is widely considered 'the Hogarth de *nos jours*', the RSC stalwart Richard Cordery had recently played Falstaff in *The Merry Wives of Windsor* (a character who might be called Hogarthian were it not a bit of an anachronism) and I am short and grumpy, like Scott (and, indeed, most men of the period).

Perusing the 4,000-odd words of Forrest's manuscript, I had found 17 separate references to eating (it was clearly all they talked about), and so I made it my business to inspire some commensurate centricity of victual-taking in our own trip.

The Hogarth party's first meal came on landing at Blackwall Reach, where they 'Eat Hung Beef and Biscuit and Drank Right Hollands'. Two paragraphs later it was 'Three Potts of Beer at an Evil House', and then, three paragraphs after that, a meal that came to haunt my imagination (and my belly) as we tramped across Southern England from one dodgy fry-up to the next: 'From One a Clock till Three, Wee were at Dinner On a Dish of Soles and Flounders with Crab Sauce, a Calves heart Stuff'd

And Roasted ye Liver Fry'd and the other appurtenances Minc'd, a Leg of Mutton Roasted, and Some Green pease, all Very Good and well Dress'd, with Good Small beer and excellent Port.'

And you thought we had had a Restaurant Revolution? We have not. We have had but a Restaurant Restoration. We have merely returned, in one or two hotspots, to something like the embarrassment of gastronomic riches we enjoyed before industrialisation spoiled everything.

In the very next paragraph our friends 'bought Shrimps and eat them' and on the next page: 'I went and bought Cockles of an Old Blind Man' – a repast which might sound rather distasteful to those unfamiliar with the prepositional peculiarities of the early 18th century. But how I would soon yearn for a well-made plateful even of old man's knackers.

Our own gastronomic tour began with cappuccinos and toasted bacon ciabattas at the Reef Cafe at Victoria Station (whence, in the absence of any skiff or small vessel, we were to board the 8.15 for Somewhere-in-Kent). No lobsters were on show. The bacon honked of poor Scott's ordurous coat. And when we enquired of our hostess whether the establishment was in possession of any tomato ketchup, she replied merely, 'Yes', and went about her business. I made a similar essay at the bar and was told once more, 'Yes'. There was again no effort made to retrieve and present any of it. Finally, I explained that the reason of my enquiry was a desire to smear a quantity of said ketchup upon my ordurous sandwich. But it was too late, for our train was due, and so the gaping maw of the swing bin got the benefit of my first meal of the day.

Our epic train journey behind us, we imposed ourselves upon the hospitality of The Old House at Home in Queenborough, a village described by Forrest as 'but One Street Situate on ye East Side of a Creek . . . no Sign of Any Trade, nor . . . many Human Creatures'.

Alas, it has lost much of its bustle since then. The inn sign creaked wolfily in the wind, as if to signal that at that very moment in heaven an angel was getting cancer. There we drank two rounds of Abbot under the silent glower of the local fishing fraternity (all six of it), enquired why the specials board was empty, and then left without being stabbed, which was something of a triumph under the circumstances.

The only other place in 'town' appeared to be a pub called The Flying Dutchman, so Falstaff, the very picture of urban bonhomie in his anorak and pendant camera, went into the only shop in town and asked the nice lady behind the counter where she would eat lunch if she were him.

'At home,' she replied.

Undaunted, he asked what if he were a stranger in town and desirous of comesting the very best that the local area had to offer by way of refection.

'The Flying Dutchman,' she said. And then, brightening up, 'The food is beautiful.'

Well, beauty is, I suppose, in the tongue of the begobbler. There was certainly range: those hundreds of dishes painted on blackboards that you see all over the boondocks where, because there are so few places to eat, your local must present a globe-trotting Marco Poloful of dishes from green curries and sushi to cow's blood mixed with milk and scampi in the basket.

Eschewing 'parcels' of this and 'pockets' of that, and dozens of 'bakes', I asked if the steak-and-kidney pie had a suet crust. The nice lady said that it did. And was it an individual pudding? It was.

It was a bit soggy, the thing that came, a bit shiny. But she did not lie. There were also such medium-sized toughish peas, hell-hot chips, gang-raped carrot and spectacularly absorbent broccoli (three stalks of this miraculous stuff could staunch a flooded basement), as you will be familiar with if you have ever eaten in an unpretentious pub (never tell me 'pretentiousness' is a bad thing in a pub). But the pie had some flavour and with 12 pints of Speckled Hen and four large Jamesons sent us on our way happily enough (and quickly).

Looking back at a photo of the pudding, a luxury Hogarth never had, I see that it resembled the imploded head of a small, sweaty bald man rather unhealthily leaking sewage from a wound to the left temple. But it did not taste that bad by any means. We walked thence to Minster, buying fireworks on the way to let off in the churchyard where Hoggy and his pals did far more pooey things. They had dined at The George. But The George was now The Prince of Waterloo ('Water-what?' Hogarth would have asked, in his pre-Napoleonic ignorance) and offered no more dinner than two rounds of IPA.

On this lightest of meals we repaired to the churchyard and let off our fireworks, unearthing more than one gaggle of local teenage crack-heads from the bushes and sending me scurrying halfway to Belgium in terror of burning hurt, of the law and of the wrath of God. We reconvened at The Highlander and drank Guinness for some hours, chortling about how outstandingly Hogarthian we were.

Thence to Rochester. By cab, of course. It's practically a mile away. What do you think this is, 1732? Gin was drunk in the ancient Cooper's Arms, low-beamed, oaky, thickly grockled. And then down the road we slid to Rochester's best (but empty) restaurant, Elizabeth's of Eastgate (which must be a part of Rochester, though why somewhere so small thinks it needs to be divided into different parts to help foreigners navigate is beyond me).

Here we were! Here we bloody were! Wobbly Tudor beams that were already quaint and pointless when Hogarth was a boy. Low pink lighting, reminder of the days when you couldn't slide a wafer between a brothel and a restaurant. Tassly lampshades of antediluvian fabrication. Ornamental copper bedpans (ordured once by Wm?) and dusty decanters for sack. And waiters from a land far, far away in time and space.

And on the menu: such, such delights of Olde England! I might mention 'melon and prawn cocktail', 'kidneys in sherry', 'fillet au stilton', and venerable, regal 'steak Diane'. To finish: 'crêpe Suzette', 'banana flambé', 'liqueur coffee'. Oh, it is 1732. It is, it is.

The kidneys were marvellous, in a sweetish way, and great things were said of the lobster thermidor (yes, indeed, lobster thermidor) by Falstaff and the Hogarth *de nos* etc, who ate it with chips. But I and Myerson went properly Hogarthian. I ate chicken Hawaii, oh yes. A breast of bird slathered with prawns, onions, ginger, pineapple, sherry and cream. A pox on yer flounders with crab sauce and ye livers fried! This was menu-making at its most rambunctious, and hang the Frenchies!

Prawns Elizabeth were cooked in cream and pernod (oh, rare Elizabeth!), the salmon Champagne simply reeked of class, but Myerson was in heaven with his 'house speciality', which was king prawns, scallops, scampi, cars and boats and planes and little houses by the sea, everything you could ever want, all together on a plate. Hurrah!

Next morning, at our lodgings with Mr and Mrs Reader (no, not you) of Salisbury House, we ate a wanton fry-up in which the black pudding was especially admirable. We walked to Upnor (indeed, 'twas Upper Upnor, I believe) and at The Tudor Rose were warned by local drinkers off the house ale, Graves-end Shrimpers. We drank of it anyway, and, finding it fine, enquired after the meaning of the warning. Apparently it was a joke. So good is the local brew that Upnorians amuse them-selves by preventing aliens from drinking it. We laughed uproariously and took our luncheon custom elsewhere.

Luckily there was November Midweek Madness at The King's

Arms just up the road. This meant whitebait, mixed grill, and bread and butter pudding for Pounds 9.95. Mad as a stoat in a stovepipe. It was all perfectly fine for three big strapping Englishmen (and me) walking in the cold on 12 pints a day, but if you'd given me a blindfold and sent in the dishes in a mystery order I could not have told you which was which. We drank three rounds of Black Sheep and a bottle of Taylor's '97 (Good Small beer and excellent Port) on which we haggled a price, and the landlady dined out for a month.

We walked to Hoo. We made jokes about it. Mostly knock-knock jokes. We snoozed in the graveyard there and then collapsed over a round of Jack Daniel's at The Three Bells as we waited for a taxicab to take us to the station. Thence home again. To now.

CROATIA

I love it when a country lives up entirely to expectations. And the sooner it does it, the better. So imagine my glee when, standing two places in front of me in the check-in queue at Heathrow for a Croatian Airlines flight to Zagreb, I saw none other than . . .

. . . wait. Surely you can guess who I saw. It's easy. If you were about to fly to Croatia for the first time, having selected it entirely randomly for a three-week summer holiday, whom would you expect to see in front of you in the check-in line?

Exactly. Goran Ivanisevic. He was just standing there, plain as your arm. Although bigger. He's an absolute whopper, is Goran. It's no wonder Tim flaked it in that Wimbledon semi in 2001. I dropped two sets just looking at him in an airport.

He was standing there, obviously, because Croatia has only one inhabitant. So if you get on a flight which is going there, he is bound to be on it. It's like the time I went to Norway and saw Morten Harket on the bus (an anecdote I will tell you in its longer form one day, although, to be frank, there isn't much else to tell).

Obviously, we got him to sign our *Lonely Planet* guide to Croatia (Goran, not Morten), on the principle that if we got into any tight spots on our travels, a gander at Goran's name would cause the locals to gasp and quiver and release us from our bonds (one has wild fantasies when travelling in unfamiliar countries).

Another area in which Croatia lived up to expectations was the language, which is practically impossible. Indeed, there was a time, I am sure you remember, when 'Serbo-Croat' was a byword for 'difficult' – as in, 'it might as well be written in Serbo-Croat'. But then Yugoslavia disintegrated, and Serbia and Croatia, once separated, ceased to be funny. And one rather forgot that they used to speak the same hilariously difficult language.

The language is called Croatian these days, except in Serbia, where it is called Serbian, and it hasn't got any easier. Chapter two of my *Teach Yourself Croatian* book was about counting to ten, and gently explained as follows: 'The number one behaves like an adjective and its ending changes according to the word which follows. The number two has different forms when it refers to masculine and neuter nouns than when it refers to feminine nouns, and is followed always by words in the genitive singular, as are the words for "three" and "four". The numbers 5–20, however, are followed by words in the genitive plural . . . '

This is why you never see Croatians in groups of more than one and less than five in a bar. Because it isn't actually possible to order the right number of beers.

Before the numbers chapter came the restaurant chapter, which claimed that the word for 'waiter' is *konobar* and that to hail one in a restaurant one merely cries '*Konobar!*' and he comes running over.

They tell you the same thing about '*Garçon!*' when you are learning French, but have you ever tried shouting '*Garçon!*' in a French restaurant? Has anyone? Can you even bear to imagine the consequences if you did? So why do the language books tell us to? Nobody has cried 'Waiter!' in an English restaurant since the Thirties.

Not that this failing of my Croatian book much mattered, because the last thing you want in a Croatian restaurant is a waiter coming over and giving you food. Ye Gods, the food.

Almost everything is made from pork. Bear meat is also popular, because it tastes like pork (unless they were telling me it tasted like pork because pork was all they had ever eaten, apart from bear). Any dish named after the place you're in (Veal Zagreb, Chicken Dubrovnik, Banana Split . . .) means 'filled with cheese and pork, breaded, deep-fried and served the day after tomorrow'. And the worst faux pas you can make is lighting a Marlboro after dinner. Because the local Marlboro are made in Serbia – one smokes Croatian-rolled Ronhill for a quiet life.

Like anywhere where the sea has been fished dry, the more familiar varieties of fish are mostly reserved for export and appear locally at 90 quid a kilo. Then there are lots of fish you have never seen before which don't look terribly appetising and turn out, when you look them up in your Collins Gem, to be called in English 'Splunk' and 'Fnottle' and 'Turgreen'. On the plus side, the extinction due to over-fishing of all predators bigger than a sardine has, as in Greece, led to a proliferation of jellyfish and squid, at least one of which is excellent eaten grilled, with salad and a cold beer. Every day.

I tried using guidebooks to find interesting places to eat, but lines such as 'the squid stuffed with ham and cheese rarely fails to disappoint' (in *The Rough Guide*'s write-up of its favourite Dubrovnik spot, Konoba Ekvinocijo) hardly breed confidence. And the place recommended by the *Lonely Planet* guide as serving the best pizza in Dubrovnik did not serve pizza at all, and never had. Which was just as well, because Croatian pizza is terrible.

A national dish called *peka*, I liked. This is a recipe in which a cheap cut of meat is lobbed in a pot with potatoes, sweet peppers, whole garlics and seasoning, and buried in the ground, whereabove a fire is kindled. It comes out after four or five hours, very tender and aromatic. Whether or not it was invented deliberately or is simply a re-enactment – in a land so regularly torn apart by war – of what one finds in the larder after digging through the smouldering rubble of what used to be one's home, I am not entirely sure.

As for the supposedly top-notch Proto in Dubrovnik, where, according to *The Rough Guide*, 'Edward VIII and Wallis Simpson ate on one of their trips in the Thirties', it reveals only that if Edward's greatest regret was never becoming King of England then he can't have ordered the Istrian sole (four fillets rolled around a prawn and stuck with a cocktail stick then baked in truffle oil and Fairy Liquid).

On the way out I noticed a sign that said 'Dalmatian Food Served Here', but had been in Croatia long enough by then to have stopped thinking that was funny.

How to Order Wine

JUST HAVE A
CONVERSATION WITH the waiter, for
Heaven's sake. Whether it is a scary Michelin-
starred swankorium with a leather-bound, hundred-
page winelist that the sommelier calls 'the Bible' with an
infuriating snigger, or a High Street Eyetie with eight badly kept
reds stacked over the bar, just explain what you like and don't like (or
better, because liking and not liking things is a bit childish, what you feel
like drinking this evening or don't feel like drinking this evening) and give a
price range. As you would do if you were buying a car or a flat or a slave.
Conversation is the key. A little chat. If he offers something more
expensive than you've suggested, you can say, 'These others are undrinkable,
are they?' It doesn't need to be firmer than that. Please don't be embarrassed
to mention the money. Wine is bought and sold by everyone for money.
Growers, makers, exporters and importers, dealers, critics, chain-shop owners,
sommeliers and restaurant buyers talk about cost all the time, in the first breath,
before anything else, so it is preposterous for all that talk suddenly to stop at
the restaurant table, and everyone be too embarrassed to talk about it. There
is value to be had away from big-named wines which command less
fashion value, and you can ask for advice if you want that sort of value.
But by and large bottles of wine end up costing more or less what they
are worth, relative to other bottles of wine.
I usually walk into a restaurant thinking, 'I fancy a twenty
quid bottle of Chianti' or 'I think I'll see if they can do a
Meursault for under fifty' or 'I'm going to get shitted on
the cheapest Riesling they have'. And it is nothing
at all to be embarrassed about. Except
maybe the last one.

LE MENU DÉGUSTATION AND A SICK BUCKET

I have eaten my last tasting menu, God willing. I suppose it is always possible that I will one day be dragged from the pavement on Camden High Street and bundled into the back of a black sedan by shouting hooded men who cosh me and cuff me, and that I will wake up in a small white room in front of an oversized piece of ornamental crockery and some posh flowers and a branded ashtray and that a man will bring me a plate with three tiny things on and describe each one (probably some crusted shellfish, a smidge of special offal, some caviar), while pointing at each item with his little finger, and then he will bring a cold soup, and another shellfish dish, and some beignets of something, perhaps turbot, then maybe a risky sorbet with an asymmetrical bowl and a glass spoon, and then the breast of some small bird with a confit (or perhaps cannelloni) of its legs, and then medallions of something organic and rare-bred accompanied by potatoes in a little tower, and then a cheeseboard which I have to eat the whole of, and then a pre-dessert, and then a hot flaky pudding with exotic fruit, and more ice-cream and then coffee.

Occasionally, in the past, I have ordered the tasting menu (or 'menu dégustation' if you have trouble eating in English) because I felt that, as a critic, I should experience a wide range of the chef's booty. But it's daft, because I never enjoy the long, drawn-out, beat-me-to-death-with-a-wooden-spoon boringness of sitting for so long with little men running backwards and forwards between me and the kitchen. Like words which, if you think of them for too long, stop sounding like real words ('hornet' and 'croon' always do that to me), it stops feeling like a real meal, and you start wondering what on earth, if it is not a meal, this experience you are having is.

At certain places, such as El Bulli (where eating 32 courses was the whole point) and The Fat Duck (where it's a more modest 20), I have had no option but to enter into the spirit. At a couple, professional diligence truly has demanded it. But otherwise, no. Starter and main course, please. Pre-starter if you must. Pudding only if I'm drunk and flagging and need the sugar.

But it isn't always that easy. I eat incognito, and usually I get away with it. But if I am exposed, as happens occasionally, they just won't take no for an answer. And if I take my refusal of the tasting menu to the point of fisticuffs, then they bring thousands of extra courses anyway, stacked around the two I have ordered. And always the richest things, too. I doubt you have any idea how depressing the sight of two lobsters dancing out of the kitchen *avec ses accompaniments de foie gras et caviar aux truffes* can be to a man who has already swallowed 11 unbidden courses and has had to make himself sick in the bogs twice just to stay in his trousers.

Interred in these lengthy repasts, I develop a mad envy of the people at other tables whom I see leaving as the evening goes on. I imagine them driving home to their little houses to have a cup of camomile tea and to read, perhaps, a chapter of *The Decameron*, before clicking off the bedside light, kissing their wives and sinking into cool goosedown to nod off to the sound of owls. Meanwhile, some bastard of a waiter is bringing me a tray of caramelised widgeon hearts to keep me busy until the stuffed udders and tripe course, which should arrive about the same time as the milkman.

HAND DRYERS

Hand dryers are bad. You can tell just to look at them. Great big metal things that get all hot and make a terrible noise. They are the motorbikes of the washroom. The coal-fired power stations of the post-piddle clean-up. You simply can't justify that much energy, that much heat and sound, that much waste, just to get your hands a little less wet.

It's not as if they actually work. They take far too long. By the time I'm halfway through a slash, I've usually got three hilarious things I've thought of that I want to rush back and tell my dining companions. By the time you've finished peeing and washing your hands, the last thing you want to see, as you worry that the conversation will have moved on and your top quip may die alone and forgotten in the windblown attic of your mind, is some rusty old box on the wall that will wheeze feebly over your frantically rubbing hands like the last, cold breath of an expiring soldier.

That's when you have to grab bog roll from one of the cubicles to dry your hands, and then they're still not quite dry, so you wipe your hands in your hair to finish off and get little pills of rolled grey paper all over your head so that everyone stares at you when you get back to the table, and you look in the mirror and shriek, and the things you were so looking forward to saying get forgotten altogether.

You can tell the really bad dryers because they're so small, and thus doubly powerless and slow. Men will often clock these on their way into the bathroom and make a decision not to wash their hands at all. And I hate to eat in a roomful of people with pee on their hands (you see them rummaging in the bread basket just before it comes to you: 'Shall I have this one or this one? Ooh, this one feels nice, too, or maybe this one?'), which is why I always hit the loo as soon as I arrive in a restaurant and, if the dryer is small, leave immediately and eat somewhere else.

There was one at a place called Frascati, a small Italian in Hampstead with okay gnocchi where in 1987 I first told a girl I loved her over lunch and meant it, which was bracketed to the wall six feet off the ground, so that when you raised your hands to receive its weedy electric fart, water ran down your sleeves into your armpits. But it closed down last year, perhaps entirely because of the unsatisfactory hand-drying arrangements in the gents. Which was a great blow struck for manual hygiene, but a shame for me in terms of possibly lucrative future London tours of my Romantic hotspots.

And if there are some dryers that do a reasonable job of drying your hands, blasting them dry with a torrent of screeching hot air only five times more slowly than you could have done it with a towel, then these are the ones whose ecological horrors are most obvious. That they are usually labelled 'World Dryer Corporation' only underlines the damage they are doing to the planet from which they have taken their name.

I'm not entirely sure what I can do about it, though. I've toyed with the idea of handing out points in my restaurant reviews for 'hand-drying facilities', in which the only way to score ten will be to install a Dyson Airblade, which uses jet-engine technology to pump out room-temperature air at 400 mph through a 0.3 millimetre slot, creating a constant sheet of air that acts like a windscreen wiper, drying both hands in 10 seconds and using 83 per cent less energy than conventional dryers.

But that might sound a bit too much like advertising. You might almost think that, back in the mid-1990s, as a struggling young journalist, I had ghost-written James Dyson's autobiography and been granted the full copyright to the great (and very generous) man's life, so that ever afterwards I have received quite decent royalty cheques on sales not only here in the UK but from editions published in France, America, Japan, Korea, Norway . . . and that the more famous he is and the more products he sells, the more copies the book sells, and the more money keeps on rolling into my numbered Swiss account, fully 15 years after I washed my hands of the copy.

So, incorruptible as I so famously am, I'll recommend a stack of nice, clean, warm, dry hand towels instead.

How to Complain about the Wine

WINE I
TRICKIER to complain abou
than food. There is such a huge, gre
area of potential unknowing, which make
it difficult to assert with confidence that yo
have been mis-served. But don't worry about tha
You do not know as little about wine as you think yo
do, and the waiter (or sommelier) does not know as muc
as he thinks he does. So never try to fake knowledge you d
not have. It's not worth it. Wine is not about knowledge, it
about pleasure. The way that we know James Bond is such a tote
bell-end (know for certain, rather than dimly intuit) is that he knows s
much about wine.

Because vast, in-depth knowledge of wine, and the skill to identif
individual types and vintage of wine from mere tasting alone, is accrue
only through years and years of application, hard work, sobriety, note
taking, studying, reading, concentrating and having no mates. Just like
great knowledge of physics, Latin and Greek or train numbers.

When Bond says, 'Ah, delicious, a Château Cheval Blanc 1873, if I'm no
very much mistaken,' it is only as cool and slick and sophisticated as squealing
'Ooh, look, it's the 17.43 from Preston, and if I'm not very much mistaken it's
Class 57 British Rail diesel-electric locomotive made by transplanting a Genero
Motors reconditioned power unit and alternator into a Class 47 bodyshe
commonly known as a "Bodysnatcher".

You do not need to know about wine to complain about it. Nobody eve
serves a wine that is not what it says on the label. And nobody has eve
tasted such a wine and contested it, ever, in the history of restaurants.

When the guy pours it out for you to taste, he is asking you only on
question. Is it corked? If, when you give it a sniff, it smells nastily (rathe
than nicely) of mouldy old books that have gone rotten in a damp cella
then it is corked. (Very, very old clarets can come out of a bottl
cellared for fifty years smelling a bit cloistered and poky but it
hardly their fault, and if you're doing thousands of pounds in
restaurant on some celebrity ancient plonk to impress you
fuckface banker mates and it isn't quite as stellar in th
mouth as you had hoped it would be then, frankly, he
ha ha ha ha ha ha hardy ha fucking ha.)

If the bottle is corked, then there is n
question about it and your firs
impression is always right.
have often though

on a second
and third sniff, that
maybe it was okay, before
drinking half a bottle of it, realising it
really was corked and regretting it hugely.

If it's corked, hand it back to the waiter and tell
him it is. He ought to just take it away, but he'll
probably sniff it himself. To mellow your annoyance at this
impertinence, try asking him for his opinion on whether it is
corked, turning his snooty gesture into a service performed on
your behalf. In 98% of places, if it is corked, he will apologise and
bring another bottle. If it is one of the other 2%, then ask him very
politely to cork it up again and give it to you to take home, because
you will be making a formal complaint with the backing of consumer
groups and your favourite restaurant critic later, and ask to see the wine
list to choose something else.

Some provisos: 'Corked' doesn't mean there are bits of cork in the wine.
The technicalities of corked wine are too boring for me ever to have paid
proper attention but, essentially it is caused by the presence of
2,4,6-trichloroanisole (TCA), and/or 2,4,6-tribromoanisole (TBA) in the wine,
which in many cases will have been transferred from the cork, but which also
can have been transferred through the cork rather than from it.

If there bits of cork floating in the wine, that is usually just down to sloppy
opening by the waiter. It seems to happen more with white wine (or maybe
it's just more visible), and doesn't matter. It doesn't look nice, and a decent
place will strain it for you into clean glasses, but it's not a fault with the wine.
Also, some white wines will come at you with crystals in the bottom that
look a bit grim but are only 'tartrates' that are the result of the house
fridge being too cold, I believe, and certain sugars crystallising, but they
don't really matter.)

When you taste the wine, the guy is not, repeat not, asking what
you think of it. There is no point saying, 'Ooh, that's delicious,'
unless he has specifically recommended something to you and
you really think it is. If he has specifically recommended
something to you, and you do not like it (but it is not
corked), you are within your rights to say so and to ask
nicely for something else (especially if it is a place
you visit regularly) but I think that's a bit
wanky and ungrateful and you should
just neck it down and have
something else for the next
bottle.

PUDDING IS FOR WIMPS

'*Ompa loompa doompety doo . . .*' God, I loved those Oompa-Loompas. As moralists, they made Samuel Johnson look liberal. If the Mel Stuart/Gene Wilder film of Roald Dahl's *Charlie and the Chocolate Factory* was the great Hollywood morality tale of 1971, the Oompa-Loompas were its Greek chorus: spooky, supernal, poetic, prophetic ('What do you get when you guzzle down sweets? Eating as much as an elephant eats.'). And did we heed them? Did we hell. We got fat because, like Augustus Gloop (the fat boy who got sucked down the chocolate tube), we wouldn't listen.

I hate chocolate. It is gacky and ugly and obvious and dumb and it wreaks palatal havoc on your mouth. I hate it and I hate people who like it. I hate puddings with names like 'Death by Chocolate' and 'Chocolate Devil' and 'Cocoa Satan-Worshipper'. I hate the implication that chocolate is in some way naughty. It is not naughty.

Flying to Sri Lanka on company time to buy boys and opium is naughty. Giving in to chocolate when there is some nutritional reason why you should not be eating it is just moral turpitude, and it is not particularly attractive.

I hate people who think that saying 'I'm a chocoholic' is in some way funnier than saying 'I'm a smack addict' – all dependence is weak and pitiful and bad. And I hate conspiratorial waitresses who, when you tell them you are too full for pudding, tell you that you must have the 'triple chocolate S&M dungeon pot' because it is simply to die for. No, luv, it is to die of. As a result of precocious myocardial infarction brought on by being too stupid to resist refined sugars and prettily coloured starch.

Chocolate is utterly pointless. It is what fat people have instead of cigarettes.

Okay I don't hate it. I eat little ascetic squares of the very dark posh stuff with a cup of peppermint tea in front of the telly late at night. But I do hate it after a meal. I do hate pudding of any sort. Which means I get endless letters complaining that my reviews never feature dessert.

I have never been a supporter of the pudding as a course in its own right. It is rationalised by mere convention and is a relic of 18th-century vanities, Antonin Carême and the heyday of service à la russe.

Nutritionally, it contains nothing of value at all. It's just sugar and starch or, at a push, a bit of fruit poached, roasted or baked to well past the point where anything useful in it is left intact. Pudding is nothing but wasted calories, meaningless sugar spike, tragic glycaemic overload.

I eat 4,000–5,000 calories a day as it is, which is twice the recommended daily intake. As a consequence, I try to exercise properly about four times a week, which is just enough to stay the right side of critically obese. If I ate pudding as well I would either have to live on a treadmill, taking my meals liquidised through a tube as I ran, or I'd have to accept swelling to the size of a Texan.

But then my fingers would be too fat to type. Each flabby-digited punch at a key would depress seven or eight letters at a time and this review would have begun: 'op.lrxfcdarxfcdajbi bvfcwraewrEWIJK.' And then you'd really have had something to write letters about.

Also, I don't have a sweet tooth. The taste for sweet things does not normally last much past puberty in men, except in those pudgy-faced, childlike fellows in *Guardian* mail-order shoes you see sitting alone by the aisle in cinemas, buried in a king-size carton of pick'n'mix, like pigs rootling in a bin.

I just can't imagine who would go to a restaurant for the puddings. Pudding is just a sugar hit for diners who have drunk too much and need a lift to get them out of the restaurant and into the car. And besides, who on earth has room for pudding after two courses of the kind of monstrous portions restaurants now provide, in response to years of heckling by their increasingly lard-arsed clientele?

I usually order three or four starters between two, for the sake of an overview, then three mains to share, and a couple of sides. My eyes, at the start of any meal (reviewing or otherwise), are bigger than my belly. But by the time I am done with my mains, my belly has caught up and is once again bigger than my eyes (which is an aesthetic blessing, if nothing else). So then, when I am sitting there stuffed as hell, they bring me another menu. And my newly small eyes just want them to go away.

But they insist, prodding it towards me. I roll my eyes and heave and fart and wave them away. But still they grovel and fawn. Sometimes I get the whine about how distraught the new pastry chef will be if I don't try her tortured sugar weasel in its raspberry cage, and I have to pull the man down to my slumping eye level and give him the full Mr Creosote.

Even then they'll bring petits fours with the coffee, which I am compelled to load on to the handle end of a spoon and then, banging the scoop end with my fat fist, launch into the chandeliers.

How to Choose a Restaurant for a Date

NOT LONG AGO a young chap I play cricket with, about 25 years old, nice-looking, rich family, clean clothes (hell, I'd go to bed with him myself), emailed me as follows:

'Hi Giles, How are you? Can I ask a quick favour of a restaurant recommendation? I'm going on a first date with a girl and I'm not really sure where to take her. There are basically no criteria other than somewhere that would be nice for a first date; sorry I know that's not helpful. Yours, Tom.'

I was about to delete it and pretend I had never seen it (as I do with most requests for help in this area from friends) but came over all avuncular and replied like this:

'Hey Tom. First off, don't take her somewhere too quiet, or too romantic. That's a bit scary for both of you. Where do you live? More importantly, where does she live? Is she into food? What are you hoping to achieve? Main thing is for you to be comfortable. I can tell you the right place but I need a tiny bit more.'

'I live in Notting Hill,' he replied. 'And she lives in Knightsbridge. I met her in the gym. I don't know what she thinks about food. I was thinking of E&O. My aim is to get to know her and get a second date.'

And I told him this:

'Do NOT go to E&O! It is a shithole and any half-classy

Doris can
sniff that from the door.
Also, do not let her see that you
cannot leave your mimsy little bourgeois
Eurotrash hood. Go to Bar Boulud, at the
Mandarin Oriental.

'When taking a chick out the crucial thing is to
be near HER home. That way she hasn't had a
hassly journey when she arrives, and she isn't just
sitting there worrying about how she's going to get
home. And on the off chance that action is on the cards
it is she who has to ask you back, not vice-versa, so you
don't come over all rapey. At the same time, there is no
danger of her being offended by your NOT asking her back.
Bar Boulud has advantage of being big and bustly so you're
not laying on a heavy romantic shtick, but the food is very
good and also plenty of scope for her, being a chick, to eat
lightly. Also getting a table isn't too hard, as long as you
give them a bit of notice.'

It's not like I think there's anything magic about that.
I'm just passing it on because Tom replied so
enthusiastically and added, 'If you have another
child, I hope you have a son, as this is choice
advice that definitely needs to be passed on.'

But I don't have a son, I have a daughter.
And if any man so much as invites her out
for a cup of coffee, EVER, before she
is 25, then I will personally cut
off his knackers.

THE HEALTH FARM

Every now and again I undertake to give up drinking. I almost always undertake to do this when I have a hangover. Which means that it rarely comes off, because great ideas conceived during a hangover are even less likely to bear fruit than ones conceived while drunk.

But it is a resolution one has to make. Because while painkillers may dull the headache, water may rehydrate and a nice bath can do away with the sweats, the really tricky bit of the hangover, the existential bit, can only be ameliorated by the making of resolutions. Tell yourself that this is the last hangover you will ever have, and it doesn't seem so bad. Say to yourself that never again will you lose all track of a perfectly nice evening around nine and wake up naked in the smouldering remains of a burned-out brothel, holding a cigarette, with a police camera in your face, and the fact that you've just done so is instantly reframed as a forgotten activity from a dim and irrelevant past.

I usually manage it for as long as three or four days. Sometimes even six or seven. But sobriety is a mixed blessing. Everything seems terribly clear and bright, it's true, but how is one supposed to get to sleep? With nothing to sleep off there is just no incentive. In my sober patches I drink tap water with my supper, go to bed almost immediately afterwards (since the two things that bore me most when sober are television and other people), then lie there and stare at the dark until morning.

In theory, you could go jogging to make yourself tired, and thus more likely to sleep. But if you're not drinking, and you don't smoke, and your diet is not all that bad, then there just isn't the guilt to motivate you. It's an odd sort of physical limbo: not doing anything bad, not doing anything good. From a health point of view, you are neutral, like Switzerland. You have nothing to fear from the health fascists and they have nothing to fear from you. Let them round up and exterminate the fat and unfit, you'll just look the other way. You'll even store their looted gold and paintings until it's over.

Last time I went on the wagon I ended up on the most cataclysmic accidental bender when, while making a broccoli and camembert soup, I forgot to cook off the alcohol from the half-bottle of white wine that went into it, and didn't realise until the second mouthful, when I noticed an unfamiliar acidity ascending through the chlorophyll and dairy notes, just before I passed out.

When I came round I decided it was time for dehab or notox, or whatever it is that people do who can't say no to a second spoonful of cheese soup. And I checked into Champneys. Totally random: Google, health spa, Champneys. I had no preconceptions, having only dimly heard of it in the past, but people I told about it said, 'Ooh, Champneys' – as if it were in some way posh or exclusive.

It turned out to be neither. First thing they did when we arrived was show us their celebrity-client wall. I looked at the signed photos of George Best, Gazza, Neil Morrissey, and felt suddenly very sad and lonely. Our room had nice tartan fabrics and views through high windows across fields and streams, but the Victorian-style ancestral portraits on the walls had the heads of dogs (posher, I suppose, than if the dogs had been playing snooker), the place was draughty as hell (which must affect the mortality rate in a place full of old wet people walking around in bathrobes) and in the dining room I had never seen people as bad with a knife and fork in my life.

So faux-genteel was the clientele that they held their knives and forks just in the tips of their fingers, so far back up the handle that they appeared not to be holding them at all. It was as if they were playing one of those fairground robo-arm clutchy games, with salad in the bottom of the booth instead of pink furry gonks.

And you know what? I think I'd rather eat a gonk. For the Champneys refectory offered old-school health food of the low-fat, high-fibre, finish-it-or-stand-in-the-corner variety. There was no nod to the post-Atkins world of glycaemic indices, complex carbohydrates and acceptable fats – largely, I guess, because Champneys wants to use its special crockery with its plates all divided up by red lines for percentages of carbohydrate, fat and protein.

Thus the lunch buffet was all dull salads with 'lite' dressings (on the principle that if it's cold and wet and tastes of nothing you will eat less and get thinner), but with heaps of potatoes, white bread, white rice and tinned sweetcorn. I didn't know anybody ate that stuff anymore. Where was the rye bread, the brown rice, the stuff your body doesn't just turn immediately into candy floss?

Two pages on the menu devoted to 'Champneys' approach to healthy eating' yielded the stunning revelation that 'there is no such thing as a "good" or "bad" food – only healthy or poor eating habits'. I beg to differ. On the first day I identified a pork curry (woeful concatenation) and asked, naturally, where the pork came from. Nobody knew. That's bad, plain and simple. Whatever your eating habits. Mine happen to forbid me from eating pork of unknown provenance.

Now, for breakfast I usually juice organic beetroots, carrots and apples with a bit of ginger, and drink a couple of espressos (yes, I'm a bit of a wanker). Here they were offering awful filter coffee (which has more caffeine and fewer antioxidants) and eight different kinds of cereal (Shreddies, Special K with dried red bits, Bran Flakes, Corn Flakes, etc), which are nothing but refined starch pepped up with hidden salts and sugars (to borrow a term from current Conservative Party demonology: stealth additives). And these fatties were chowing down like they thought the Kellogg's Challenge wasn't a cynical joke played by marketing men on the weakest people in society. And with milk! From a cow! Like they hadn't noticed that even a calf, which has four stomachs, stops drinking milk after about eight weeks.

There was no bacon – as if that were worse for you than a white bread roll – but you were allowed eggs. Alas, these did not claim to be either organic or free-range. You may get thin, but you'll also develop tits and an immunity to penicillin.

Supper was better. At least it was served at one's table in the bizarre Romanesque triclinium with its *trompe l'oeil* triforium and gardens. But they still went for the small-portion, low-calorie school of diet food which just doesn't work, because you get hungry later. In fact, if you are a growing lad like me and are served the uniform portion that is also considered healthy for the tiny anorexic nonagenarian at the next table, you actually get more hungry as you eat.

Furthermore, I was eating exclusively vegetarian options for the first time in my life because there was just no information on the meat at all. Indeed, when I asked about the 'turkey steaks' the waitress came back with the news that 'chef says there is no information about them'. I've just seen too many documentaries about where turkey steaks come from to accept that.

And so I ate little tiny portions of couscous with asparagus on them (the asparagus is year round at Champney's, because these people have paid for a posh spa and they want to see 'posh' things like asparagus on the menu whether they have been grown in Kenya, frozen and air-freighted in all their tasteless glory or not) and minuscule Caesar salads (made with Iceberg lettuce, so help me – as if it had fewer calories than Romaine) and, for the first time in my life, a mushroom vol-au-vent for a main course – a single one (actually not bad). Oh, and I ordered the cheese course once but the Wensleydale had a seam of cranberry relish running through it – some sort of special sugary treat for the troops that I could neither understand nor stomach.

On the plus side, Champneys did have a better steam room, sauna, swimming pool and masseurs than most restaurants, which at least enabled me, for the first time in ages, to sleep.

If only I'd had something to sleep off.

Be Nice to the Staff

JUST BE
NICE TO THEM, that's
all. You should always be nice to
everybody. But if you're not, and are
generally a mean, pompous, self-regarding, vain,
argumentative shitbag, then make being nice to the
staff in restaurants your only exception. It will pay back a
thousandfold in ways you can only dimly intuit. If you do not
understand how then read *A Christmas Carol* again. (And also
the chapter here on my time as a waiter.)
By the way, don't flirt with waitresses, they're fed up with it.
DO flirt with waiters, they can't get enough of it.
Don't try and speak French to them, they don't give a shit that you
have a house in Provence and can just about make yourself understood
when talking about salad dressing.
Don't ask them where they're from, especially if you suspect them of
being Polish. Nobody wants to be grilled on their country of birth. Nobody
wants it pointed out to them that they are immigrants. And most of the
people serving you will have come from countries where being asked
such a question was generally a prelude to interrogation, torture and
death. They can't be sure that you are not from the Home Office.
So just smile, say please and thank you, look at them when you
are ordering (especially, you, ladies, those of you at least who
have a tendency to tell the nearest man at your table what
you want to eat for no earthly reason, regardless of
the waiter standing right by your side) and
then shut up and eat.

THE SUPERSIZERS GO . . .

Time present and time past
Are both perhaps present in time future,
And time future contained in time past.
If all time is eternally present
All time is unredeemable.

But the least you can do is TRY. The least you can do is travel back through time with the help of some willing chefs, a small BBC budget for costumes and a lot of draughty castles, and do your very best to eat your way through the ages of Man, find out what we have learned, and what we have lost, and live for a short while in the past, present and future all at the same time, just like T.S. Eliot said.

After several years eating pretty much everything that is available to eat on earth, the time eventually came to eat everything that no longer is. And the only place you can do something like that, something completely impossible, is on television.

I had done a tiny bit of telly already – the first series of *The F-Word* with Gordon Ramsay; a not-very-good documentary series for Channel Four about bio-technology in the food industry; a controversial (to those who noticed it) anti-obesity film for More4 called *Tax the Fat*; and a film review series for Channel Five called *Movie Lounge* (or, as an Old Etonian friend of mine preferred to refer to it, 'Film Drawing Room') – and I thought it was all a fine old lark.

So when they asked if I fancied doing a sort of Morgan

Spurlock rip-off, set in the Edwardian Period, I thought, 'Yup, sure, fine, no problem.' Well, strictly I first thought, 'I wonder how much they'll pay me.' But it's not very much in my sort of telly (BBC, factual, not really watched by anybody) so I soon got over worrying about that.

Initially, they suggested I present the show with my sister. But she screamed with horror at the mere thought of it. And she had just won a million quid in a poker tournament, so wasn't too fussed with working at the time. They said, 'Well, who else then?'

I thought through all the women I knew in television, which was Sue Perkins, and suggested I do it with her. We'd met a few weeks before when she was a guest on my movie show and rather hit it off, in the sense that I quite fancied her and she told my sister (who was a friend of hers) that if, at gunpoint, she had to do it with a man, I would narrowly make the top half of her list. (I'm saying 'my movie show' like I'm Jonathan Ross or Barry Norman or something, when in fact it was a no-budget Channel Five bag of cock that went out during the deadly 'Hollyoaks slot' at 7 p.m. and its highlight, for the four months it lasted, was 0898 calls people made to answer a ridiculously easy question about movies – 'was Jaws a shark, a pig, or a doughnut or?' – in the hope of winning a telly. And when that didn't work we changed it to a cash prize of a few hundred quid instead of a telly, but even that couldn't save it.

And so history was made.

In the sense that we made a show about history.

The Edwardian era, from the death of Queen Victoria in 1901 to the expiration of her obese but happy son Edward VII (who announced his mother's passing with the words 'Gentlemen, you may smoke') from a not entirely surprising double heart attack in 1910, was the Golden Age not just of cricket, motoring, amateurism and one-piece swimsuits for chaps, but of eating.

Unlike his famously stay-at-home mum (who set the tone for our current Royal Family with her 'simple and British is best' philosophy), Edward VII loved French food and loved eating out. Where he went, the more well-off of his admiring subjects followed, generating the first great restaurant boom, an explosion of new and exciting dishes, the arrival of the celebrity chef (bleurgh), and the birth, in the shape of the *Pall Mall Gazette*'s Lieutenant-Colonel Newnham-Davis, of the restaurant critic (hooray!).

There can have been no better time for a chap like me to be alive. And if the BBC needed someone to live, dress, exercise, eat and drink like an Edwardian man of means – to find out what it did to his girth, his arteries, his inner organs, his digestion, his mood, his very soul – then really that man could only be me.

Some guinea pigs might have been daunted by the prospect of four whopping meals a day, rivers of grog and hardly any fruit, vegetables or water for an entire week. But not I. I couldn't wait for them to Edwardian Supersize Me.

In advance of this week of quite possibly hazardous consumption, I was sent to Dr Richard Petty in Harley Street for a check-up, partly to get some 'before' levels for the sake of comparison later, and partly to check, just check, that I would be able to handle it.

I was in bullish mood, assuming myself to be just about the healthiest example of a 37-year-old man you could possibly hope to encounter, proffering my arm to the nurse's needle and saying to the director, 'I've never had any sort of check-up before. Wouldn't it be funny if I am in such bad shape that I can't actually do the diet at all?'

Hilarious. It turned out that my cholesterol was through the roof, my liver produces too much bile, and I have gout. Or if not gout exactly, then the very high level of uric acid in my blood that will lead me eventually to get gout. And all I can do to prevent it is to avoid offal, shellfish and alcohol – the very core elements of the Edwardian diet. As were the red meat, dairy products and fried food that Dr Petty says I must eschew for the sake of my heart.

Suddenly, I wasn't so keen to go Edwardian. All my good mood, all my thrill at the prospect of the coming week, evaporated. At news like this, a chap may not necessarily change his diet forever, but it is a fair bet that he will consume nothing but fish and greens for at least the first week, before lapsing into his old ways.

But to go straight from the doctor's to a gigantic breakfast and on into a week of 12-course dinners, riotous alcoholism and pork chops the size of tennis rackets was so counter-intuitive as to seem suicidal. For the first time in my life, and just when it all seemed to be coming together, I truly didn't want to eat.

To give him a chance to impose a sense of perspective, I asked the doctor if this experiment could actually kill me. 'Well,' he said, not pooh-poohing the notion with nearly enough vigour for my liking, 'I wouldn't do it for more than a week.'

So I didn't.

DAY 1

Breakfast: *Porridge, sardines, curried eggs, grilled cutlets, coffee, hot chocolate, bread, butter, honey.*

The meal is served at the Edwardian house in Barnes in which I am residing with Sue, and is cooked, as all our meals here will be, by Sophie Grigson from a weekly menu taken from an Edwardian housekeeping book. I go at it full tilt, using the age-old technique of 'surprising my stomach' by getting as much as possible down before it realises I am full. I do myself proud and end by wiping my fifth cutlet in the remaining curry sauce from my eggs. Sue, who I've heard in the past claiming to be a vegetarian, has not fared so well, going green halfway through her first sardine.

We discuss briefly how income tax at the preposterously low rate of 5 per cent freed up plenty of cash for eating, but are interrupted by Sophie ringing the bell to announce lunch.

Lunch: *Sauté of kidneys on toast, mashed potatoes, macaroni au gratin, rolled ox tongue.*

Good stuff, this. Toast all mulched with kidney fat and blood, macaroni good and rich, tongue gigantic and purple. It is exactly what Dr Petty wants me to avoid.

Afternoon tea: *Fruit cake, Madeira cake, hot potato cakes, coconut rocks, bread, toast, butter.*

High tea was invented by the Edwardians to stave off hunger during the endless minutes between lunch and dinner. Everything is very brown.

Dinner: *Oyster patties, sirloin steak, braised celery, roast goose, potato scallops, vanilla soufflé.*

Oysters, the gouty man's nemesis. I swallow eight in my patties. I carve the goose, as the man of the house always did, and find that it is not easy in the stiff-fronted shirt I am wearing with my white tie, nor can I properly incline my neck to observe my work, what with the three-inch-high stiff separate collar I am wearing, and thus very nearly lose a thumb. Sue says that I can shut up until I have worn a corset. Apparently her spleen and kidneys have already been forced up into her ribcage (a recognised problem of the Edwardian lady) and her stomach, contained in a waist now narrowed to the width of a toddler's thigh, is no longer allowing ingress of food.

And so to bed. But up again an hour later for a midnight snack of roast chicken and Madeira. King Edward always took a roast chicken to bed with him, so it seems only right. Alas, after my chicken, I do not get back to sleep. I have consumed 5,000 calories in a single day, well over Dr Petty's recommendation of 1,800, and toss and turn and rumble until dawn.

DAY 2

Breakfast at Simpson's-in-the-Strand: *Smoked haddock, scrambled eggs, kippers, cold cuts, one roast pheasant, fruit, bacon, sausages, devilled kidneys, scones and kedgeree.*

I feel good walking into Simpson's in my impeccable morning dress and top hat, but after scoffing a fair portion of everything I spend the rest of the day wishing I was dead. This was the sort of breakfast available in country houses all over England and died out only with the decline in domestic staff and the introduction of cereal from America. In short, we gave it all up for Frosties.

Lunch at Rules, Covent Garden: *Oysters, foie gras terrine, roast cod with asparagus, mutton hotpot, pink Yorkshire rhubarb and clotted cream.*

A stonking meal in London's oldest restaurant. But alas, Sue and I are being taught the chew-chew diet, or Fletcherism, the dieting system devised by Horace Fletcher which compelled diners to bow their heads and chew each mouthful for one minute, until it had liquefied and could be simply absorbed by the mouth. After each minute's chew is up, a bell is rung and one is allowed to swallow. We look ridiculous, and it makes the food taste revolting, but it does result in my eating less. Or perhaps that was because I have had 2,500 calories at breakfast and haven't pooed in two days.

Dinner party at home with several guests, including Roy Hattersley: *Melon glacé, mock turtle soup, sole au gratin, crab and asparagus mousse in aspic, boiled mutton with caper sauce, quail pudding, punch romaine.*

Awesome. Mock turtle soup was made with a calf's head to imitate the gelatinous quality of turtle meat and now all I want is the real thing. Quail pudding was a cheeky little dish, too – each bird wrapped in thinly sliced fillet steak before getting its suet crust. We drink lots of champagne, as they did back then, and also a lot of hock (liebfraumilch, really) and youngish claret. Then, when Roy has gone, we have a food fight.

A society hostess would have thrown at least two parties a week like this for up to 20 guests. Ours was for eight and would have cost £24, or £2,000 in today's money.

DAY 3

Breakfast: The usual, plus a nice fat Cuban cigar. King Edward, in his final illness, took his doctor's advice and promised to limit himself to two cigars before breakfast.

Lunch at Simpson's Chophouse on Cornhill: Beloved of Thackeray, Dickens and Newnham-Davis himself (who reviewed it on one occasion when he had been caught out in the evening in morning dress and dared not be seen in his club improperly attired for the hour). It's been here since 1757 and I eat with some very old fellows. Have steak and kidney pudding with a giant sausage, then a huge pork chop and then stewed cheese served fizzling in a little tin tray with toasted bread triangles on the side. Also lots of claret.

Simpson's opened its doors to women only in 1916, and since I'm living in 1907, I've left Sue behind. The chaps and I discuss the good old days, when men were men and the sort of women who made trouble about it were generally chained to railings somewhere out of earshot.

Dinner: More of the same, to be honest. And when I get a little queasy I am invited to prepare a famous Edwardian remedy for indigestion called 'beef tea', which I make by putting two teaspoons of mashed beef into a jam jar with three teaspoons of cold water, and leaving in a warm place to macerate. Then I strain and drink. And after that it all comes, as it were, rushing back.

Days 4, 5 and 6 roll on much the same. I gradually recover the ability to sleep and poo, so crucial to the enjoyment of life, and generally adjust to the Edwardian life. We have gigantic picnics of lobster and foie gras on Hampstead Heath; Sue takes me to a vegetarian restaurant. They were very popular at the time, being the only places that women could eat unaccompanied, and were thus a hotbed of suffragette sedition.

Finally, we come to the last supper, a dinner cooked for us by the head chef at The Savoy, recreating, to the molecule, an original nine-course banquet served there on the evening of January 14, 1905.

In full evening formal wear, starched to the eyeballs and with my corseted consort, Sue, at my side, along with six other guests including the great Anton Mosimann, I eat:

1. Beluga Caviar and native and rock oysters – £1,000 worth.
2. Pot au feu Henry IV – the shoulder, shank, rib and tail of beef braised all day and served in their broth with a blob of béarnaise.
3. Sole cardinale and whitebait, which was meant to be an either/or.
4. Chicken d'Albufera, in which the roasted bird is served in a sauce of boiled cream, triply-reduced, with mushrooms and black truffles and quenelles of veal tongue and chicken.
5. Saddle of lamb with spring vegetables and parsley potatoes.
6. Pressed Rouen ducklings, in which four birds killed specially for us in France are roasted and their bones and organs crushed in a solid silver duck press before our eyes, the resultant juice then reduced at the boil in a silver dish to produce a sauce for the meat which Sue called 'slightly bummy duck's blood'.

7. Asparagus hollandaise, which the Edwardians loved as a pre-dessert but is apparently murderous for the gouty.
8. Peach Melba served in a hand-carved ice-swan as big as a ten-year-old child.
9. Canapés à la Diane, which, I confess, I cannot remember.

I imagine Vita Sackville-West must have recently eaten a meal a bit like that when she wrote in *The Edwardians*: 'Those meals! Those endless, extravagant meals, in which they all indulged all year round! Sebastian wondered how their constitutions and their figures could stand it; then he remembered that in the summer they went as a matter of course to Homburg or Marien-bad, to get rid of the accumulated excess, and then returned to start on another year's course of rich living. Really there was very little difference, especially, between Marienbad and the vomitorium of the Romans.'

As for Dr Petty, he was not amused. He found that although I had put on only a pound in weight, my body fat had increased by an extraordinary 10 per cent over the week, with corresponding declines in muscle mass and water content. My haematology showed excess blood urea due to an excess of protein and dangerous signs of dehydration from the excess booze and lack of water. And my cholesterol, from an already worrying 5.8 (modern quacks like to see a result below 4), had in seven days skyrocketed to 6.6!

On a diet like that, he reckoned, a chap with my heredity would do well to live till he was 42.

With a prognosis of that nature, and after a week like that, you might have thought I'd be desperate to get my mouth round a bit of salad and a bottle of water. And, in a way, I was. But the thing is, I had got rather used to my Edwardian way of life: the great clothes, the staggering food, the not having anything much to do, and I was reluctant to let it go.

If it really were 1910, I think I would very probably have carried on with it, and hang the death sentence. After all, in four years' time I'd be on the Western Front, running at the German guns.

And, indeed, a few months later we were back. On BBC2 this time and up for six, count them six, journeys back in time. And this time the results were very different.

Six times over 12 weeks, with a week off between each to recover, I was once again dressed up in the costume of the period, sent first to the doctor for a check-up and then packed off with Sue to a period house, built, decorated and gastronomically set up in the era to which we were 'travelling'. There was often some shock at the sudden immersion, but by the end of each week the doctors were getting some astonishing results.

The Age of Shakespeare

The earliest period into which we lunged, and the most immediately shocking. For a start, I was dressed in big, puffy knee-length trunk hose and tights with a giant codpiece, all attached to my doublet so that I couldn't wee without getting totally naked: less of a problem than you might think, since I wasn't drinking a single cup of tea or coffee, neither having yet arrived in England.

At first, it was terrible. Up at dawn to go hunting and not so much as a sniff of espresso. Irritability during the day quite terrible, not to mention the headaches. To offset these, a lot of ale and sack (sherry) is drunk, which gradually makes me much less irritable, and not in the least bit bothered about being sleepy all the time. By day five, I'm not even missing the coffee.

Dr Tom Van Den Bossche, a GP specialising in nutrition, has looked at the diet and predicted constipation and weight gain, but dishes such as calf's foot jelly are too grey and sad to eat.

Likewise, a dish containing 16 live frogs falls to bits when its contents go AWOL and an hour of frog-hunting burns off all the roast piglet and swan.

As for the rest of the diet, well, who's actually going to finish a supper of sheep's head mulled in cloves? Or even start it. Straight to bed with no eyeballs: minus 1,000 calories.

Then there is treacle tart filled with pickled mackerel and herring, so barf-inducing that once again Sue and I end up ingesting precious little of this newly fashionable 'sugar' we have heard so much about.

There's pumpkin pie, meat pottage, stewed mutton, boiled pigeon, calf's lungs, meat custard, numble pie (made with deer's testicles) . . . all sorts of delicious stuff. But in 1590, the fork has yet to be invented, and we find that eating with your hands, and feeling your digits grow stickier and smellier by the second, seriously reduces the amount you feel like shovelling in. Hey nonny, nonny.

At the end of a week in which we've consumed three times the recommended intake of protein, not to mention zero fibre and our own weight in ale and wine, Dr Van Den Bossche finds that I've lost three kilos and kicked my caffeine habit.

I have never felt better in my life. Might even write a play. Or maybe just a sonnet.

The Restoration

High protein again, and no water AT ALL to reflect people's habits at this time of dangerous contamination of the Thames. Dirk Budka, an expert in nutrition and bacteriology at the Wellman Clinic, anticipates constipation (again – no wonder they didn't invent the flushing toilet for another 200 years: chaps in the olden days clearly never pooed) and perhaps, with the dehydration and all the offal and booze, the beginnings of a kidney or bladder stone of the kind that nearly killed Samuel Pepys.

And so we sit down to such delights as neat's tongue in a caul (the tongue of an ox in the amniotic sack of a calf) and a 10 kg 'coffin pie' with pastry an inch thick and a reusable lid, full of coxcombs, sweetbreads, sheep's tongue, bone marrow, chicken, veal, pigeon breasts, oysters and nutmeg, which will last us a week – although by the end it is starting to go a bit green.

At first, it is awful not drinking water. Headaches and a general sluggishness ensue. But small beer (weak ale, basically) is a decent substitute, and eight pints a day of the stuff keep me in excellent spirits. After four or five days the headaches and sluggishness subside and I realise that they were just psychosomatic. The received wisdom that we should all drink two litres of water a day is just modern urban vanity, and complete rubbish: a big Puritan con designed to stop anyone having any fun that seems to have lasted 350 years.

By the end of the week, once again, I am feeling terrific. Is it the absence of fast food, and candied fruit instead of chocolate? Can it be that the 24-hour head sauna I am getting from my 5-lb full-bottomed Samuel Pepys wig is keeping my brain light? Sure, my pee is like treacle and I have the breath of a necrophiliac on hunger strike, but my weight is down four or five pounds and my belly, empty of water, is hard as a rock. I am likely, apparently, to live to at least 80 – unless I get syphilis.

The Regency

Ah, the era of Jane Austen, of balls and dresses and, ah, balls and, um, dresses. They don't really eat in the books, do they? That's why they all look so good in frock coats and riding breeches. And I make a pretty awesome Mr Darcy, too. Sue can hardly keep her hands off.

I spend much of the time wearing a corset (as Beau Brummel often did, and no doubt Mr Darcy too, the old queen) and so cannot really force down much of the food – which in this period is a combination of patriotic roast beef eaten in defiance of the perfidious French and, conversely, poncy, heavily sauced French food, of the kind cooked for aristocrats by top chefs fleeing France as their noble patrons were beheaded.

I visit Dr Petty again for this one, and he predicts great digestive discomfort and an attack of gout (the man is obsessed) from the purine in all the port I'll be drinking: during the Napoleonic wars claret was not available, so we got stinko on the sticky stuff instead, imported from our old allies, Portugal.

But I have the time of my life. Determined to keep looking rakishly handsome in my fine clothes, I burn up thousands of calories stalking my estate with a blunderbuss, firing at poachers robbing my rabbits in defiance of the Enclosures Act.

Breakfast having just been invented, I make that my main meal. But it is so recently invented that it comprises only bread, so I don't eat much of it.

Pineapples are newly available too but, you know, who gives?

As for lunch, that doesn't seem to have been invented either. But they do have a thing called 'nuncheon', which is most often cheese served deliberately with the maggots who live in it. I dine only on the occasional sandwich at the casino tables (invented by the Earl of Sandwich for that very purpose) and so go to bed reasonably hungry – a good way to stay slim.

At the end of this immersion I do, in fact, have dangerously high uric acid, indicating the imminence of an outbreak of gout. But I am in terrific shape on the surface.

The Victorian

As a wealthy industrialist living in a big house in Barnes and wearing a stovepipe hat at all times, I live on brown Windsor soup, cold meat pie and mutton chops. The fear is obesity, heart attack and general moral calamity.

Darwin is big in this period, not just because he was a great student of animals, but because he was a big eater of them. He ate hawk, bittern and owl, puma ('tastes like veal') and giant tortoise. Sue and I do our best, avoiding endangered species and chomping down squirrel, maggot, fox, donkey, Pomeranian and even lettuce (bleurghh!).

Then there were the first curries, the first fish and chips, the first restaurant boom, fast food stalls for The Great Exhibition and a megaton Christmas involving ten courses, several whole animals, mince pies full of actual mince, and a layered pie of 24 carcasses.

But by the end of the week I have, astonishingly, lost weight. This is probably down to a sort of Atkins' effect from the meat-only diet. Furthermore, the total absence of additives or preservatives compared with a modern diet suggests that I could live for ever. This natural stuff, though leaden, is just so much easier to digest. Also I cycle everywhere on my penny-farthing, so I am fitter than ever.

Interestingly, all the protein has made me randy as hell, which is tedious, because in the Victorian era sex was, of course, illegal.

The Second World War

Who do you think you are kidding, Mr Hitler, if you think I'm eating that? Everything in the 1940s seems to have been the colour of a manila envelope: the food, the clothes, the women's legs (Sue's are stained with Bovril to look like she's wearing stockings – and are about the meatiest thing I lick all week).

We live on 'national loaf', which is bread made from whatever you make bread from when there is no wheat – I'm guessing pea flour, brick dust and hair. We also eat a lot of 'national sausage'. Known at the time as Hitler's secret weapon, it was made from 3 per cent pig bits (sphincter, eyelid, sinus) and 97 per cent national loaf (see above, brick dust, etc). So you can just imagine how exciting a sausage sandwich is. Like eating loft insulation that might or might not have been slept on by a pig.

Then there's ersatz coffee, powdered egg, mock duck, mock ham, mock chicken, mock chocolate and Spam, which, alas, was not mock. Spam is truly a horror. If you fattened a weasel on axle-grease, skinned it and then pressed it into a cube, you'd get something like it, but a little bit nicer.

Otherwise it's just veg, veg, veg. Sue and I get an allotment and 'dig for victory', and with all that digging, and Home Guard drilling, and bayoneting ersatz Hun, the 100 per cent stodge diet converts into pure muscle.

We get heavier, yes, but when tested with callipers our fat mass is found to have gone down, and when put through our paces on a treadmill in a hypoxic chamber we seem to have developed the stamina of supermen. It was clearly the stodge wot won it.

The Seventies

Mark Hix, the chef who made The Ivy great, is our cook for the week, and lays before us on the first morning the food we will be eating at home. There isn't a fresh or a green thing in sight. Everything is in plastic or tin: boil-in-the-bag cod mornay, Findus crispy pancakes, frozen faggots, Angel Delight.

With all this processed food my gastroenterologist at UCH predicts totally ungroovy traffic jam in colon. And what would happen to my weight? In the 1970s we ate, on average, 750 calories a day more than we do now, and yet obesity rates were a fifth of what they are today. I usually hover around 12 stone most of the time, and at 5 foot 9 that means my BMI is at the top end of healthy. A few extra pounds and I tip into overweight – which leads to self-hatred, and running. And we don't want that.

But down I chow, nonetheless. At home it is the unfeasible gunk described above, plus Mark's fantastic flambéed steak

Diane with crinkle-cut chips. And then there's duck à l'orange, cheese fondue, chocolate fondue, coronation chicken, school dinners of liver and Smash followed by grey chocolate pudding with custard (skin on, of course). There's a 'swingers' dinner' of Fanny Craddock recipes where everything is shaped like penises and vulvae . . .

And at the end of the week – guess what? I'm skinny as a pencil, and now look absolutely bang on period in my skintight tank-tops and flares. Far from slowing down, my digestion has gone into overdrive. My body, used to the lush life of the restaurant critic, just isn't used to all this artificial and pre-fabricated stuff and simply doesn't recognise it as food. It's just passed right on through without being absorbed. Maybe that's what happened in the 1970s.

Widely acclaimed (by me) as a revolution in television food programming, the show was called back for another series the following year, and we piled straight in, in our gloriously logical and methodical way, to the food and lifestyle of Revolutionary France, the Fifties, the Norman Conquest, the Eighties, the Twenties and, er, how many is that? I'm sure there was another one. Oh yes, Ancient Rome, by Jupiter. Eating hay-roasted dormice in a toga. In Northumberland. In February.

And it all began to get rather discombobulating. It wasn't just that from one week to the next I didn't know which town, country, house, cave, day, month or century I was living in, it was that, even when I did, I didn't know what time it was. Because the camera, which never lies, nonetheless never does anything in the right order.

'Right,' says the director, as you stumble down off the Eurostar at 7 a.m., bleary-eyed and boggy from train coffee and stale croissant. 'It's the last days of Robespierre, we're doing the 28-course turkey banquet with six French historians and a burlesque dancer at the Musée de la Decouverte, so we need you in the Marie Antoinette costume pronto. And don't forget to shave.'

Then at lunchtime you do four different 18th-century breakfasts, two more banquets in the evening (one of them with a live pig and three antiques dealers), and shoot a night-for-day picnic lunch at two in the morning. Then for the next three days you have no meals at all, because you've got to be filmed walking in and out of various buildings you have not yet eaten in (but will have done, you are told, by 1791). Then you do a let-them-eat-cake bit from 1789 which is filmed last but will be shown first, and then, finally, back at the Gare du Nord for the trip home, you do your 'arriving in France, looking forward to the week ahead' scene.

It fair does your head in. The whole notion of cause-and-effect, the very idea of sequentiality, falls apart and corrupts the rest of your life. When I got home after my week away, the first thing I said to my wife was, 'How was it for you?' And only when she said, 'How was what?', did I remember that I hadn't yet so much as kissed her hello.

So I went upstairs and did the teeth-brushing and putting on pyjamas scene, and then I nipped out to the pub. Next morning I got up, had dinner, drank a couple of large brandies and went to buy the newspapers to read over breakfast. After breakfast I got undressed and went for a run on the Heath.

And so Sue and I decided that was it. Apart from anything else, there weren't really any other eras for us to murder. If we'd known at the beginning how popular it was going to be we might have proceeded chronologically, breaking eras down into their component parts and preparing for 20 or 30 shows. But when you've covered, say, 1066–1485 in one show, as we did in the medieval episode, or the whole of the long and complex Victorian period in a single hour, you screw yourself a bit: you can't go back and do little bits from each when you realise people want to see more, and the tiny corners of history you have left yourself between the big periods (the bit between 1485 and the Age of Shakespeare, say, or the 1930s not counting the War, or the nondescript gap between 1616 and 1640) rather pale by comparison with what has gone before.

We thought about a Stone Age one, with us living off weeds in a cave and me occasionally whacking Sue over the head with a club, but she didn't fancy it. We might have gone biblical, we might have gone into the future or into space. But we couldn't be arsed.

So we knocked it on the head. And gave thanks for small mercies.

If I learned anything, it was that every single period I ate in had made me healthier. Sure, these were always the diets of the relatively wealthy, and, yes, I would probably have been stricken down young with some sort of terrible disease long ago. But as long as I did live, and had money to feed myself, I think I would have been healthier and fitter at any time in the past than I am now. We all would. And we'd all be happier, too. The food chain has become poisoned, corrupted, bastardised with bad practice, profiteering and snide science. It was better when it was simpler.

We can't escape backwards in time, unfortunately. We have to escape forwards, into a different future, where they do things better and simpler than we do now. And I get to wear a codpiece.

Take a Doggy Bag

... NOT with you to the restaurant, that's overkill. But away with you afterwards if there is anything at all you can' finish but might eat later.

Years of grumbling from British consumers has led to a ludicrous inflation of portion sizes in restaurants (although you will more often hear and read comments about portions being too small than too big, because fat people are more grumpy than thin people, on account of being so wheezy and uncomfortable all the time and not sleeping properly because of their fat necks cutting off their windpipes, and so are much more likely to complain, and the thing that upsets them most is not getting enough food to overfill their fat faces and get even fatter), so that these days I, a fairly gluttonous adult male pushing thirteen stone, can very rarely finish everything on my plate in a restaurant, and have not had room for pudding in seven or eight years. And half of all restaurant diners are women, and thus likely (on average) to eat far less than me.

So for God's sake, take the excess away. It may not seem very classy, or elegant, or British. You might worry that it looks a bit povvo, scuttling away from The Ivy after a special trip you've saved up for years for and had to book three months in advance (for a bad table in the middle of a weekday afternoon) with a bag of leftovers to eat 'free' later. You may worry that the other diners, with their diamonds and Rolexes and their stupid Italian cars parked on the zigzag outside might think you are poor or common. But there are four ways to deal with this.

1) Think, 'fuck 'em'.

2) Pretend (to yourself, your guests, and even your surrounding diners if you want to make a thing of it) that the food really is for your dog. And that it will only eat foie gras because it is such a posh

expensive
bloody dog.

3) Do it because the millions of
ons of perfectly good food that restau-
ants throw away every year that has been left
on plates (quite apart from the waste that goes off
before it is eaten, or even cooked) is a ruinous, ruinous
waste, contributes to the landfill crisis, global warming (maybe), and is just shit and wrong.*

4) Think, 'fuck 'em'. (That's really the main one, which is why I've
put it twice).

Personally, I always take a doggy bag away with me. Especially from
ethnic restaurants. Poncy French frilly Michelin food may look a bit ropey the
next morning but there is nothing on earth so delicious as a big bag of Singapore noodles (Hokkien mee, say, or char kway tiow) fried up for lunch the next
day, maybe with some fresh chilli chopped in and a squeeze of lime to perk it
up. Or the bare dregs of four or five different curry dishes all smooched together in a saucepan and heated up fiery hot and tossed over a well-buttered
baked potato. In some ways I'd be happiest to cut out the boring hours of sit-
ing there at the table with the tedious waiters coming up and interrupting my
conversation all the time and just get every meal I had put in a bag to take
away and enjoy in the comfort of my own home.

Just a word on that environmental element. I have been asked by a number of
roups, such as the Sustainable Restaurant Association and others, to back
ampaigns to make restaurants offer doggy bags, and to generally push to
romote them as an ecological move but have resisted for the perverse, but I
ink reasonable reason that I do not want doggy bags to become so
niversally thought of as a necessity at the end of a meal that we get the
rt of escalation they have had in America – the world's fattest
ountry – where the already giant portions that engendered the
oggy bag fad have had to be expanded to ensure that
eople can always take a bag, and where people, giant
t people, actually complain if they have been
le to eat everything on their plates and
ve nothing to take away.

DON'T YOU EVER GET BORED OF EATING IN RESTAURANTS?

Yes, obviously I do. Doesn't everyone?

Don't you get fed up with having to get in the car and worry about how much you're going to drink and who's going to drive home, and hoping you'll be able to find the restaurant easily enough when you get there, and that you will be able to park, and that you won't be too late and that they'll give your table away and just shrug and look at their watches when you come panting in, and tell you that you can take a seat at the bar and maybe something will come up in half an hour or so?

Don't you get fed up with wondering what to have for a starter – I mean, what in the world is the point of starters? – and of everybody faffing over what to have, and then when the waiter comes he has to stand there for hours while your boring friends natter on about their boring lives and don't pay him the respect even of stopping to acknowledge him?

And don't you get fed up with the women at the table going, 'Er, what, me? Ooh, I haven't looked yet,' like it's the first time they've ever been to a restaurant? Like they don't know that the women will be invited to speak first?

The men have always decided what to have. Why haven't the women? How did society so arrange itself that the sex that is invited to order first is the one that never wants to? ('Why don't you go first, while I decide?') It's mental. Why don't we just swap over now, and make it the men who order first ('Soup, steak, wine'), and the women who go second when they've had a bit more time? ('I'm not very hungry, is it okay if I just have two starters? Do you think that'll be enough? And if I have the soufflé with the 15-minute waiting time first instead of second, does that mean everyone will have to wait longer for their starters? Or can you stagger it so that it comes a little bit after theirs but then, because I'm only having a salad, then that can come out at the same time as their mains?')

Bored with going to restaurants? Of course! Aren't you?

'Well, er, I suppose. But, you know, it's your job. I don't get to go to them all that often, whereas you probably go to them all the time. You must get fed up with it.'

I suppose, but may I ask what you do?

'I'm a teacher/shopkeeper/banker/murderer.'

And do you ever get fed up with that?

'Oh yes, all the time.'

Well, it's the same. The point here is that it's my job. And I've been doing it for 10 or 15 years now and a lot of the time it is just very, very repetitive and boring. Jobs are, by their very nature, awful. That's why they're called 'jobs'. Five million Englishmen play football for fun every weekend of the year, but have you ever seen a professional footballer who looked like he was enjoying himself?

What I wouldn't give to be a footballer instead of a restaurant critic. Oh God, the hell of it all.

The hell of the obsequious greeting (multiplied by a factor of squillions if they rumble I'm here for work); the automatic seating of my group at the worst table in the house (*unless* they rumble I'm here for work), which all restaurants do because someone has to sit there and you might as well try it on everyone who comes in because some town-struck grockle is eventually going to accept without a squeak; the laborious business of the menu you've seen a thousand times before trying to pretend it is new and interesting; all the misspellings; the 'Have you eaten at Chez Van Kerr before? May I explain how the menu works?' . . .

And then the stupid *amuse-bouche* – if it's somewhere posh – slimy, lukewarm and insubstantial as a sick dog's cough; the sitting and waiting; and waiting and waiting; then the mild disappointment of the food; the vile spotlighting that makes everyone look 100 years old, and throws weird shadows on your plate when you lean forwards to eat and makes you feel like you're having a stroke; the achy back from sitting so long; the insistence on pudding (but I'm not an eight-year-old, why would I want to eat cakes at bedtime?); the endless dawdle over the bill and the gigantic size of it . . .

And then the tedious schlep home through traffic (where are they all going? It's practically midnight.); the tricky night's sleep on all that food; the small-hours wake-up to wee from all that drinking; the bilious morning; the 80–20 chance of mild squits from some filthy bum-scratching thumb in the kitchen poking your tian back into shape after someone sneezed on it . . .

Of course I'm bored with it. I wouldn't care if I never went to another restaurant again as long as I live.

TEXT ACKNOWLEDGEMENTS

Extract from *The Edwardians* by Vita Sackville-West, is reproduced with permission of Curtis Brown Group Ltd, London, on behalf of The Estate of Vita Sackville-West.
Copyright © Vita Sackville-West, 1930.

The poem, *Dooley is a Traitor* by James Michie, is taken from the book: 'Possible Laughter' by James Michie, published by Hart-Davis and used by permission of David Higham Associates. © James Michie.

'Burnt Norton' taken from *Four Quartets* © Estate of T.S. Eliot and reprinted by permission of Faber and Faber Ltd.

The best books can be about discovery. The ones whose pages open new views on the world, make you think differently – or more deeply.

If you would like to discover more, join us at www.hodder.co.uk, or follow us on Twitter @hodderbooks, and you can tap in to a community of people who believe that life is about learning new things every day.

Whether you want to find out more about this book, discover more about a particular author or subject area, watch trailers and interviews, have the chance to win early limited editions, or simply browse our expert readers' selection of the very best books, we think you'll find what you're looking for.

And if you don't, that's the place to tell us what's missing.

We love what we do, and we'd love you to be part of it.

www.hodder.co.uk

@hodderbooks

HodderBooks

HodderBooks